Teaching Reading and Writing

Teaching Reading and Writing

Improving Instruction and Student Achievement

edited by

Brett Miller, Ph.D.
Eunice Kennedy Shriver National Institute
of Child Health and Human Development
National Institutes of Health
Bethesda, Maryland

Peggy McCardle, Ph.D., M.P.H.
Peggy McCardle Consutling, LLC
Bethesda, Maryland

and

Richard Long, Ed.D.
International Reading Association
Washington, D.C.

·P A U L·H·
BROOKES
PUBLISHING CO.®

Baltimore • London • Sydney

Paul H. Brookes Publishing Co.
Post Office Box 10624
Baltimore, Maryland 21285-0624
USA

www.brookespublishing.com

Typeset by Scribe, Philadelphia, Pennsylvania.
Manufactured in the United States of America by
Sheridan Books, Chelsea, Michigan.

Cover image ©iStockphoto.com/GlobalStock

The following were written by a U.S. Government employee within the scope of his or her official duties and, as such, shall remain in the public domain: Chapters 1, 5, and 14. The opinions and assertions contained herein are the private opinions of the authors and are not to be construed as official or reflecting the views of the U.S. Government.

The views expressed in this book are those of the authors and do not necessarily represent those of the National Institutes of Health, the Eunice Kennedy Shriver National Institute of Child Health and Development, the U.S. Department of Health and Human Services, or the International Reading Association.

Library of Congress Cataloging-in-Publication Data
Teaching Reading and Writing: Improving Instruction and Student Achievement / edited by Brett Miller, Ph.D., Peggy McCardle, Ph.D., M.P.H., and Richard Long, Ed.D.
    pages   cm
Includes bibliographical references and index.
ISBN 978-1-59857-364-0 (pbk. : alk. paper) — ISBN 1-59857-364-0 (pbk. : alk. paper) — ISBN 978-1-59857-446-3 (epub) — ISBN 1-59857-446-9 (epub)
1. Language arts. 2. Reading. 3. English language—Study and teaching. I. McCardle, Peggy D. II. Long, Richard, 1953- III. Title.

LB1576.M515 2013
372.6—dc23   2013030363

British Library Cataloguing in Publication data are available from the British Library.

2017   2016   2015   2014   2013

10   9   8   7   6   5   4   3   2   1

Contents

About the Editors

Brett Miller, Ph.D., Program Director of the Reading, Writing, and Related Learning Disabilities Research Program in the Child Development and Behavior branch of the *Eunice Kennedy Shriver* National Institute of Child Health and Human Development (NICHD); Rockville, Maryland; millerbre@mail.nih.gov.

Dr. Miller oversees a research program focused on developing and supporting research and training initiatives to increase knowledge relevant to the development of reading and written-language abilities for learners with and without disabilities. This program supports research that includes work with diverse groups and a range of ages.

Peggy McCardle, Ph.D., M.P.H., former Chief of the Child Development and Behavior branch at the *Eunice Kennedy Shriver* National Institute of Child Health and Human Development (NICHD); currently Consultant/President, Peggy McCardle Consulting, LLC; Annapolis, Maryland; pmccardle@yahoo.com.

Dr. McCardle has been a classroom teacher, university faculty, and hospital clinician. In addition to leading the NICHD branch, she directed the research program on language, bilingualism, and biliteracy, which addressed all aspects of typical language development as well as cross-linguistic and bilingualism research related to typical learning and learning disabilities. She now writes and consults independently in all these areas.

Richard Long, Ed.D., Director of Government Relations for the International Reading Association and Executive Director for Government Relations for the National Title I Association; Washington, DC; rlong@reading.org.

With a doctorate in education counseling from the George Washington University, Dr. Long brings to his work in education and literacy a special interest in policy. He has written on improving literacy education for struggling readers, key issues for improving education reform, as well as the role of the federal government in professional development. In addition, he is writing a book on education policy, *The Hidden Cauldron: The Paradox of American Education Reform.*

About the Contributors

Unber Ahmad, B.S., Carolina Institute for Developmental Disabilities, University of North Carolina (UNC) School of Medicine; Chapel Hill, North Carolina; unber.ahmad @cidd.unc.edu. Ms. Ahmad is conducting assessments and interventions for a U.S. Department of Education, Institute of Education Sciences project devoted to using strategy-based interventions for middle-school students at risk for writing disabilities.

Yusra Ahmed, M.S., Researcher 4, Texas Institute for Measurement Evaluation and Statistics (TIMES), University of Houston; Houston, Texas; Yusra.ahmed@times.uh.edu. Ms. Ahmed is completing her doctoral degree in Developmental Psychology from Florida State University. Her dissertation is a meta-analytic structural equation model of written composition (as measured by curriculum-based, qualitative, and sentence-writing measures) using multiple literacy and language predictors. Other research areas include structural equation models, literacy and language acquisition in typically developing students and students with learning disabilities, identification and classification of learning disabilities, and language development in Spanish-speaking English language learners.

Kim Atwill, Ph.D., Professor, Department of World Languages and Literatures, Portland State University; Portland, Oregon; katwill@pdx.edu. Dr. Atwill is a former classroom teacher. Her current research focuses on the impact of instructional practice on language and literacy development among at-risk learners.

Sara Ballute, M.A., Lead Teacher of Social Studies, High School for Service and Learning at Erasmus Hall; Brooklyn, New York; sballute@schools.nyc.gov. Prior to NYC, Ms. Ballute spent 2 years teaching in Montego Bay, Jamaica. She earned her bachelor's degree in social studies education from Ithaca College and her master's degree in anthropology from Hunter College. In 2009, Ms. Ballute was named by the *New York Times* as a "Teacher Who Makes a Difference." For 2 years Ms. Ballute has been involved with New Visions for Public Schools, using the Literacy Design Collaborative to incorporate reading and writing into the social studies curriculum.

Jay Blanchard, Ph.D., Professor Emeritus of Reading Education, Mary Lou Fulton Teachers College, Arizona State University; Tempe, Arizona; currently Director of Reading, National Assessment of Educational Progress (NAEP), Educational Testing Service; Princeton, New Jersey; jsblanchard@ets.org. Dr. Blanchard is a former classroom teacher and the author of numerous books and articles about technology and reading education beginning in 1979 with *Computer Applications in Reading*. For the last 10 years, he has assisted teachers of language minority and American Indian children with early literacy education through U.S. Department of Education Early Reading First grants. Dr. Blanchard is also a former board member of the International Reading Association.

Devon Brenner, Ph.D., Professor of Reading and Language Arts and head of the Department of Curriculum, Instruction, and Special Education in the College of Education, Mississippi State University; Mississippi State, Mississippi; devon@ra.msstate.edu. Dr. Brenner's research focuses on policy and practice in literacy education and teacher education.

Megan C. Brown, Ph.D., Research Scientist and Project Manager, Language and Literacy in High Risk Populations Lab, Georgia State University; Atlanta, Georgia; MBrown151@gsu.edu. Dr. Brown studies the relationships between dialect variation, language knowledge, and literacy using experimental and quantitative methods. Her current research addresses how language disabilities intersect with dialect variation to complicate acquisition of language and literacy skills.

Joanne F. Carlisle, Ph.D., Professor Emerita, School of Education, University of Michigan; Ann Arbor, Michigan; jfcarl@umich.edu. Dr. Carlisle's research interests include the relation of language and literacy development, effective language and literacy instruction, and professional development for elementary literacy teachers. Her current work focuses on the development of an interactive web-based professional development program (Case Studies of Reading Lessons) and studies of a video analysis system focused on teachers' support for students' learning from texts. She oversaw the evaluation of the Reading First program in Michigan and served as coeditor of *Elementary School Journal* and *Learning Disabilities Research and Practice.*

Carol McDonald Connor, Ph.D., Professor, Department of Psychology, and Director, Early Learning Research Initiative Center, Learning Sciences Institute, Arizona State University; Tempe, Arizona; carol.connor@asu.edu. Dr. Connor is also a distinguished Research Associate at the Florida Center for Reading Research. Her research focuses on children's language and literacy development, including writing, and the multiple sources of influence that affect this development, including the classroom learning environment and child characteristic × instruction interactions. Her research also focuses on children with dyslexia and other learning disabilities and on the efficacy of interventions designed to improve children's literacy and language skills.

Lara-Jeane Costa, M.A., Research Specialist, Carolina Institute for Developmental Disabilities, University of North Carolina School of Medicine; Chapel Hill, North Carolina; lara-jeane.costa@cidd.unc.edu. Ms. Costa has worked with students with disabilities as a classroom teacher, camp counselor, and clinician. During her graduate studies at the University of North Carolina (UNC) Chapel Hill, she received training as part of the Leadership Education in Neurodevelopmental Disorders (LEND) program and Maternal and Child Health Bureau Leadership program. Currently, Ms. Costa is a doctoral candidate in the UNC School of Education, examining the impact of an evidence-based instructional model for students who struggle with written expression.

Paul Deane, Ph.D., Principal Research Scientist in Research and Development, Educational Testing Service (ETS); Princeton, New Jersey; pdeane@ets.org. Dr. Deane's current research interests include automated essay scoring, vocabulary assessment, and cognitive models of writing skill. During his career at ETS he has worked on a variety of natural language processing and assessment projects, including automated item generation, tools to support verbal test development, scoring of collocation errors, reading and vocabulary assessment, and automated essay scoring. His work currently focuses on the development and scoring of writing assessments for the ETS research initiative, Cognitively Based Assessments for Learning.

Jennifer Lucas Dombek, M.S., Doctoral Candidate in Reading Education and Language Arts, Florida State University; Tallahassee, Florida; jdombek@fcrr.org. Ms. Dombek began working at the Florida Center for Reading Research in 2006, where she is currently an associate in research. While at the Florida Center for Reading Research she has worked on curriculum development, as an interventionist has provided teachers with professional development, and has coordinated multiple research studies with students in various local elementary schools. Her current research interests include grade retention, content area literacy instruction, and the assessment of writing in elementary-age students.

Julie Dwyer, Ph.D., Assistant Professor of Education, Early Childhood Department, Boston University; Boston, Massachusetts; dwyerj@bu.edu. Dr. Dwyer holds an M.Ed. in Language and Literacy from Harvard University and a Ph.D. in Language, Literacy, and Culture from the University of Michigan. Her research focuses on early language and literacy learning and teaching. She specializes in conceptual knowledge, vocabulary development, and vocabulary instruction. She is on the editorial board of *Reading Research Quarterly*. She has published papers in *Reading Research Quarterly, Early Childhood Research Quarterly, The Reading Teacher,* and *Early Childhood Education Journal.*

Crystal Edwards, B.A., Research Associate, Carolina Institute of Developmental Disabilities, UNC School of Medicine; Chapel Hill, North Carolina; crystal.edwards@cidd .unc.edu. Ms. Edwards is conducting assessments and interventions for a U.S. Department of Education, Institute of Education Sciences project devoted to using strategy-based interventions for middle school students at risk for writing disabilities.

Joanna S. Gorin, Ph.D., Director of the Cognitive and Learning Sciences Group, Educational Testing Service; Princeton, New Jersey; jgorin@ets.org. Dr. Gorin's research interests are in applications of cognitive science principles to assessment design, development, scoring, and validation. She has particular interest in the innovative use of technology to enhance the meaningfulness and instructional utility of educational assessment scores.

Steve Graham, Ed.D., Mary Emily Warner Professor, Mary Lou Fulton Teachers College, Arizona State University; Tempe, Arizona; steve.graham@asu.edu. Dr. Graham's research focuses on writing development and instruction. He is a former editor of *Exceptional Children* and *Contemporary Educational Psychology* and current editor of *Journal of Writing Research.* He authored *Handbook of Writing Research, Handbook of Learning Disabilities, Writing Better, Best Practices in Writing Instruction, Making the Writing Process Work,* and *Powerful Writing Strategies for All Students.* Dr. Graham also authored *Writing Next, Writing to Read,* and *Informing Writing* for the Carnegie Corporation. He served as an editor on the three-volume series, *American Psychological Association Educational Psychology Handbook.*

Karen R. Harris, Ed.D., Mary Emily Warner Professor, Division of Educational Leadership and Innovation, Mary Lou Fulton Teachers College, Arizona State University; Tempe, Arizona; karen.r.harris@asu.edu. Dr. Harris has worked in the field of education for more than 35 years as a teacher, teacher educator, and researcher. Her research focuses on theoretically based interventions for the development of academic and self-regulation abilities among students who are at risk and those with severe learning challenges, as well as approaches to professional development in writing that result in sustainable changes in the quality of writing instruction in schools. She is the developer of the Self-Regulated Strategies Development approach in writing.

Stephen R. Hooper, Ph.D., Professor of Psychiatry, UNC School of Medicine; Chapel Hill, North Carolina; stephen.hooper@cidd.unc.edu. Dr. Hooper is Director of Education and Training at the Carolina Institute for Developmental Disabilities (CIDD), as well as Director of the CIDD Child and Adolescent Neuropsychology Consultation Service. For more than 25 years he has worked in child neuropsychology, focusing on neurologically based disorders, including children and adolescents with learning disabilities.

Sarah Ingebrand, M.S., developmental psychology graduate student, Florida State University, and Predoctoral Interdisciplinary Research Training Fellow through the Florida Center for Reading Research; Tallahassee, Florida; ingebrand@psy.fsu.edu. Ms. Ingebrand graduated from Northwestern University with a bachelor's of science in communication sciences and disorders and psychology. She began pursuing her Ph.D. at Florida State, where her research focuses on the development of reading, writing, and spelling skills in older elementary and middle school students. She finished her master's thesis in the spring of 2013 under her advisor Dr. Carol Connor and will complete her doctoral degree at Arizona State University.

Young-Suk Kim, Ed.D., Assistant Professor, Florida State University; Tallahassee, Florida; ykim@fcrr.org. Dr. Kim is a former classroom teacher in primary and secondary schools and community college in California. Dr. Kim's research areas involve language and literacy acquisition and instruction, including early literacy predictors; reading fluency and comprehension; and writing for children from various language backgrounds such as English, Korean, and Spanish. Dr. Kim is currently the principal investigator and co-investigator of several studies funded by the Institute of Education Sciences, U.S. Department of Education, and the National Institutes of Health.

Julie E. Learned, M.Ed., Doctoral Candidate in Literacy, Language, and Culture in Educational Studies, University of Michigan; Ann Arbor, Michigan; jlearned@umich.edu. Prior to pursuing her degree, Ms. Learned worked as a secondary reading specialist and special education teacher in Seattle-area public schools. Her research examines the role of social, institutional, and instructional contexts in adolescent literacy learning, particularly for youth identified as struggling readers. She holds a master of education in learning and teaching from Harvard University and a master of education in special education from the University of Washington.

Timothy A. Lent, M.A., high school history teacher and curriculum designer; Brooklyn, New York; TLent2@schools.nyc.gov. Mr. Lent started using the Literacy Design Collaborative (LDC) tools in the winter of 2011 to integrate the Common Core State Standards into his curriculum. Over the last 3 years, he has led LDC-related professional development sessions in his school, district, and at national conferences. In addition to his participation with the LDC, Mr. Lent is Student Achievement Partners Core Advocate and a New York City Department of Education Common Core Fellow.

Tenaha O'Reilly, Ph.D., Research Scientist, Educational Testing Service; Princeton, New Jersey; toreilly@ets.org. Dr. O'Reilly's research interests are in assessment, reading comprehension, reading strategies, metacognition, and the role of background knowledge in understanding and learning. He is currently involved in projects aimed at designing and evaluating innovative measures of reading comprehension for students in pre-K–12 settings.

P. David Pearson, Ph.D., Professor of Language and Literacy and Human Development, former Dean, School of Education, University of California Berkeley; Berkeley, California; ppearson@berkeley.edu. Dr. Pearson conducts research on reading curriculum, pedagogy, and policy practices in K–12 educational settings. His most recent work focuses on a research and development project in which reading, writing, and language serve as tools to promote the acquisition of knowledge and inquiry skills in science.

Katherine T. Rhodes, M.A., Doctoral Student, Developmental Psychology Program, Georgia State University; Atlanta, Georgia; krhodes1@student.gsu.edu. Ms. Rhodes is a language and literacy fellow with research interests centering on understanding mathematics achievement difficulty as it relates to symbol acquisition, language, reading, assessment biases, and minority achievement disparities. Her current research focuses on children's linguistic skills as predictors of mathematics performance on standardized achievement assessments.

John Sabatini, Ph.D., Principal Research Scientist in the Research and Development Division, Educational Testing Service; Princeton, New Jersey; jsabatini@ets.org. Dr. Sabatini's research interests and expertise are in reading literacy development and disabilities, assessment, and educational technology. Dr. Sabatini is lead editor of two books on innovation in reading comprehension assessment. Currently, he is the principal investigator of a grant to develop pre-K–12 comprehension assessments and serves as coinvestigator on projects exploring the reading processes of adolescents, English language learners, and students with reading-based disabilities.

Yi Song, Ph.D., Associate Research Scientist, Cognitive and Learning Sciences Group, Educational Testing Service; Princeton, New Jersey; ysong@ets.org. Dr. Song's research interests and expertise are in the field of argumentation, including argumentative writing, argumentation learning progressions, and argumentation strategies. Currently, she is collaborating closely with researchers, assessment development staff, and classroom teachers to validate argumentation learning progressions, to develop formative assessments aligned to the progressions, and to create teacher support materials.

Dorothy S. Strickland, Ph.D., Samuel DeWitt Proctor Professor of Education, Emerita, Rutgers University; New Brunswick, New Jersey; dorothy.strickland@gse.rutgers .edu. Dr. Strickland is the former president of the International Reading Association and Reading Hall of Fame. She received the International Reading Association's Outstanding Teacher Educator of Reading Award, the National-Louis University Ferguson Award for Outstanding Contributions to Early Childhood Education, and the William S. Gray Citation of Merit. She served on the Common Core State Standards Validation Committee. Her publications include *Essential Readings on Early Literacy, Literacy Leadership in Early Childhood, Bridging the Literacy Achievement Gap: 4–12,* and *Administration and Supervision of Reading Programs.*

Jacquelyn M. Urbani, Ph.D., Assistant Professor of Special Education, Dominican University of California; San Rafael, California; jacquelyn.urbani@dominican.edu. Dr. Urbani completed her Ph.D. at the University of California, Berkeley in human development and special education. Her interests in literacy achievement began when she was a teacher at the Pennsylvania School for the Deaf, where she taught for 12 years. She is also interested in pre- and in-service teacher education and is currently engaged in research exploring the roles of doctoral programs and hiring institutions in developing quality educators. Specifically, she is examining the features of institutions that assist in developing content and pedagogical knowledge across disciplines.

Sarah Vanselous, B.A., Research Associate, Carolina Institute of Developmental Disabilities, UNC School of Medicine; Chapel Hill, North Carolina; sarah.vanselous@cidd .unc.edu. Ms. Vanselous is conducting assessments and intervention for a U.S. Department of Education, Institute of Education Sciences project devoted to using strategy-based interventions for middle school students at risk for writing disabilities.

Richard K. Wagner, Ph.D., Robert O. Lawton Distinguished Research Professor of Psychology and W. Russell and Eugenia Morcom Chair, Florida State University; Tallahassee, Florida; rkwagner@psy.fsu.edu. Dr. Wagner also is a cofounder and the current associate director of the Florida Center for Reading Research. He earned a Ph.D. in cognitive psychology from Yale University in 1985. He previously earned a master's degree in school psychology from the University of Akron. His major areas of research interest are dyslexia and the normal acquisition of reading. He currently is the principal investigator of the Multidisciplinary Learning Disability Center funded by NICHD.

Julie A. Washington, Ph.D., Professor, Department of Educational Psychology and Special Education, Georgia State University (GSU), Program in Communication Disorders; Atlanta, Georgia; jwashington@gsu.edu. Dr. Washington is also an affiliate faculty of GSU's Language and Literacy Initiative, a unique research initiative focused on the challenges of acquiring language and literacy. Her work focuses on understanding cultural dialect use in African American children, emphasizing language assessment, literacy attainment, and academic performance. Her work with preschoolers has focused on understanding and improving the emergent literacy skills necessary to support later reading proficiency in high-risk groups, with a focus on the needs of children growing up in poverty.

Donna Carlson Yerby, M.Ed., Educational Specialist, UNC; Chapel Hill, North Carolina; Donna.yerby@cidd.unc.edu. Ms. Yerby is involved in research, clinical evaluations, and outreach services at the Carolina Institute for Developmental Disabilities at the UNC School of Medicine. She taught Grades K–12 and was formerly a clinical instructor at the UNC School of Education. As Director of Professional Development at All Kinds of Minds Institute, she developed instructional materials for understanding learning differences and trained clinicians in dynamic assessment methods. Ms. Yerby has published and presented on learning disabilities, differentiation of instruction, postsecondary education initiatives, and educational reform.

Foreword

In September 2001, I launched a statewide reading effort, *Just Read, Florida!*, which had the man-on-the-moon goal of "all children reading on grade level or higher by 2012." This was a year after the National Reading Panel report was released, and as a data nerd, I was excited to have research to drive our reading reforms. The initiative was announced at Dover Shores Elementary School in Orlando, Florida, because then-Principal Irma Ross was doing some fantastic things to make reading a priority in her school. One of her approaches was to make sure that reading and writing instruction were intertwined.

While we did not achieve our man-on-the-moon goal in 2012, Florida students have made tremendous progress in reading. I have not given up on that goal for Florida's children—or America's children, for that matter. With the advent of the Common Core State Standards, we have the opportunity to reach beyond the moon when it comes to student learning. The English/Language Arts Common Core State Standards are focused on what matters: teaching our children how to be successful communicators so that they can compete globally. These standards shift the focus from developing a written response based on experiences—stories of how vacations were spent or question responses that can be lifted directly from text—to purposeful writing that is based on what students have read, using and synthesizing text evidence to support reasoning, and building and defending arguments.

How can we make sure that we have a nation of principals like Irma Ross, who focus on the reading–writing relationship to truly change education—from instruction to policies? As this edited volume underlines, research-based instruction is vital because teachers must be equipped with the best tools and methods. Technology must also be an integral component of both instruction and assessments. This volume helps illuminate the current status of the evidence base we do have, how technology might play a role, and what is still left undone in order to develop an even stronger evidence base for use in classrooms.

Several of the researchers that contributed to this volume are the same researchers whose work we used to craft Florida's reading policy in 2001. I am thrilled to know that this group continues to work on the most important skill a child can have—literacy.

Jeb Bush
Governor of Florida from 1999–2007 and
Chairman of the Foundation for Excellence in Education

Preface

Bridges—connecting structures that span between two places, often over something treacherous. They are carefully structured and engineered to absorb the demands of the traffic imposed on them throughout the day. They are made up of small parts and large parts, steel parts and cement parts, flexible parts and rigid parts. Yet each and every part of a design structure is essential to the function of the bridge. So if you were to ask the engineer which part of the bridge was essential or most important for the structure to be sound, the answer would be that they are *all* important because if any one piece—large or small—gives way, the structure weakens and eventually topples; they are inextricably linked. Such it is with reading and writing and the teacher's role in planning and implementing the curriculum. Both reading and writing are complex processes made up of various skills and components, but each piece—from a minilesson on word meaning or choice to a larger one on synthesizing texts—is absolutely essential to building a strong literacy foundation.

When we think of bridges, some terms come to mind that are analogous to the reading–writing connection. A *tower foundation* is the tall pier or frame supporting the cable of a suspension bridge. In terms of literacy, one of these towers is reading, and the other is writing. The relationship of these two structures has been pondered for years, yet for some reason, reading always seemed to be considered the more essential of the two. Now, for the first time, writing is standing tall and is not simply beside reading but is working synergistically with reading as a matching literacy partner, absorbing as much of the weight and responsibility. In order for these tower foundations to be equally strong, time must be allocated for explicit instruction in reading, and similarly, for instruction that is specific and intentional to writing.

The connection between reading and writing, the importance of instruction in both, and their reciprocal influences on one another have been the topics of a major panel activity sponsored in partnership by the International Reading Association (IRA) and the *Eunice Kennedy Shriver* National Institute of Child Health and Human Development (NICHD), which culminated in a summary document (International Reading Association & the *Eunice Kennedy Shriver* National Institute of Child Health and Human Development [IRA/NICHD], 2012) and now, fortunately, this edited volume. The relevance and timeliness of this work is heightened by what is happening in literacy education today.

The Common Core State Standards for English Language Arts (National Governors Association Center for Best Practices, Council of Chief State School Officers [NGA/CCSSO], 2010) is having a profound influence on today's literacy education, and reading and writing development forms an integral part of these standards. For the first time, these literacy partners are working together to support literacy learning that allows for the transfer of knowledge within and among all content areas. In the standards, reading is being used to advance writing and writing to enhance reading. For example, students discover the author's craft during reading that they then apply in their own writing; they use evidence of what they read to support what they write in both informational and argumentative texts; and they use writing to demonstrate understanding of what was read. Just as the cables connect two tower foundations, reading and writing are interwoven and connected as well.

Teachers responsible for the engineering of this new structure must plan for and build strong tower foundations through the explicit teaching of reading and writing, both independent of one another and as integrated subjects of instruction. Planning for the construction via explicit and well-formulated intentional lesson plans and then moving forward to install the cables that link these two foundations is a new challenge for teachers and may require time for them to build their own understanding of the reading–writing connection. This book provides detailed insights into many of the intricate parts of this connection with the following basic principles being essential elements necessary to maintaining a strong structure:

- Students must be immersed in literacy—lots and lots of reading and writing daily.

- Reading and writing must both be *taught*—students don't just "catch them."

- Strategies and skills of reading and writing must be taught explicitly—knowledge and process relationships made as concrete as possible.

- Instruction must be scaffolded—modeled, shared, and independent—all with an awareness of where each student is within the process.

- Students must talk about their reading and writing—accountable talk creates deeper meaning in the text being read or written.

- Students must be actively engaged in the process—students are drivers instead of passengers because reading and writing are "wide-awake" processes as opposed to passive ones.

- Students must read and write for different purposes—transporting different vehicles of text over the literacy bridge.

- Genre characteristics must be taught—knowing each genre helps guide the reading of text and helps writers include more appropriate details and evidence.

- Students need to read and write different kinds of texts—recognizing the unique characteristics of text helps a reader analyze and predict and helps a writer know what elements must be present.

- Vocabulary and the role words play in the process of reading or writing must be taught—words and their roles are important, as they help the reader "read between the lines" and help writers improve coherency.

- Critical thinking must be intentionally taught—reading and writing are thinking activities, and readers and writers need to see beyond the obvious.

These basic principles represent practices that have been used for some time in reading and in writing instruction but that can be even more effective when used in the simultaneous teaching of reading and writing. The chapters within this book further explore the intricacies of the reading–writing connection, each one making a statement of its own yet all integrally connected and addressing these principles.

Bridges—connecting structures made of various parts, all essential to the design and function. Reading and writing—complex processes made up of various skills and components, all essential to the development of literacy. Teachers—the engineers and construction workers on the job responsible for installing the cables that link the tower foundations of reading and writing and who customize literacy bridges in a way that will service students the best. This book—a vehicle of information to help guide teachers in their efforts to build strong literacy bridges of reading and writing that support academic achievement and life success.

Carrice Cummins
Former President, International Reading Association and
Professor of Curriculum, Instruction, and Leadership,
Louisiana Tech University

REFERENCES

International Reading Association & the *Eunice Kennedy Shriver* National Institute of Child Health and Human Development (IRA/NICHD). (2012). *The reading–writing connection.* Retrieved from http://www.reading.org/Libraries/resources/reading-writingconnection_final.pdf
National Governors Association Center for Best Practices & Council of Chief State School Officers (NGA/CCSSO). (2010). *Common core state standards: English/language arts standards.* Washington, DC: Authors.

Acknowledgments

We wish to acknowledge the dedication, commitment, and energy that our authors put into getting the chapters in this volume accomplished so well in so short a time and we offer a special thanks to those who served on the original panel that gave rise to this volume. All these individuals gave of their time and talents because they believe so strongly in the importance of creating a nation of truly literate children and youth who can read and write, enabling them to contribute to their schools and communities and to ultimately replace us all as the teachers, administrators, and researchers of the future—who will carry on the quest of making sure that teachers are well trained, that students are well educated, and that administrators are well informed about the needs of both students and teachers.

Thanks to those at the *Eunice Kennedy Shriver* National Institute of Child Health and Human Development and the International Reading Association who made possible the partnership under which our reading and writing panel was convened, for recognizing the importance of such relationships, and for making research accessible to educators who use it in classrooms.

We also must thank our wonderful editors at Paul H. Brookes Publishing, Sarah Shepke and Sarah Kendall, who guided, assisted, and encouraged us through the conceptualization and the realization of this volume. Thanks also to everyone at Paul H. Brookes Publishing behind the scenes—their production process made it possible for us to have this book in readers' hands much sooner than most anticipated. Working with all of them was terrific!

*Reading and writing are among the very few things that
we all do for work, that we also use functionally at home,
and that most of us are lucky enough to love doing when we are on
vacation! This volume is dedicated not only to today's teachers, education
administrators, and students but also to those of tomorrow and beyond. May
this book contribute to helping them ensure that more children and youth learn to
read and write and that all come to love these activities, in both their work and their play.*

1

Introduction

Brett Miller, Peggy McCardle, and Richard Long

Both reading and writing development begin in early childhood and are linked in daily function and in classroom activities from prekindergarten and kindergarten through high school and beyond. They form an integral part of the now widely adopted Common Core State Standards (CCSS) for English Language Arts (National Governors Association Center for Best Practices & Council of Chief State School Officers, 2010). Reading has been recognized as an essential ability for all school children, and reading instruction has been a longstanding key focus of instruction in the early grades. The focus on writing instruction is more recent, but increasingly, *literacy* means both reading and writing. In addition, changes in early childhood education have resulted in a greater emphasis on early literacy development that includes oral language development, reading, and writing. An expanded emphasis on graduation rates also resulted in a greater emphasis on both reading and writing in middle and high school. But the reciprocal influences and the critical interface between reading and writing have been less well recognized. Although few would argue with the claim that reading and writing are related in important ways, there is little research addressing that relationship or when and how best to integrate these two critical areas instructionally.

In 2012, a panel of individuals with expertise in reading, writing, instruction, intervention, assessment, and research methods was convened under a partnership activity of the International Reading Association (IRA) and the *Eunice Kennedy Shriver* National Institute of Child Health and Human Development (NICHD) to discuss these topics. To be able to focus on the connection between reading and writing, rather than on how each person defined the two, it was agreed that they would define these two terms simply, a priori: *Reading* was defined as the ability to decode written text quickly and accurately and to comprehend what is read; *writing* was defined as the ability to produce connected text (sentences, paragraphs, and documents)—either by handwriting or by keyboarding—that communicates an idea or information. The results of that discussion are published in a summary document, *The Reading–Writing Connection* (IRA/NICHD, 2012). The widespread interest in delving more deeply into this topic led the group to propose an edited volume to lay out in much greater detail what we know in order to assist educators in addressing these areas within the CCSS and other initiatives as well as to explore the potential for productive additional research.

A substantial body of research on reading has existed for some time—its components, instruction, and intervention—and was documented more than a decade ago in two national reports focused primarily on K–3 but with some studies ranging into middle school–age students (Snow, Burns, & Griffin, 1998; NICHD, 2000). More recently, researchers have also been studying the effects of reading instruction and intervention for older students (preadolescent and adolescent as well as young adult). While intervening at these ages is more challenging, there have been some noteworthy successes (e.g., Calhoon, 2005; Edmonds et al., 2009; Vaughn et al., 2011).

For writing and writing instruction, there is less research, but there are some promising findings. Recent studies and syntheses examining both instruction and remediation have revealed aspects of intervention that have improved both the quality and quantity of student writing (e.g., Graham & Perin, 2007; Rogers & Graham, 2008; Sandmel & Graham, 2011) and the potential positive impact of writing instruction on reading comprehension (Fitzgerald & Shanahan, 2000; Graham & Hebert, 2010, 2011; Moats, 2005/2006; Neville & Searls, 1991; Tierney & Shanahan, 1991). Reading and writing exhibit interesting similarities; both require some depth of vocabulary knowledge (including word-internal morphology and meaning in context), grammatical knowledge (including complex sentence structure and usage), and genre knowledge. Successful writing and reading are both complex skill sets that require extensive self-regulation of flexible, goal-directed, problem-solving activities and the ability to effectively use strategies (e.g., Harris, Graham, Brindle, & Sandmel, 2009).

In this volume, authors—many of whom served on that initial panel—with expertise in reading, writing, instruction, intervention, assessment, and research methods provide insights into what is known about the interactions of reading and writing and what instructional approaches seem most promising. The volume presents these authors' thinking on instructional issues, technology, and assessment approaches. The three chapters in Section 1, *The Basis*, address how we currently approach reading and writing instruction. Connor

What is the nature of the connection between the two interrelated disciplines of reading and writing? This is the basic question that the panel convened by the IRA and NICHD explored. The panel developed a series of recommendations as to the nature of the reading and writing connection that reflected a wide range of disciplines. Among the key findings are the following five:

1. Reading has received more research attention than writing.
2. There is a significant need for more research on how and when to teach reading and writing together.
3. Most elementary-school writing instruction is focused on story writing. More attention needs to be given to persuasive and expository writing.
4. There is a need for an enhanced focus on the development of assessments examining common and unique skills that contribute to reading and writing in order to inform instruction.
5. While technology is a significant part of instruction, research is needed on the reading and writing connection that is specific to the use of technology.

Overall, the panel found that there is a need to understand reading and writing both as separate and as integrated endeavors.

To access the panel's document, go to http://www.reading.org/Libraries/resources/reading-writingconnection_final.pdf

and colleagues (Chapter 2) and Costa and colleagues (Chapter 3) offer parallel chapters addressing the reading–writing connection from the reading and writing sides, respectively, whereas the team of Harris and Graham (Chapter 4) tackle both reading and writing and the history behind the relative disparity of attention that has been given to writing.

In Section 2, *Applying What We Know,* authors discuss applying what is already known and how this might be used as schools move forward to implement the CCSS. McCardle and Miller (Chapter 5) first tackle the issue of what we know and how we know it—what actually constitutes an evidence base and when that evidence can and should be used in practice. The chapter reviews past major sources of evidence as well as efforts that have been made to move that evidence to practice and discusses what should guide instruction in the classroom when sufficient, solid evidence does not exist. The next chapters in this section cover professional development and how reading and writing instructional practices are taught, with thoughts on directions for better preparing teachers to integrate reading and writing in their classrooms to better address the CCSS (Brenner, Chapter 6); the role of linguistic differences, including nonmainstream dialect and English as a second language, and how these factors have an impact on reading and writing (Washington and colleagues, Chapter 7); and the use of reasoning and analytic ability for interpreting texts and for presenting information and ideas orally and in writing, skills emphasized in the CCSS (Carlisle and colleagues, Chapter 8). Urbani and colleagues (Chapter 9) discuss what is known about project-based learning, reading, and writing across the disciplines and how these may relate to implementation of the CCSS. Finally, Strickland (Chapter 10) discusses efforts to integrate literacy activities into the CCSS and cautions about the application and potential misapplication of evidence in classrooms.

This book is not only about reading and writing but also about the intersection or connection between reading and writing. With this in mind, Section 3, *Preparing for Change,* as its title clearly indicates, addresses the intersection of theory, measurement, and technology with instruction as they relate to the intersection of reading and writing. Gorin and colleagues (Chapter 11) address measurement, including both formative and summative assessment as well as the possibility of integrating both reading and writing assessment into research and instruction. Technology has become omnipresent in life both inside and outside the classroom. Atwill and Blanchard (Chapter 12) tell us how technology can be used to enhance reading and writing and project where they think the field of educational technology is heading, and ramifications that current and future technologies have for classroom practice. In the last chapter in this section, Ahmed, Kim, and Wagner (Chapter 13) explain how models of reading and writing can elucidate the connections between reading and writing and why this should be important to teachers.

In the final chapter, we offer some thoughts that emerged during discussions with our panel and in broader discussions with the field through town hall meetings and presentations at association meetings about issues to consider in moving the field toward more fully understanding the nature and importance of the reading–writing connection, as well as summarizing areas for future research.

REFERENCES

Calhoon, M.B. (2005). Effects of a peer-mediated phonological skill and reading comprehension program on reading skill acquisition of middle school students with reading disabilities. *Journal of Learning Disabilities, 38*(5), 424–433.

Edmonds, M.S., Vaughn, S., Wexler, J., Reutebuch, E.K., Cable, A., Tackett, K.K., & Schnakenberg, J.W. (2009). A synthesis of reading interventions and effects on reading comprehension outcomes for older struggling readers. *Review of Educational Research, 79*(1), 262–300. doi:10.3102/00346543025998

Fitzgerald, J., & Shanahan, T. (2000). Reading and writing relations and their development. *Educational Psychologist, 35*(1), 39–50.

Graham, S., & Hebert, H. (2010). *Writing to read: Evidence for how writing can improve reading* [A report from the Carnegie Corporation of New York]. Washington, DC: Alliance for Excellent Education.

Graham, S., & Hebert, M. (2011). Writing to read: A meta-analysis of the impact of writing and writing instruction on reading. *Harvard Educational Review, 81*(4), 710–744.

Graham, S., & Perin, D. (2007). *Writing next: Effective strategies to improve writing of adolescents in middle and high schools* [A report from the Carnegie Corporation of New York]. Washington, DC: Alliance for Excellent Education.

Harris, K.R., Graham, S., Brindle, M., & Sandmel, K. (2009). Metacognition and children's writing. In D. Hacker, J. Dunlosky, & A. Graesser (Eds.), *Handbook of metacognition in education* (pp. 131–153). Mahwah, NJ: Erlbaum.

International Reading Association (IRA) & the *Eunice Kennedy Shriver* National Institute of Child Health and Human Development (NICHD). (2012). *The reading-writing connection.* Retrieved from http://www.reading.org/Libraries/resources/reading-writingconnection_final.pdf

Moats, L. (2005/2006). How spelling supports reading: And why it is more regular and predictable than you may think. *American Educator,* Winter, 12–22, 42–43.

National Governors Association Center for Best Practices & Council of Chief State School Officers. (2010). *Common Core State Standards: English language arts standards.* Washington, DC: Authors.

National Institute of Child Health and Human Development (NICHD). (2000). *Report of the National Reading Panel. Teaching children to read: An evidence-based assessment of the scientific research literature on reading and its implications for reading instruction: Reports of the subgroups.* (NIH Publication No. 00-4754.) Washington, DC: U.S. Government Printing Office.

Neville, D., & Searls, E. (1991). A meta-analytic review of the effects of sentence-combining on reading comprehension. *Reading Research and Instruction, 31,* 63–76.

Rogers, L., & Graham, S. (2008). A meta-analysis of single subject design writing intervention research. *Journal of Educational Psychology, 100,* 879–906.

Sandmel, K., & Graham, S. (2011). The process writing approach: A meta-analysis. *Journal of Educational Research, 104,* 396–407.

Snow, C., Burns, S., & Griffin, P. (Eds.). (1998). *Preventing reading difficulties in young children.* Washington, DC: National Academies Press.

Tierney, R., & Shanahan, T. (1991). Research on the reading-writing relationship: Interactions, transactions, and outcomes. In R. Barr, M. Kamil, P. Mosenthal, & D. Pearson (Eds.), *The handbook of reading research* (Vol. 2; pp. 246–280). New York, NY: Longman.

Vaughn, S., Wexler, J., Leroux, A.J., Roberts, G., Denton, C.A., Barth, A.E., & Fletcher, J.M. (2011). Effects of intensive reading intervention for eighth-grade students with persistently inadequate response to intervention. *Journal of Learning Disabilities, 45,* 515–525. doi: 10.1177/0022219411402692

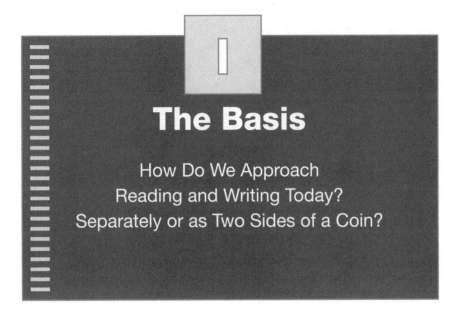

I

The Basis

How Do We Approach
Reading and Writing Today?
Separately or as Two Sides of a Coin?

The Reading Side

Carol McDonald Connor, Sarah Ingebrand, and Jennifer Dombek

There has been increasing recognition among reading researchers and practitioners that writing has been largely ignored as a topic for either research or instruction and that this is a serious lacuna (Mehta, Foorman, Branum-Martin, & Taylor, 2005; National Institute of Child Health and Human Development [NICHD], 2000; Parodi, 2007; Snow, 2001; Tierney & Shanahan, 1991). At the same time, reading research and practice have explicitly or implicitly included writing for both assessment (e.g., responses to open-ended questions to test comprehension) and instruction (e.g., graphic organizers, summarizing across texts). For example, the National Assessment of Educational Progress (NAEP; 2011), considered the gold standard for assessing literacy, incorporates questions that require students to provide a written response to exhibit their understanding of passages they read. Thus students' reading and writing abilities are conflated in the national test results, which show that almost one third of fourth-grade students fail to achieve basic levels of literacy. This percentage is even higher for children living in poverty or who come from certain racial/ethnic groups. What is less clear is whether the lack of proficiency has more to do with weak writing skills than with weak reading comprehension skills and how much of the effect is reciprocal.

Although reading and writing instruction have been treated rather separately in the past, as the Common Core State Standards (CCSS) are adopted across states, there will be increasing focus on students' ability to understand *and* generate coherent text. The mission statement of the CCSS reads,

> The standards are designed to be robust and relevant to the real world, reflecting the knowledge and skills that our young people need for success in college and careers. With American students fully prepared for the future, our communities will be best positioned to compete successfully in the global economy. (http://www.corestandards.org)

Indeed, reading–writing connections are typified in the introduction of the "Reading: Foundation Skills" portion of the CCSS. The description states, "These standards are

We thank the Individualizing Student Instruction (ISI) and Reading for Understanding (RFU) project teams and the children, parents, teachers, and school participants. Funding was provided by the *Eunice Kennedy Shriver* National Institute of Child Health and Human Development (NICHD): R01HD48539 and P50 HD052120; and the U.S. Department of Education, Institute of Education Sciences: R305F1000027, R305H04013, and R305B070074.

directed toward fostering students' understanding and working knowledge of concepts of print, the alphabetic principle, and *other basic conventions of the English writing system*" [emphasis added] (National Governors Association Center for Best Practices, Council of Chief State School Officers, 2010, p. 15). Whereas this set of skills is listed as a major component of the reading standards, the introduction reveals the overall goal focuses not simply on basic reading skills but also on understanding and learning about writing concepts while reading. It is likely that these standards will serve to encourage a more symbiotic connection between reading and writing instruction.

In this chapter, we first review research that explicitly considers the reading–writing connection, the construct of literacy, and whether writing is part of or separate from reading. Then we explore instruction in early elementary grades and its impact on reading comprehension and writing by presenting data from our ongoing research on individualized literacy instruction and the types of writing instruction that are observed during the dedicated block of time devoted to reading instruction in first and third grade. We also examine the role of writing in reading instruction and in teachers' beliefs regarding reading and writing instruction as a possible explanation for the variability in writing instruction observed across classrooms.

READING AND WRITING: ONE CONSTRUCT OR SEPARATE CONSTRUCTS?

Accumulating research reveals the reciprocal nature of the reading–writing connection. Skills gained in one area have the potential to support the development of the skills in the other and vice versa (Abbot & Berninger, 1993; Fitzgerald & Shanahan, 2000; Shanahan, 2006). Reading and writing development arguably depend on the similar knowledge domains (Shanahan, 2006). *Content or domain knowledge* about the topic being read or written about can greatly aid a reader's and writer's ability to successfully complete tasks because prior knowledge provides a starting point from which to make connections to new information. *Metaknowledge* about reading and writing—that is, knowledge about the purpose of reading and writing, which includes such features as the author's purpose—may aid readers and writers in understanding the role of written language. *Knowledge of written language*—specifically areas such as phonological knowledge, syntactic knowledge, morphological knowledge, and semantic knowledge—can aid the reader in decoding and comprehending text and the writer in spelling words and conveying meaning by creating a comprehensible text. Finally, *procedural knowledge*, which includes "knowing how to use, access, and generate information during reading and writing" (Shanahan, 2006, p. 176), is critical to both reading and writing success. Moreover, the nature of reading–writing connections appears to change over time (Shanahan, 1984). For younger students, spelling and decoding provide important links between reading and writing. Then, as students' reading skills become more proficient, sophisticated vocabulary and story structure become more important to writing achievement.

There are a number of theoretical models proposed for understanding reading and writing connections. For example, Shanahan and Lomax (1986, 1989) compared three theoretical models of the reading–writing relationship: the interactive model, the reading-to-writing model, and the writing-to-reading model. The interactive model allows for a reciprocal connection between reading and writing skills, whereas the reading-to-writing and writing-to-reading models propose one-way directional connections. Testing these models revealed that the interactive model fit the reading and writing data better than did the reading-to-writing model for second grade and better than the writing-to-reading model for both second and fifth grades.

Notably, the writing-to-reading model was a better fit for the data than the reading-to-writing model (Shanahan & Lomax, 1988). The authors note that "significant knowledge transfer takes place in both directions, even at relatively low levels of literacy attainment" (p. 208).

Given this clear evidence of reading–writing reciprocal and inclusive connections, a key question among researchers is whether writing is an integral part of the construct of literacy or a separate but related construct. Although reading researchers have tended to define literacy more narrowly, broadly defined, literacy can apply to any number of capabilities—computer literacy, economic literacy, and so forth—with the implication that literacy includes developing knowledge and skills that support learning (Morrison, Bachman, & Connor, 2005). Literacy within this broader definition should clearly include writing. However, one consideration when deliberating about reading and writing research and practice is whether writing is part of the multidimensional construct of literacy when more narrowly defined. Although, as reviewed earlier, there are a number of studies that show high correlations among students' reading and writing skills (see also Vellutino, Tunmer, Jaccard, Chen, & Scanlon, 2004), this does not necessarily mean that reading and writing are the same thing; there is ongoing debate in the field.

For example, Mehta and colleagues (Mehta et al., 2005) used multilevel, multitrait analyses to examine whether writing was part of the construct of literacy and how classroom instruction had an impact on the components of literacy, including writing; these authors define literacy as a "multifaceted phenomenon that includes numerous dynamically evolving components including phonological awareness, word recognition, spelling, reading comprehension and writing" (p. 88). This analytic strategy allowed them to examine literacy at the classroom level and at the individual student level, simultaneously using data from a large sample of children attending higher-poverty schools. They found that at both student and classroom levels, writing was an integral part of literacy but that it was loaded less strongly than the other components of literacy included in the model, including spelling. These investigators concluded that literacy *is* a unitary construct that includes writing. The second finding, however, suggested more dimensionality at the classroom level; they found that the quality of teaching that students received *did* predict students' writing outcomes but *not* their phonological awareness, word recognition, spelling, or reading comprehension. There are a number of possible reasons for this finding. It might be that writing is more responsive to instruction than the other components of literacy, which would tend to suggest that writing is somehow different from the other components. It may be that the malleability of the components changes over time as students become more proficient readers and, hence, instructional effects change as well. Another explanation not considered by the authors is that there was more variability in the amounts and quality of writing instruction than in the instruction targeting the other components. In other words, virtually all students received sufficient instruction in the other literacy components, but some students did not receive sufficient writing instruction where others did, and this variability in instruction predicted variability in writing outcomes.

This interpretation is in line with other observations that there is not much explicit writing instruction taking place in classrooms during the time typically devoted to literacy instruction but that this varies tremendously across teachers (Ingebrand, Snyder, & Connor, in review). For example, in a report by Applebee and Langer (2006), NAEP results revealed that, in 2005, almost 50% of eighth graders spent anywhere from 11% to 40% of their time in language arts class on writing, according to their teachers. Eleven percent spent less than that. If we figure that a typical eighth-grade language arts block is 60 minutes long, that means teachers reported anywhere from 6 minutes to 24 minutes spent in writing instruction. Moreover, from 2002 to 2005, there was a small decrease in the amount of time devoted to writing. This is important because the researchers also found that, for the 2002 data, students who reported writing at least "a few times per year" or more had stronger writing scores than did students who reported that they "never or hardly ever" wrote during language arts (p. 9). These results are also in line with surveys conducted by Graham and Harris (2009).

WRITING DURING THE "READING BLOCK"

With the passage of No Child Left Behind (PL 107-110), there was increasing focus on using research-based practices to teach reading in the early elementary grades (U.S. Department of Education, 2004), with an important focus on teaching children the alphabetic principle and how to decode text fluently (Adams, 2001; NICHD, 2000). As part of Reading First, many schools began to utilize a daily block of time devoted solely to reading instruction and activities, based on evidence from a series of "beat-the-odds" studies about schools where many students achieved stronger reading skills than might be expected given school demographics, including poverty (Wharton-McDonald, Pressley, & Hampston, 1998). From 2005 to 2011, we conducted a series of randomized controlled trials testing whether child characteristics interacting with instruction (characteristic X instruction interactions) were causally implicated in students' varying response to kindergarten through third-grade literacy instruction (i.e., individualizing student instruction [ISI]; Connor, 2011; Connor et al., in press). As part of these studies, we recorded the amounts and types of instruction each student received during the literacy block, including writing instruction (Connor, Morrison, et al., 2009; Ingebrand et al., in review).

Here we discuss findings from our first- and third-grade studies, conducted in 2006 through 2007 ($n = 202$ first graders) and 2008 through 2009 ($n = 338$ third graders) of students who attended 25 different classrooms scattered across 7 different schools. The schools served an economically and ethnically diverse student body with about half the students qualifying for the U.S. Free and Reduced Lunch program, a widely used indicator of poverty. About 50% of the students were White and about 40% were African American; the remaining belonged to other ethnicities. One hundred of the students were in both first- and third-grade samples. Students' literacy skills were assessed in the fall and spring of each year and included decoding, word reading, reading comprehension, expressive vocabulary, and writing fluency (Woodcock, McGrew, & Mather, 2001) in first and third grade, with the addition of the Gates-MacGinitie reading tests (GMRT) in third grade (MacGinitie, MacGinitie, Maria, & Dreyer, 2000). Using hierarchical linear modeling (HLM; Raudenbush & Bryk, 2002), because students were nested in classrooms, we found that students' fall reading comprehension, expressive vocabulary, and writing fluency skills significantly predicted their spring writing fluency in first grade (see Table 2.1). Notably, there was no

Table 2.1. First-grade hierarchical linear modeling (HLM) results predicting spring writing fluency (WF) W scores

	Coefficient	SE (df)	P-value
Fitted mean spring WF	471.67	.85 (24)	< .001
Fall passage comprehension	.255	.07 (173)	< .001
Fall picture vocabulary	.269	.10 (173)	.007
Fall writing fluency	.424	.06 (173)	< .001

Note: W scores, computed from raw scores, are similar to Rasch scores and have equal intervals so they can show score gains.

significant classroom level variability. HLM results, however, differed for third grade (see Table 2.2). In third grade, both fall reading comprehension measures predicted writing fluency, but expressive vocabulary did not. Moreover, there was significant classroom level variance. These results support other study findings on the interdependence of reading comprehension and writing and how associations among components change as children develop more proficient literacy skills.

But what was the impact of writing instruction on students' outcomes? The ISI coding system (Connor, Morrison, et al., 2009) examines the instruction individual students receive across three dimensions: 1) grouping—whole class, small group, and one-on-one; 2) role of the teacher—teachers interacting with students (teacher/child-managed [TCM]) or students working independently or with peers (child-managed [CM]); and 3) content of instruction. These dimensions operated simultaneously to define the various types of literacy instruction observed (see Table 2.3 for instructions defined by grouping and role of the teacher). (For examples of types of writing instruction coded, contact the corresponding author.) Classrooms were observed and videotaped in the fall, winter, and spring. Coding was conducted in the laboratory directly from the video using Noldus Observer Pro software.

Using this conceptualization, we examined the amounts of writing instruction observed during the 90-minute literacy blocks with instruction measured in minutes per day. In first grade, the amount of writing instruction increased overall from fall to spring, with the amount of CM writing (both peer and independent) increasing and the amount of TCM whole class instruction decreasing from fall to spring (see Figure 2.1). However,

Table 2.2. Third-grade hierarchical linear modeling results predicting writing fluency (WF) W scores including the Gates-MacGinitie Reading Tests—Reading Comprehension (GMRT-RC)

	Coefficient	SE (df)	P-value
Fitted mean spring WF	495.43	.58 (30)	< .001
Fall passage comprehension	.103	.06 (314)	< .001
Fall picture vocabulary	−.049	.043 (314)	.260
Fall writing fluency	.365	.051 (314)	< .001
GMRT-RC	.048	.012 (314)	< .001

Classroom level variance = 3.61, p = .043.

Table 2.3. Types of instruction observed across grouping and teacher-role dimensions

Writing instruction (whole-class instruction)
- **Teacher/child managed:** Teacher is actively interacting with children and providing guidance in how to write
- **Child/peer managed:** Children are writing independently or working with peers.

Small group
- **Teacher/child managed:** Teacher is working with a small group of children
- **Child/peer managed:** Peer-managed

Individual
- **Teacher/child managed:** One-to-one writing instruction
- **Child/peer managed:** Independent

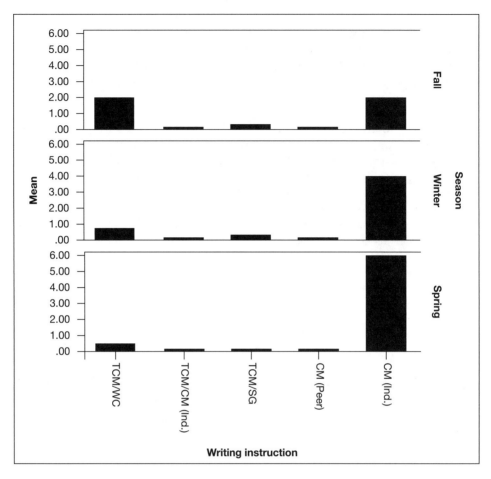

Figure 2.1. First-grade writing instruction (mins/day) out of the 90-minute literacy block for teacher-child managed (TCM), whole-class (WC), small-group (SG), peer, and child-managed (CM) writing instruction.

overall amounts were quite modest, with only about 4 minutes per day observed in the fall and 6 minutes per day in the spring. Moreover, the range of amount observed was wide, with some teachers providing substantial time for writing opportunities (about 25 minutes) and some providing none at all. In addition, the amount of time students spent in writing activities represented only 4% of the instructional time in the fall, 5% in the winter, and 7% in the spring.

In third grade, the picture did not improve. Far less of the 90-minute literacy block was devoted to writing with only about 3 minutes in the fall (3%), 3.5 minutes in the winter, and less than a minute per day on average (1%) in the spring (see Figure 2.2). Again, there was a substantial amount of variability both within and across classrooms, with some teachers never observed providing writing instruction during the literacy block. Moreover, unlike first grade, where the opportunities for writing increased from fall to spring, there was a marked reduction in writing during the spring of third grade (perhaps because the focus was on preparing for the state-mandated tests, which did not include any writing).

In first grade, writing instruction significantly and positively predicted students' gains (residual change) in writing fluency (see Figure 2.3). Specifically, the more first graders

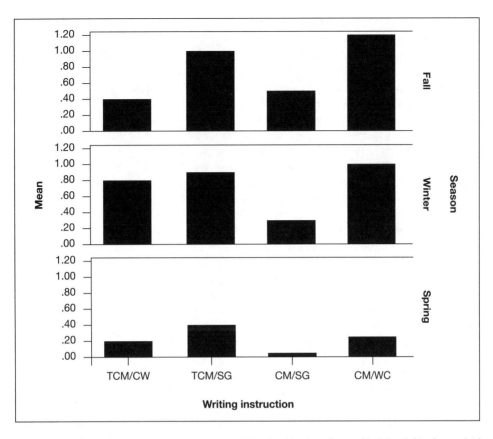

Figure 2.2. Third-grade writing instruction observed during the 90-minute literacy block in min/day for teacher/child-managed (TCM), whole-class (WC), small-group (SG), and child/peer-managed (CM) writing instruction.

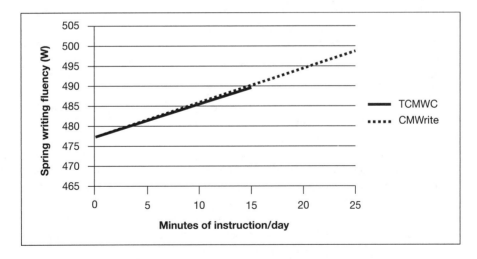

Figure 2.3. Hierarchical linear modeling results examining the effect of first-grade writing instruction on spring writing fluency W scores controlling for fall writing fluency. Specifically teacher/child-managed, whole-class writing instruction (TCM/WC) and child-managed writing instruction (CM).

participated in TCM whole-class (WC) writing instruction as well as CM opportunities to write independently, the greater were their gains in writing fluency. These effects were large, comparing children who received 0 minutes per day (25th percentile for the sample) versus more (the 75th percentile for the sample; TCM WC d = 1.4; CM Write d = .8).

Moreover, the more one-to-one time students spent with their teacher in writing instruction, the stronger were their reading comprehension gains (d = .4). This is similar to the size of the effects reported in the meta-analysis conducted by Graham and Hebert (2011). The observed amount of this instruction ranged only from 0 to about 2 minutes per day (the 75th percentile of the sample), suggesting the potentially powerful effect of such individualized writing instructional strategies. We conjectured that, because the more time first-grade (and third-grade) students spent in small group, TCM meaning-focused activities (e.g., discussion, text reading, comprehension activities), the greater were their reading comprehension gains (Connor et al., 2011; Connor, Piasta, et al., 2009), we might find similar results for gains in writing fluency. However, time spent in small group, TCM meaning-focused instruction did not predict first graders' writing fluency gains. In addition, when we examined the relation of other components of literacy instruction (comprehension, oral language, phonological awareness, morphological, fluency, etc.) to spring writing, we found no significant correlations except morpheme instruction, which was negatively correlated (r = −.143, p = .036). Thus we see some specificity with regard to writing-instruction effects on writing fluency (that writing instruction predicts writing skill gains) as well as more widespread effects of writing instruction, which predicts both reading comprehension and writing fluency gains.

We (Ingebrand et al., in review) investigated third-grade writing instruction with the ISI sample using a more complex model of writing, adapting models presented by Flower and Hayes (1981; Hayes & Flower, 1987). The Flower and Hayes model is among the most influential models of writing instruction. In this recursive model, students work through phases that include planning, instruction, composing (i.e., writing), revising, and publishing. Notably, reading is implicitly woven into the iterative process of composing, particularly during the revising and editing stage, when students reread what they have written, evaluate it, and then revise their text. We added the role of the teacher into this model by distinguishing when the teachers were interacting with students (TCM) and when students were working independently (CM; see Figure 2.4). Even averaged across the school year, only modest amounts of writing instruction were observed (about 6% of the literacy block) with most of the opportunities in either direct instruction (TCM instruction) or independent writing (CM writing) with substantial variability both within and between classrooms.

When we examined whether amounts during each phase of writing instruction predicted third-grade writing fluency, we found that TCM revising/editing positively predicted writing fluency gains (see Figure 2.5), which was considered part of TCM instruction in the first-grade analyses. However, unlike first grade, simply providing students with opportunities to write did not predict gains in writing fluency. Surprisingly, the more time students spent with their teacher in TCM planning, the smaller were their writing fluency gains. It is not clear why TCM planning was negatively associated with students' writing outcomes, because other studies clearly indicate that such planning can strengthen students' writing skills. It may be because so very little planning was observed, and when it was, it was primarily in the fall. It might also be the generally poor quality of the planning activities. For example, one teacher was observed simply asking students what they were going to write about (e.g., *what animal are you going to write about?*) and did not provide any

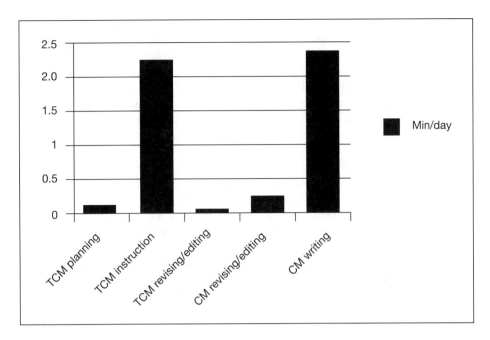

Figure 2.4. Mean writing instruction amounts in minutes per day for teacher/child-managed (TCM) planning, instruction, revising/editing, and child/peer-managed (CM) revising/editing and writing.

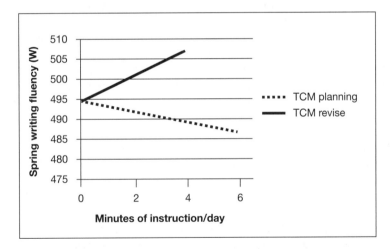

Figure 2.5. Spring third-grade writing fluency as a function of fall writing fluency and writing instruction types including teacher/child-managed (TCM) planning and TCM revising/editing.

guidance with regard to expanding their ideas (one-word responses were accepted without comment), organizing their thoughts, or structuring their essays. In contrast, the TCM revising/editing observation related directly to the text students had written with a focus on reading the text they generated, improving and expanding their ideas, improving sentence construction, and organizing their essays.

In contrast to first grade, none of the third-grade variables predicted students' reading comprehension gains. Nor did time spent in small group, TCM meaning-focused instruction significantly predict gains in writing fluency. Of note, virtually all the writing observed was narrative writing in response to a prompt, which is similar in structure to the state-mandated writing assessment students take the following year in fourth grade.

There are a number of possible reasons why so little writing instruction was observed during the first- and third-grade literacy blocks. First, these results are based on direct observation rather than teacher or student reports (e.g., Applebee & Langer, 2006; Graham & Harris, 2009). Next, it might have been an artifact of the coding system we used. Content was coded based on the focus of the instruction, so only instruction that was explicitly intended to improve students' writing skills was coded as a writing activity. That means that writing in the service of learning spelling (e.g., putting spelling words in a sentence), vocabulary (writing definitions of words), and comprehension (writing a summary of a book just read) would not have been coded as writing instruction but would have been coded as word encoding, vocabulary, or comprehension, respectively. Thus there was likely a good amount of writing happening that was not captured with this system.

Indeed, in two separate reading-for-understanding interventions that we developed—one for content-area literacy, the Content Area Literacy Instruction intervention (CALI; Connor et al., 2010), and the other to improve students' awareness of non-mainstream dialects, the Dialect Awareness Study intervention (DAWS; Connor & Lonigan, 2012)—writing was an integral part of these multicomponent literacy interventions. For example, in the DAWS intervention, second through fourth graders who used either African American English or Southern Vernacular English were randomly assigned to a business-as-usual control or to receive the DAWS intervention. DAWS was designed to bring the largely unconscious ability to shift between mainstream School English and nonmainstream Home English to students' conscious awareness by using the analogy of formal clothing (e.g., what they would wear to a wedding) versus informal clothing (what they might wear at home or to play with friends). They were also taught to edit Home English to School English when writing, with the understanding that School English was nearly always expected in writing texts (e.g., story characters might use Home English in dialog, but then it would be in quotes) but might not necessarily be expected in conversations.

Results revealed that students who received the DAWS intervention were better able to edit Home English to School English and used substantially less nonmainstream dialect in an open-prompt writing task compared with students in the control group. We hypothesized that, by improving students' awareness of Home versus School English, we would improve their reading comprehension indirectly through greater awareness of the morphological system of School English (a component of oral language). We also found a direct effect on reading comprehension, which we conjectured was related to the emphasis on writing as the context for building dialect awareness. This illustrates that, directly and indirectly, writing instruction may support better comprehension and that many teachers may be providing reading instruction that incorporates writing even if they do not think of this instruction as writing instruction. This observation is supported by other studies. For example, the meta-analysis by Graham and Hebert (2011) revealed that four types of writing activities supported comprehension, including summary writing, notetaking, and generating and answering questions.

Another reason teachers might not provide as much instruction in writing during the literacy block is because of their beliefs and understanding about the reading–writing connection. A teacher's influence over classroom instruction hinges partially in his or her own beliefs about the subjects he or she is teaching. These personal beliefs can manifest themselves in a number of ways, including classroom instruction and skill assessment. For example, calling the dedicated block of time devoted to literacy the "reading block" may unconsciously instill the belief that reading—and not writing—is taught during this time. In addition, teachers who do not feel like adequate readers or writers themselves are less likely to focus on instruction in the area in which they feel less competent (Applegate & Applegate, 2004). With regard to assessment, when teachers are required to assess a student's abilities, their primary focus will likely be on areas they consider most important. For example, teachers might consider reading comprehension—not writing—to be the goal of literacy instruction and thus may develop their assessments and instructional activities around this belief (Brindley & Schneider, 2002; Brooks, 2007).

Teachers often have very strong opinions relating to their classrooms and lessons. This emotional attachment can make them resistant to change, even when introducing evidence-based literacy curricula, particularly in writing (Wiebe Berry, 2006). Brindely and Schneider (2002) interviewed fourth-grade teachers to gain insight into how teachers' beliefs and personal abilities as readers and writers might affect their teaching. They found that teachers had a tendency to be empathetic toward students about the areas with which they personally struggled, including writing, and did not always demand that their students work hard to improve their skills in these areas. The teachers' responses also revealed a tendency to assume that students had learning styles similar to their own. Teachers gravitated toward activities that made sense to them, which, if they were uncomfortable with writing, meant fewer writing learning opportunities.

Researchers conducted interviews to more directly gauge how teachers decided which aspects of the writing process to focus on during instruction. This type of data collection can also illuminate how teachers' personal opinions and experiences with writing may influence how they view the writing process as a whole (Brooks, 2007; Wiebe Berry, 2006). For example, some teachers felt that the purpose of writing instruction was to present writing as a highly structured process. These teachers used explicit instruction and concrete writing tools that presented writing as a step-by-step process fairly divorced from reading. Other teachers felt that the purpose of writing instruction was to provide students with a communication tool rather than a specific skill set. These teachers emphasized creativity and more abstract writing concepts in their instruction.

Another reason teachers may not focus on writing is that it is difficult to evaluate writing quality, whereas there are many formative assessments for components of reading (Graham, Harris, & Hebert, 2011). For example, studies have shown that a fairly accurate reflection of students' writing abilities can be obtained by collecting multiple samples of a student's work, allowing him or her to compose the writing sample in whatever form he or she prefers (computer or hand written), and minimizing any unintentional bias due to misspellings or handwriting legibility. Unfortunately, most teachers do not implement these practices. Taken together, these findings present emerging evidence that, when teachers do not consider writing to be part of the construct of literacy or misunderstand reading–writing connections, they are much less likely to incorporate writing into their literacy instruction. With implementation of the CCSS and wider dissemination of research on reading–writing connections, hopefully more teachers will understand the importance of writing instruction in the context of literacy instruction and begin to implement more effective instruction.

CONCLUSIONS

Whether explicit or not, writing is an integral part of reading instruction and assessment, particularly for reading comprehension. Indeed, the tasks of reading and writing can never be fully separated. As we have discussed, literacy assessments require students to write about what they have just read. Even when the task is "pure" writing, writers read what they have just written. In fact, better writers use particular patterns of reading what they write; better writers are more likely than weaker writers to read at the point of inscription and to read recently composed sentences than are less proficient writers (Beers, Quinlan, & Harbaugh, 2010). Plus, many multicomponent reading interventions incorporate writing activities. This helps to explain why, when tested empirically, reading and writing might be considered to comprise one multidimensional construct, *literacy* (Mehta et al., 2005; Shanahan, 2006; Shanahan & Lomax, 1989).

At the same time, writing acquisition appears to be more influenced by high-quality instruction than other components of reading, such as spelling and decoding. As discussed, this may be for a number of reasons—writing instruction might be more variable, the skill of writing might be more malleable, or writing might be somehow different from other components of literacy. Our results also suggest that simply providing meaning-focused instruction (e.g., discussion, text reading) without a specific emphasis on writing does not predict writing outcomes. Taking all this together, from a reading perspective, writing can certainly be considered an integral part of literacy. The more teachers understand the reading–writing connection, the more likely writing is to be part of effective literacy instruction. Ongoing research on the role of writing as a means to stronger literacy skills and on improving writing outcomes will be increasingly important for ensuring that all students meet the CCSS and are college and career ready.

REFERENCES

Abbot, R.D., & Berninger, V.W. (1993). Structural equation modeling of the relationships among developmental skills and writing skills in primary- and intermediate-grade writers. *Journal of Educational Psychology, 85*(3), 478–508.

Adams, M.J. (2001). Alphabetic anxiety and explicit, systematic phonics instruction: A cognitive science perspective. In S.B. Neuman & D.K. Dickinson (Eds.), *Handbook of early literacy research* (Vol. 1; pp. 66–80). New York, NY: Guilford Press.

Applebee, A.N., & Langer, J.A. (2006). *The state of writing instruction in American's Schools: What existing data tell us.* Albany: University at Albany, The State University of New York.

Applegate, A.J., & Applegate, M.D. (2004). The Peter effect: Reading habits and attitudes of preservice teachers. *The Reading Teacher, 57*(6), 554–563.

Beers, S.F., Quinlan, T., & Harbaugh, A.G. (2010). Adolescent students' reading during writing behaviors and relationships with text quality: An eyetracking study. *Reading and Writing, 23*(7), 743–775. doi:10.1007/s11145-009-9193-7

Brindley, R., & Schneider, J.J. (2002). Writing instruction or destruction: Lessons to be learned from fourth-grade teachers' perspectives on teaching writing. *Journal of Teacher Education, 53*(4), 328–341.

Brooks, G.W. (2007). Teachers as readers and writers and as teachers of reading and writing. *Journal of Educational Research, 100*(3), 171–191.

Connor, C.M. (2011). Child by instruction interactions: Language and literacy connections. In S.B. Neuman & D.K. Dickinson (Eds.), *Handbook on early literacy* (3rd ed., pp. 256–275). New York, NY: Guilford Press.

Connor, C.M., Kaya, S., Luck, M., Toste, J., Canto, A., Rice, D.C., . . . Underwood, P. (2010). Content-area literacy: Individualizing student instruction in second-grade science. *Reading Teacher, 63*(6), 474–485.

Connor, C.M., & Lonigan, C.J. (2012). *Examining key components of comprehension: Developing targeted interventions.* Paper presented at the Society for Research in Education and Evaluation, Washington, DC.

Connor, C.M., Morrison, F.J., Fishman, B., Crowe, E.C., Al Otaiba, S., & Schatschneider, C. (in press). A longitudinal cluster-randomized controlled study on the accumulating effects of individualized literacy instruction on students' reading from first through third grade. *Psychological Science.* doi:10.1177/0956797612472204

Connor, C.M., Morrison, F.J., Fishman, B., Giuliani, S., Luck, M., Underwood, P., . . . Schatschneider, C. (2011). Classroom instruction, child X instruction interactions and the impact of differentiating student instruction on third graders' reading comprehension. *Reading Research Quarterly, 46*(3), 189–221.

Connor, C.M., Morrison, F.J., Fishman, B., Ponitz, C.C., Glasney, S., Underwood, P., . . . Schatschneider, C. (2009). The ISI classroom observation system: Examining the literacy instruction provided to individual students. *Educational Researcher, 38*(2), 85–99.

Connor, C.M., Piasta, S.B., Fishman, B., Glasney, S., Schatschneider, C., Crowe, E., . . . Morrison, F.J. (2009). Individualizing student instruction precisely: Effects of child by instruction interactions on first graders' literacy development. *Child Development, 80*(1), 77–100.

Fitzgerald, J., & Shanahan, T. (2000). Reading and writing relations and their development. *Educational Psychologist, 35*(1), 39–50. doi:10.1207/S15326985EP3501_5

Flower, L., & Hayes, J.R. (1981). Process-based evaluation of writing: Changing the performance, not the product. Paper presented at the annual meeting of the American Educational Research Association.

Graham, S., & Harris, K. (2009). Almost 30 years of writing research: Making sense of it all with the *Wrath of Khan. Learning Disabilities Research, 24*(2), 58–68.

Graham, S., Harris, K., & Hebert, M.A. (2011). Informing writing: The benefits of formative assessment. In *A Carnegie Corporation Time to Act* Report. Washington, DC: Alliance for Excellent Education.

Graham, S., & Herbert, M. (2011). Writing to read: A meta-analysis of the impact of writing and writing instruction on reading. *Harvard Educational Review, 81*(4), 710–744.

Hayes, J.R., & Flower, L.S. (1987). On the structure of the writing process. *Topics in Language Disorders, 7*(4), 19–30.

Ingebrand, S., Snyder, L., & Connor, C.M. (in review). Third-grade writing instruction and reading and writing outcomes.

MacGinitie, W.H., MacGinitie, R.K., Maria, K., & Dreyer, L.G. (2000). *Gates-MacGinitie reading test* (4th ed.). Itasica, IL: Riverside.

Mehta, P.D., Foorman, B.R., Branum-Martin, L., & Taylor, W.P. (2005). Literacy as a unidimensional multilevel construct: Validation, sources of influence, and implications in a longitudinal study in grades 1 to 4. *Scientific Studies of Reading, 9*(2), 85–116.

Morrison, F.J., Bachman, H.J., & Connor, C.M. (2005). *Improving literacy in America: Guidelines from research.* New Haven, CT: Yale University Press.

National Assessment of Educational Progress (NAEP). (2011). *The nation's report card.* Retrieved from http://nces.ed.gov/nationsreportcard

National Governors Association Center for Best Practices, Council of Chief State School Officers (NGA/CCSSO). (2010). *Common Core State Standards: English language arts standards.* Washington, DC: Authors.

National Institute of Child Health and Human Development (NICHD). (2000). *Report of the National Reading Panel. Teaching children to read: An evidence-based assessment of the scientific research literature on reading and its implications for reading instruction: Reports of the subgroups.* (NIH Publication No. 00-4754.) Washington, DC: U.S. Government Printing Office.

Parodi, G. (2007). Reading-writing connections: Discourse-oriented research. *Reading and Writing, 20*(3), 225–250. doi:10.1007/s11145-006-9029-7

Raudenbush, S.W., & Bryk, A.S. (2002). *Hierarchical linear models: Applications and data analysis methods* (2nd ed.). Thousand Oaks, CA: Sage.

Shanahan, T. (1984). Nature of the reading-writing relation: An explanatory multivariate analysis. *Journal of Educational Psychology, 76*(3), 446–477.

Shanahan, T. (2006). Relations among oral language, reading, and writing development. In C.A. MacArthur, S. Graham, & J. Fitzgerald (Eds.), *Handbook of writing research* (pp. 171–183). New York, NY: Guilford Press.

Shanahan, T., & Lomax, R.G. (1986). An analysis and comparison of theoretical models of the reading-writing relationship. *Journal of Educational Psychology, 78*(2), 116–123.

Shanahan, T., & Lomax, R.G. (1988). A developmental comparison of three theoretical models of the reading-writing relationship. *Reading in the Teaching of English, 22*(2), 196–212.

Snow, C.E. (2001). *Reading for understanding.* Santa Monica, CA: RAND Education and the Science and Technology Policy Institute.

Tierney, R., & Shanahan, T. (1991). Research on the reading-writing relationship: Interactions, transitions, and outcomes. In R. Barr, M. Kamil, P. Mosenthal, & D. Pearson (Eds.), *Handbook of reading research* (Vol. 2; pp. 246–280). Mahwah, NJ: Lawrence Erlbaum.

U.S. Department of Education. (2004). No child left behind: A toolkit for teachers. Washington, DC: U.S. Department of Education, Office of the Deputy Secretary.

Vellutino, F.R., Tunmer, W.E., Jaccard, J., Chen, R., & Scanlon, D.M. (2004). Components of reading ability: Multivariate evidence for a convergent skills model of reading development. *Scientific Studies of Reading, 11*(1), 3–32. doi:10.1207/s1532799xssrl101_2

Wharton-McDonald, R., Pressley, M., & Hampston, J.M. (1998). Literacy instruction in nine first-grade classrooms: Teacher characteristics and student achievement. *Elementary School Journal, 99*(2), 101–128.

Wiebe Berry, R.A. (2006). Beyond strategies: Teacher beliefs and writing instruction in two primary inclusion classrooms. *Journal of Learning Disabilities, 39*(1), 11–24.

Woodcock, R.W., McGrew, K.S., & Mather, N. (2001). *Woodcock-Johnson-III tests of achievement.* Itasca, IL: Riverside.

The Writing Side

3

Lara-Jeane Costa, Unber Ahmad, Crystal Edwards,
Sarah Vanselous, Donna Carlson Yerby, and Stephen R. Hooper

Writing is a complex, multifaceted process that has been the subject of an increasing amount of research over the past several decades. One of the major thrusts for this increase in research has been to conceptualize written expression as a cognitive process. Researchers began to study written expression through the lens of cognitive psychology in the 1960s, and this led to a significant increase in the subsequent scientific literature on the topic (Hooper, Knuth, Yerby, Anderson, & Moore, 2009). It is critical that the scientific foundations of writing research continue to develop, as difficulty with written expression is a highly prevalent issue (Lerner, 2000; National Center for Education Statistics [NCES], 2012). For instance, the NCES's National Assessment of Educational Progress (NAEP) data from 2002, 2006, and 2011 indicated that about two thirds of students demonstrated limited mastery of prerequisite information and skills that are essential for proficient writing at their given grade. Specifically, only 27% of U.S. students in 8th and 12th grades scored at or above proficient on the 2011 NAEP assessment (NCES, 2007, 2012). In contrast to its literacy partner, reading, where significant scientific advances have been asserted for underlying components, assessment of these components, and instruction for both typical and atypical readers (National Reading Panel [NRP], 2000), the literature for writing has lagged behind. This is not an accident or oversight but rather reflects the challenge of studying the inherent complexities of written expression. Even more challenging is how these components interrelate with the processes of reading and how these interrelationships may affect instruction.

This chapter is a companion to Chapter 2 in this text, "The Reading Side." As such, a brief overview of the contemporary findings pertaining to written expression will be presented. This will include a brief discussion of definitional issues, two key conceptual models for written expression, underlying cognitive functions, and related intervention approaches. In addition, a major section devoted to the writing–reading connection is provided, with

This project was conducted with support from the Institute of Education Sciences (R305H060042; R305A110622), Administration of Developmental Disabilities (#90DD043003), and Maternal and Child Health Bureau (#MCJ379154A).

preliminary findings from the North Carolina Writing Skills Development Project being presented to address this interrelationship.

WRITTEN EXPRESSION

Definition

Writing comprises three basic tasks: handwriting, spelling, and translation. Although each of these components of writing is critical to successful written expression, for this chapter we will focus on the component of translation. Translation—or written expression—can be defined as the production of connected text (e.g., sentences, paragraphs) in order to communicate an idea or thought, descriptive or procedural information, or more general knowledge. This process requires a marriage of many skills including the ability to comprehend structure (i.e., paragraph, sentence), content (i.e., the author's thoughts), and purpose (i.e., the audience, the author's intentions). Other cognitive functions (i.e., processes that rely on underlying brain function) are considered important to translation as well (e.g., language, executive functions; Hooper et al., 2013) and can serve to facilitate or hinder the translational process. Hayes (2012) noted, "What we most commonly think of as writing is the activity of producing text to be read by other people, for example, writing articles or school essays. I will call this formal writing" (p. 18). We agree with Hayes and will highlight this component of writing in the examination of written expression and the writing–reading connection.

Cognitive Models

The cognitive models of writing feature the writer taking an active role in the writing process, focusing on language use, solitary cognitive processes (e.g., language, memory, attention, executive functions), and the writer's own self-efficacy. Cognitive models propose that writing is recursive, where backtracks and loops are not only frequent but necessary. In addition, although the social constructivist theory places writing inside a larger context of the writer's social identity and the social context within which he or she is writing, cognitive models hone in on the individual experience between the writer and his or her creative process (Hidi & Boscolo, 2006).

    Hayes and Flower Model   Hayes and Flower (1980) proposed a cognitive model of writing more than 30 years ago that stimulated a significant amount of research in written expression. The model has recently been updated (Hayes, 1996, 2000, 2012) and continues to be one of the most influential models in writing research. This model includes three main components: planning, translating, and revising. It is based on research with adult participants and illustrates writing as a complicated problem-solving procedure that operates within the writer's 1) task environment and 2) long-term memory.

    The task environment comprises the social environment (i.e., collaborators and the audience) and the physical environment (i.e., the writing tool and the text-written-so-far; Hayes, 2012). The individual interacts with the task environment using cognitive processes and motivation. The cognitive processes include the planner, which represents the thought processes in preparation for writing (e.g., goal setting); the translator, the process by which the lexical and syntactic choices are made; the memory resources, which include utilizing the author's buffers that hold output; the evaluator, which assesses goal progress; the transcriber, which physically creates new written or spoken text; and the text-written-so-far, which is the previously written text. These processes and the task environment come together to form a finished written product. This model is conceptualized within a problem-solving approach due to the need for the individual to navigate through the steps and processes by strategizing and solving problems to achieve the writing goal.

Not-So-Simple View of Writing Twenty-six years later, after Hayes and Flower first presented their model, Berninger and Winn (2006) proposed a different model that applies specifically to children's writing. The basic components of the Not-So-Simple View of Writing include transcription, executive functions, and text generation. Simultaneously, working memory activates both short-term and long-term memory, bringing planning, composing, reviewing, and revising knowledge from long-term memory and activating the short-term memory during reviewing and revising. These functions work in synchronicity and recursively to support the translation process. Using their model, the researchers make the case that externalizing cognition (i.e., students relying on more capable others to aid their executive function) can overcome some limitations in internal working memory. They have also supported their model with evidence concerning word storage and processing units (i.e., orthographic, phonological, and morphological), a phonological loop, and executive supports for controlling attention, including both focused and shifting attention. Other functions that contribute to this process include metalinguistic and metacognitive awareness, cognitive presence, and cognitive engagement (Berninger & Hayes, 2012).

Cognitive Underpinnings

Based on the previously mentioned theoretical models, as well as others (e.g., Kellogg, 1996), there are several clear cognitive functions that have been identified as being important to children's written expression. Fine-motor, attention, language, visual processing, memory, and executive functions all hold potential significance for written expression. Given the language-based aspects of written expression, targeted linguistic functions have been deemed critical to successful written expression. For example, phonemic awareness is essential to both writing and reading acquisition (Juel, Griffith, & Gough, 1986), and Berninger, Abbott, Nagy, and Carlisle (2010) found that linguistic functions such as phonological, orthographic, and morphological processing also are critical to written expression, particularly in young elementary school children. The nuances and interrelationships between these core linguistic functions are complex, each having their own developmental trajectories, but suffice it to say that if these functions are disrupted, children will struggle in their written expression. Hooper and colleagues (2011) demonstrated the overwhelming importance of language functions (e.g., phonological processing) for both first and second graders' written language, and in a related study documented preschool language and phonological processing abilities as significant predictors of later growth in written language in grades 3, 4, and 5 (Hooper, Roberts, Nelson, Zeisel, & Kasambira Fannin, 2010). These language-related functions appear to be critical to early written expression, and it is suspected that these functions will serve as mediators of writing development.

Another cognitive domain that has been deemed important for children's written expression is executive function. Executive functions comprise multiple cognitive abilities, including working memory, planning, problem solving, inhibitory control, and set shifting, and have been shown to be important in the process of written expression. Hooper, Swartz, Wakely, de Kruif, and Montgomery (2002) and other research groups (e.g., Vanderberg & Swanson, 2007) found that poor writers in elementary school were less proficient in some executive functions than good writers. Specifically, poor writers had greater difficulties in the initiation and set-shifting functions but not in sustaining and inhibitory control abilities. Altemeier, Jones, Abbott, and Berninger (2006) found executive functions to be important to notetaking and report-writing and implicated these functions in the reading–writing connection. Further, although a writer may have good spelling and handwriting skills, executive functions (e.g., planning) may hinder the child's ability to translate thoughts to paper. For example, a student proficient in spelling and handwriting may experience significant difficulties organizing ideas; consequently, this student's ideas will not be translated effectively in the essay without significant outside effort by teachers and others.

Finally, working memory functions have been deemed critical to the writing process. These functions underlie the active maintenance and simultaneous management of multiple ideas, the retrieval of grammatical rules from long-term memory, and the recursive self-monitoring that is required during the act of writing (Kellogg, 1996; Vanderberg & Swanson, 2007). More generally, working memory has been found to make both general and domain-specific (e.g., verbal vs. visual-spatial) contributions to the writing process (Vanderberg & Swanson, 2007). Further, a variety of studies have indicated that poor writers typically have reduced working memory capacity or inefficient working memory that could undermine the entire translational process. How developmental change in this system contributes to deficits or facility in the translation process remains to be determined.

With respect to the cognitive underpinnings of written expression, it is important to note that the manner in which these abilities affect written production as well as the development of written expression is only beginning to be understood. In this regard, Berninger and Amtmann (2003) have placed within a neurodevelopmental framework several key cognitive functions that unfold in a hierarchical fashion, thus mediating the development of written language. Specifically, they noted that the written expression of early elementary school students will be constrained by factors related to fine-motor output (e.g., letter formation) and then linguistic capabilities—including memory for letters and words (Berninger et al., 2002; Berninger & Winn, 2006)—with executive functions emerging later in development. In addition, recent work has shown that task requirements in school curricula change in later grades, as children are expected to integrate reading and writing during translation, making the translation process for writing more complex as age increases (Altemeier, Abbott, & Berninger, 2008; Altemeier et al., 2006).

Writing Interventions

At present, evidence does not support a single, comprehensive method for teaching writing across the elementary and secondary school years, although 72% of primary grade teachers use the process approach to teach writing to their students (Cutler & Graham, 2008). Teachers who use the process approach focus on a cycle of brainstorming, editing, and translating (Graham & Harris, 2009). Teachers not only are using related methods to teach writing, but they also have their students write the same types of compositions. In most elementary classrooms, students are primarily engaging in narrative writing as opposed to expository writing (Cutler & Graham, 2008). Indeed, Chapter 2 highlights that little time is spent in the direct instruction of written expression in a broader literacy curriculum, and it remains unclear how this might change with the adoption of the Common Core State Standards.

In addition, almost one third of teachers believe that they are not sufficiently prepared to teach writing in the classroom (Cutler & Graham, 2008). Even if teachers may provide lessons on spelling and grammar daily, they do not spend much class time teaching written expression to their students. It is estimated that students spend only about 105 minutes per week (i.e., 21 minutes per day) writing, with all writing components (e.g., brainstorming, revising, drafting) being included in this time. Despite students not receiving much time in the classroom to write, writing assignments for homework are not uncommon. This disconnect undoubtedly will hinder homework performance and production, particularly with writing demands increasing with advancing grades, and how this disconnect will affect the implementation of the Common Core State Standards remains to be determined (e.g., How will writing be incorporated to facilitate the standards of English or science?).

The expansion of the scientific understanding of the writing process has developed concurrently with efforts to intervene with students showing writing difficulties. A variety of interventions, such as self-talk, talk through, and various forms of technology, have proven successful in improving the struggles in writing faced by children. These types of intervention have been shown to increase metacognitive capabilities, self-regulation, self-efficacy, and active learning (Englert, 2009; Graham, Harris, & Mason, 2005; Hooper, Wakely, de Kruif, & Swartz, 2006; MacArthur, 2009; Rogers & Graham, 2008). For example, Klein (2000) found that thinking aloud while writing a journal entry for science class had a greater impact than the amount of text that the students wrote. Similarly, Green and Sutton (2003) found that writing skills improved when children considered both the audience and the purpose of their writing. In general, the evidence to date indicates that, for students with writing difficulties, explicit writing instruction appears to be essential (Berninger, 2009; Hooper et al., 2009; Troia & Graham, 2002). In addition to improving transcription skills, explicit instruction has been shown to improve planning capabilities that, in turn, have produced increased length, better organization, and improved quality of students' compositions (Baker, Chard, Ketterlin-Geller, Apichatabutra, & Doabler, 2009; Graham & Harris, 2009). In general, the magnitude of the treatment effects has ranged from small (Berninger et al., 2002; Hooper et al., 2011) to large (Englert, 2009; Graham & Perin, 2007), depending on the outcome variables used, instructional formats employed, ages of the students, and specific interventions that were implemented.

In conjunction with the information given earlier, interventions to improve written expression have often utilized targeted strategies. Early work applying strategy instruction to difficulties in written expression was foundational in strategy-based intervention research (Graham, 2006). Advanced planning strategies have demonstrated improvement in writing quality, composition length, and increased time taken for planning (Troia & Graham, 2002). One of the most researched approaches using strategies to improve written expression is the Self-Regulated Strategy Development (SRSD) method. The SRSD method can be used by classroom teachers to explain various learning strategies to students. When using SRSD, the instructors teach the students strategies for writing and explain how and when to use the strategies (Graham & Harris, 2009). SRSD is not only a method for teaching writing; SRSD instruction promotes the student's ability to monitor and manage his or her own writing and encourages students to develop positive attitudes and beliefs about writing and about themselves as writers. The effectiveness of SRSD also has been shown to be quite positive across different ages and different types of learners. In a series of meta-analyses examining writing instruction, SRSD instruction yielded a larger average effect size (ES = 1.14) than non-SRSD instruction (ES = 0.62; Graham & Perin, 2007). SRSD instruction is applicable not only to typically achieving students but also to students who struggle with writing and to students with learning disabilities (Graham & Harris, 2009). Furthermore, SRSD is effective with students in varying grade levels, from elementary school to high school, and across genres (e.g., expository and narrative writing). The results of several meta-analyses that evaluated the use of SRSD in studies to improve writing have continued to show the utility of SRSD (Graham, 2006; Graham & Harris, 2003; Graham, McKeown, Kiuhara, & Harris, 2012; Graham & Perin, 2007). This work also has led to explicit recommendations for writing instruction that appear to be specific to the development of the writing process. Berninger (2009) also offered a similar set of recommendations.

WRITING–READING CONNECTION

In Chapter 2 of this text, Connor and colleagues provided an intriguing set of findings detailing how reading and writing interact in an instructional setting under the broader construct of literacy. They concluded that writing is an important component of reading assessment and intervention—particularly reading comprehension—but that the development of writing skills may require a different type, or perhaps quality, of instruction than reading (e.g., decoding) due to its inherent complexity. This conclusion is in line with findings by Mehta, Foorman, Branum-Martin, and Taylor (2005), who found that writing was an important component of the larger literacy construct but that the quality of instruction was related to the quality of the written expression. Despite these initial findings, though, we are only beginning to understand the nature of the writing–reading connection (Graham & Hebert, 2011).

Shared Underlying Functions and Shared Instructional Benefits

With Chapter 2 focusing on a number of key instructional issues pertaining to the relationship between writing and reading within a broader literacy curriculum, there also has been a growing body of evidence indicating that writing and reading share a reciprocal and beneficial relationship in literacy development (Shanahan, 2006), with the existing literature pointing to many of the same preschool variables that have been found to predict later reading skills—also predicting later writing skills. In addition to socioeconomic status and classroom literacy, these variables include receptive vocabulary, letter-word knowledge, invented spelling, phonological processing, orthography, letter naming, letter writing, ideational fluency, and exposure to print concepts (Diamond, Gerde, & Powell, 2008; Juel et al., 1986; Mäki, Voetens, Vauras, & Poskiparta, 2001). The development of these early skills during the preschool years, particularly phonological awareness and letter knowledge, has been associated with significant gains for at-risk preschoolers in reading (Dickinson, McCabe, Anastasopoulos, Peisner-Feinberg, & Poe, 2003) and, perhaps, in written language (Lonigan, Anthony, Bloomfield, Dyer, & Samuel, 1999). Further, the consolidation of the alphabetic principle is critical to early literacy, and its automaticity likely frees up cognitive resources for higher-level text generation (Jones & Christensen, 1999). This increased automaticity, in turn, likely facilitates the writing–reading interaction.

With these potentially shared cognitive underpinnings, there may be shared benefits for both reading and written expression. Emergent research has noted a powerful association between reading and writing in the classroom setting (Graham & Herbert, 2011), thus it seems logical that written expression can help to improve reading. Further, reading comprehension and reading fluency can be improved by writing about the subject of the text that has been read by using techniques such as notetaking and concept mapping. The process of creating text also should make the writer more thoughtful in reading text from others. In this regard, Graham and Hebert (2011) recommended four effective writing tasks to improve reading comprehension: extended writing, summary writing, notetaking, and answering/generating questions. Graham and Hebert (2011) also reported that teaching spelling and sentence construction skills improved reading fluency for students in grades 1 through 7, and spelling instruction improved word reading for students in grades 1 through 5. Given their interrelationship, the demands on connecting reading and writing in school curricula undoubtedly increase with advancing grades (Altemeier et al., 2008); consequently, there is an inherent need to understand this relationship to a greater degree.

The North Carolina Writing Skills Development Project

The North Carolina Writing Skills Development Project (WSDP) was unique in that we used a longitudinal design to examine writing performance and response to instruction. We followed students for 4 years, examining the relationships and developmental stability of fine-motor speed, language, short-term memory, long-term memory, and a number of executive functions. The participants included 205 students from a single school district, with approximately two thirds of the students being defined as having a writing disability (i.e., falling in the bottom quartile). To date, this study has documented the relative stability of key cognitive constructs in written expression (i.e., fine-motor, language, executive functions; Hooper et al., 2013) and has shown modest effects for selected Process Assessment of the Learner (PAL) lesson plans for written language in a randomized, controlled intervention trial (Costa, Hooper, McBee, Anderson, & Yerby, 2012; Hooper et al., 2011). These findings notwithstanding, the WSDP also provides an opportunity to examine the interrelationship between early writing skills and word reading in young elementary school students with writing problems. Our data allow a closer look at the co-occurrence of word reading problems in a sample of students with writing disabilities (WD) in grades 1 through 4; the probability of having a reading disability (RD) at different grades in the presence of an already-established WD; similarities and differences in the cognitive contributors to WD-only versus WD + RD; and finally, a peek at how word reading skills might change when students with WD participate in a targeted writing intervention using selected PAL lesson plans. Taken together, these data may provide additional clues as to the nature of the writing–reading connection.

Rate of Co-Occurrence of Reading Disability in Students with Writing Disabilities Although the rate of co-occurrence of writing and reading problems has been speculated to be high, to date there are few empirical data documenting this rate and certainly no data documenting this rate over multiple grade levels. The WSDP collected both writing and reading scores for each year of the 4-year longitudinal project and has generated some preliminary data showing the rate of co-occurrence of these problems in elementary school students at risk for writing difficulties. For this initial examination, a disability was defined by a score on the Wechsler Individual Achievement Test-II (WIAT II) written expression and/or word reading subtests falling within the bottom quartile.

As can be seen in Figure 3.1, for first-grade students with WD, there was approximately a 27% rate of co-occurring RD. For second-grade students with WD, the rate of co-occurring RD increased to approximately 35%. The rate continued to climb to 42% for third-grade students and to 46% for fourth-grade students. These preliminary findings point to a significant and potentially increasing rate of co-occurrence of RD in students with WD; however, the data also suggest that reading and writing are largely separate problems, particularly in the early elementary school years. Conversely, it is suspected that these rates of co-occurrence are driven, in part, by early deficits in phonological awareness and orthographic structures of words. It remains unknown, however, if these rates would replicate in a sample of students with RD (Hooper et al., 2013).

The Probability of an Reading Disability in Typically Developing Writers and Students with Writing Disabilities We have also looked at the North Carolina WSDP data to examine the relationship between writing and reading with respect to the

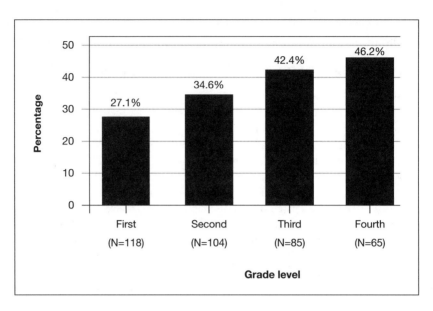

Figure 3.1. Percentages of children with a writing disability and concomitant reading disability in grades 1 through 4.

probability of having a reading problem in the presence of a writing problem at different points in time. The primary question here is if being classified as a struggling writer in earlier grades (i.e., first, second, and third) is predictive of the likelihood of being classified as a struggling reader in subsequent grades (i.e., second, third, and fourth). Students were classified as WD or RD as noted earlier (i.e., age-based standard scores falling in the bottom quartile). Results indicated that two of the models (i.e., first grade predicting second grade and third grade predicting fourth grade) were perfectly predictive of later success. Further, our data showed there to be a 26% chance that students who were struggling with writing in first grade would struggle with writing and reading in third grade, whereas typical students in first grade had only a 5% chance of struggling with writing and reading in third grade. As well, there was a 23% chance that students who were struggling with writing in first grade would struggle with writing and reading in fourth grade, whereas typically developing first-grade students had only a 6% chance. Similarly, we found there to be a 25% chance that students who were struggling with writing in second grade would struggle with writing and reading in third grade, whereas typical students had only a 5% chance. Finally, we found there to be a 26% chance that students who were struggling with writing in first grade would struggle with writing and reading in third grade, whereas typical students had only a 4% chance.

Writing Disabilities-Only versus Writing Disabilities + Reading Disability: Cognitive Comparisons
With respect to the writing–reading connection, another important question pertains to the cognitive burden that might be present for students with WD-only versus those with WD + RD. Using the WSDP data, we compared the performance of these subgroups of second graders in addition to a typically developing group of second-grade students across measures of fine-motor, language, and executive functions. As can be seen in Table 3.1, after adjusting for chronological age and maternal education, significant group differences were obtained across each of the three cognitive domains, with most of the individual tasks showing the suspected better performance for the typically developing group versus the two disability groups. Of

Table 3.1. Neuropsychological burden for typically developing, writing disability-only (WD), and writing disability + reading disability (WD + RD) second-grade students

Measures	Typical (1)M (SD)	WD-only (2)M (SD)	WD + RD (3)M (SD)	F-value	Partial eta^2	Pairwise comparisons
Fine-motor	F (6, 298) = 9.03, p < .001					
PAL alphabet writing	−0.30 (.76)	−1.22 (.48)	−1.00 (.71)	28.67***	0.28	1 > 2, 1 > 3
Sequential finger movements (D)	−0.17 (.45)	−2.67 (.44)	−0.21 (.54)	1.22	0.02	—
Sequential finger movements (ND)	−0.19 (.43)	−2.14 (.43)	−0.24 (.61)	1.66	0.35	—
Language	F (6, 132) = 9.39, p < .001					
PAL word choice	0.64 (.72)	−0.33 (1.22)	−1.62 (1.12)	26.48***	0.44	1 > 2, 2 > 3
PAL syllables	0.13 (.59)	−0.41 (.75)	−0.86 (.86)	3.85*	0.10	1 > 3
PAL phonemes	0.52 (.79)	−0.38 (.75)	−0.97 (.70)	18.36***	0.35	1 > 2, 1 > 3
Executive functions	F (14, 284) = 4.28, p < .001					
Vigil CPT omissions	42.63 (20.93)	45.41 (16.73)	55.43 (25.94)	2.50	0.21	—
Vigil CPT commissions	66.32 (57.50)	85.72 (66.73)	81.61 (78.18)	1.72	0.03	—
WJ-III planning	105.47 (8.02)	103.22 (8.40)	96.54 (11.93)	8.42***	0.10	1 > 3, 2 > 3
WJ-III retrieval fluency	101.37 (12.13)	96.00 (13.38)	87.07 (21.14)	7.21**	0.09	1 > 3
RAN letters/digits	12.27 (2.52)	10.75 (2.85)	8.68 (3.56)	19.76***	0.21	1 > 2, 2 > 3
WISC-IV digits reverse	10.80 (2.54)	9.28 (3.99)	9.07 (3.73)	3.15*	0.05	1 > 2, 1 > 3

Note: Process Assessment of the Learner (PAL), Continuous Performance Test (CPT), Woodcock Johnson (WJ), Rapid Automatized Naming (RAN), Wechsler Intelligence Scale for Children (WISC).

* = p < 0.1
** = p < 0.05
*** = p < 0.01

importance to the writing–reading connection, however, is whether the cognitive burden is greater, or perhaps different, for the WD + RD group than the WD-only group. Within the fine-motor domain, there were no differences noted between these groups; however, significant group differences were noted in the language and executive functions domains. Specifically, the WD-only group performed significantly better on tasks measuring orthographic processing, planning, and rapid naming, perhaps reflecting the influence of key reading-related skills. In contrast, the groups performed similarly in phonological processing, attention regulation, and inhibitory control. These findings suggest that, within a group of young elementary students with writing problems, those who have co-occurring reading problems show poorer performance in selected reading related skills, but there does appear to be an overlap for other core reading skills, with attention-regulation capabilities appearing to be similar between the groups. Taken together, these findings suggest that reading and writing share some underlying cognitive abilities at this developmental

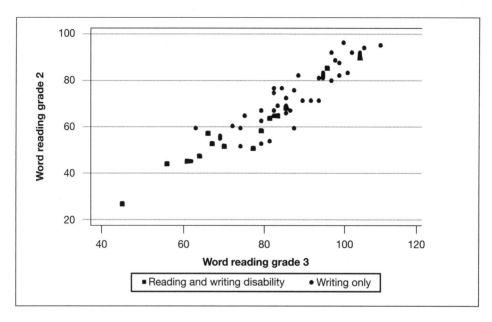

Figure 3.2. Reading skill gains in response to a written expression intervention in grade 2 for writing disability–only versus writing disability + reading disability groups in grade 3.

level, as suspected; however, there does appear to be a dissociation between other underlying skills (Hooper et al., 2013).

WD-Only versus WD + RD: Reading Growth in Response to a Written Expression Intervention A final question related to the writing–reading connection pertains to how reading changes for students with WD-only in a writing intervention when compared to those with WD + RD. For the second-grade children who went through the PAL intervention, an Analysis of Covariance (ANCOVA) was conducted to evaluate the participants' word reading scores preintervention versus postintervention for the WD-only group ($n = 49$) versus the WD + RD group ($n = 16$). These findings are depicted in Figure 3.2. After controlling for preintervention scores on reading, the results indicated no significant main effects for the subgroups, $F(1, 62) = 1.00$, $p = 0.329$, and no significant interaction between subgroup status and word reading scores postintervention, $F(3, 62) = 1.40$, $p = 0.271$; however, the effect size was large (partial eta^2 = 0.84), suggesting that significant postintervention changes might have been present with a larger sample size. These preliminary findings indicate that students who participated in a targeted intervention for written expression and have either a WD-only or a WD + RD will benefit similarly in their reading skills from the PAL intervention; however, it remains unconfirmed whether the reading skills for one group benefits more from the PAL intervention than the other group, or how response to treatment may change with age or another type of writing intervention.

CONCLUSION

This chapter has approached the writing–reading connection from the writing side of the fence. Several key conceptual models for written expression were presented, which provide a necessary foundation for how writing and reading interrelate. For example, within the Hayes

(2012) model, it is clear that reading is a critical part of the writing process, as reading what one has written contributes to the recursive nature of the writing process. This is nicely illustrated by the text-written-so-far component of the model wherein the individual must read and comprehend what has been written so as to make edits and adjustments to the written text. The Not-So-Simple View of Writing model provides an even more explicit linkage to reading by noting specific linguistic skills that subserve both writing and reading, including word storage, orthographic, phonological, and morphological capabilities. The developmental nature of this model and its associated components also provides an avenue for increasing our understanding of how both writing and reading develop from the preschool years and beyond.

Although there appears to be a significant overlap in a number of cognitive abilities that appear critical to both reading and writing skills, how these evolve over time in tandem with reading and written expression remains to be determined. The interventions that have been proposed to improve written expression may positively affect reading, especially those that contain instructional components for phonological and orthographic processing, but even the strategy development approaches may affect reading. Preliminary data from our elementary school students in the WSDP provided some initial evidence examining the writing–reading relationship in a sample of students identified as at risk for writing disabilities and suggested that writing and reading, although they share a number of commonalities, should be treated differently from an instructional perspective. The findings indicate the need for ongoing examination of the writing–reading connection with respect to topography, etiology, prognosis, and response to intervention, with a particular focus on how these core academic skills converge and diverge over the course of development. Although the scientific basis of the writing–reading connection is only beginning to be examined, future findings should contribute to improved instruction for this literacy component.

REFERENCES

Altemeier, L., Abbott, R.D., & Berninger, V.W. (2008). Executive functions for reading and writing in typical literacy development and dyslexia. *Journal of Clinical and Experimental Neuropsychology, 30*, 588–606.

Altemeier, L., Jones, J., Abbott, R., Berninger, V.W. (2006). Executive factors in becoming writing-readers and reading-writers: Note-taking and report writing in third and fifth graders. *Developmental Neuropsychology, 29*, 161–173.

Baker, S.K., Chard, D.J., Ketterlin-Geller, L.R., Apichatabutra, C., & Doabler, C. (2009). Teaching writing to at-risk students: The quality of evidence for self-regulated strategy development. *Exceptional Children, 75*, 303–318.

Berninger, V.W. (2009). Highlights of programmatic, interdisciplinary research on writing. *Learning Disabilities Research and Practice, 24*, 69–80.

Berninger, V.W., Abbott, R.D., Nagy, W., & Carlisle, J. (2010). Growth in phonological, orthographic, and morphological awareness in grades 1 to 6. *Journal of Psycholinguistic Research, 39*, 141–163.

Berninger, V.W., & Amtmann, E. (2003). Preventing written expression disabilities through early and continuing assessment and intervention for handwriting and/or spelling problems: Research into practice. In H.L. Swanson, K. Harris, & S. Graham (Eds.), *Handbook of research on learning disabilities* (pp. 345–363). New York, NY: Guilford Press.

Berninger, V.W., & Hayes, J.R. (2012). Longitudinal individual case studies of 20 children on writing treks in grades 1–5. In M. Fayol, D. Alamargot, & Berninger, V. (Eds.). *Translation of thought to written text while composing: Advancing theory, knowledge, methods, and applications*. New York, NY: Psychology Press/Taylor Francis Group/Routledge.

Berninger, V.W., Vaughan, K., Abbott, R., Begay, K., Byrd, K., Curtin, G., . . . & Graham, S. (2002). Teaching spelling and composition alone and together: Implications for the simple view of writing. *Journal of Educational Psychology, 94*, 291–304.

Berninger, V.W., & Winn, W. (2006). Implications of advancements in brain research and technology for writing development, writing instruction, and education evolution. In C. MacArthur, S.

Graham, & J. Fitzgerald (Eds.), *Handbook of writing research* (pp. 96–114). New York, NY: Guilford Press.

Costa, L.-J., Hooper, S.R., McBee, M., Anderson, K.L., & Yerby, D.C. (2012). The use of curriculum-based measures in young at-risk writers: Measuring change over time and potential moderators of change. *Exceptionality, 20,* 1–19.

Cutler, L., & Graham, S. (2008). Primary grade writing instruction: A national survey. *Journal of Educational Psychology, 100*(4), 907–919.

Diamond, K.E., Gerde, H.K., & Powell, D.R. (2008). Development in early literacy skills during the pre-kindergarten year in Head Start: Relations between growth in children's writing and understanding of letters. *Early Childhood Research Quarterly, 23,* 467–478.

Dickinson, D., McCabe, A., Anastasopoulos, L., Peisner-Feinberg, E., & Poe, M. (2003). The comprehensive language approach to early literacy: The interrelationships among vocabulary, phonological sensitivity, and print knowledge among preschool-aged children. *Journal of Educational Psychology, 95,* 465–481.

Englert, C.S. (2009). Connecting the dots in a research program to develop, implement, and evaluate strategic literacy interventions for struggling readers and writers. *Learning Disabilities Research and Practice, 24,* 104–120.

Graham, S. (2006). Strategy instruction and the teaching of writing. In C. MacArthur, S. Graham, & J. Fitzgerald (Eds.), *Handbook of writing research* (pp. 187–207). New York, NY: Guilford Press.

Graham, S., & Harris, K.R. (2003). Students with learning disabilities and the process of writing: A meta-analysis of SRSD studies. In H.L. Swanson, K.R. Harris, & S. Graham (Eds.), *Handbook of learning disabilities* (pp. 323–344). New York, NY: Guilford Press.

Graham, S., & Harris, K.R. (2009). Almost 30 years of writing research: Making sense of it all with the *Wrath of Khan. Learning Disabilities Research and Practice, 24,* 58–68.

Graham, S., Harris, K.R., & Mason, L. (2005). Improving the writing performance, knowledge, and self-efficacy of struggling young writers: The effects of self-regulated strategy development. *Contemporary Educational Psychology, 30,* 207–241.

Graham, S., & Hebert, M. (2011). Writing to read: A meta-analysis of the impact of writing and writing instruction on reading. *Harvard Education Review, 81*(4), 710–744.

Graham, S., McKeown, D., Kiuhara, S., & Harris, K.R. (2012, July 9). A meta-analysis of writing instruction for students in the elementary grades. *Journal of Educational Psychology, 104*(4), 879–896. doi:10.1037/a0029185

Graham, S., & Perin, D. (2007). A meta-analysis of writing instruction for adolescent students. *Journal of Educational Psychology, 99*(3), 445–476.

Green, S., & Sutton, P. (2003). What do children think as they plan their writing? *Literacy, 37,* 2–38.

Hayes, J.R. (1996). A new framework for understanding cognition and affect in writing. In C.M. Levy & S. Ransdell (Eds.), *The science of writing: Theories, methods, individual differences, and applications* (pp. 1–27). Mahwah, NJ: Lawrence Erlbaum.

Hayes, J.R. (2000). A new framework for understanding cognition and affect in writing. In R. Indrisano & J.R. Squire (Eds.), *Perspectives on writing* (pp. 6–44). Newark, DE: International Reading Association.

Hayes, J.R. (2012). Evidence from language bursts, revision, and transcription for translation and its relation to other writing processes. In M. Fayol, D. Alamargot, & V.W. Berninger (Eds.), *Translation of thought to written text while composing* (pp. 15–25). New York, NY: Psychology Press.

Hayes, J.R., & Flower, L.S. (1980). Identifying the organization of writing processes. In L.W. Gregg & E.R. Steinberg (Eds.), *Cognitive processes in writing* (pp. 3–30). Mahwah, NJ: Lawrence Erlbaum Associates.

Hidi, S., & Boscolo, P. (2006). Motivation and writing. In C. MacArthur, S. Graham, & J. Fitzgerald (Eds.), *Handbook of writing research* (pp. 144–157). New York, NY: Guilford Press.

Hooper, S.R., Costa, L.-J., Ahmad, U., Edwards, C., Vanselous, S., & Yerby, D.C. (in press). *The writing-reading connection in young elementary school students: Rates of co-occurrence, probabilities, and neuropsychological features.* Manuscript submitted for publication.

Hooper, S., Costa, L.-J., McBee, M., Anderson, K., Yerby, D., Childress, A., & Knuth, S. (2013). A written language intervention for at-risk second grade students: A randomized controlled trial of the process assessment of the learner lesson plans in a tier 2 response-to-intervention (RtI) model. *Annals of Dyslexia, 63*(1), 44–64.

Hooper, S.R., Costa, L.-J., McBee, M., Anderson, K.L., Yerby, D.C., Knuth, S.B., & Childress, A. (2011). Concurrent and longitudinal neuropsychological contributors to written language expression in first and second grade students. *Reading and Writing: An Interdisciplinary Journal, 24,* 221–252.

Hooper, S., Knuth, S., Yerby, D., Anderson, K., & Moore, C. (2009). Review of science-supported writing instruction with implementation in mind. In S. Rosenfield & V. Berninger (Eds.), *Handbook on implementing evidence-based academic interventions* (pp. 49–83). New York, NY: Oxford University Press.

Hooper, S.R., Roberts, J.E., Nelson, L., Zeisel, S., & Kasambira Fannin, D. (2010). Preschool predictors of narrative writing skills in elementary school. *School Psychology Quarterly, 25,* 1–12.

Hooper, S.R., Swartz, C., Wakely, M., de Kruif, R., & Montgomery, J. (2002). Executive functions in elementary school children with and without problems in written expression. *Journal of Learning Disabilities, 35,* 37–68.

Hooper, S.R., Wakely, M., de Kruif, R., & Swartz, C. (2006). Aptitude-treatment interactions revisited: Effect of metacognitive intervention on subtypes of written expression in elementary school students. *Developmental Neuropsychology, 29,* 217–241.

Jones, D., & Christensen, C.A. (1999). Relationship between automaticity in handwriting and students' ability to generate written text. *Journal of Educational Psychology, 91*(1), 44–49.

Juel, C., Griffith, P., & Gough, P. (1986). Acquisition of literacy: A longitudinal study of children in first and second grade. *Journal of Educational Psychology, 78,* 243–255.

Kellogg, R. (1996). A model of working memory in writing. In C. Levy & S. Ransdell (Eds.), *The science of writing theories, methods, individual differences, and applications* (pp. 57–71). Mahwah, NJ: Lawrence Erlbaum.

Klein, P.D. (2000). Elementary students: Strategies for writing-to-learn in science. *Cognition and Instruction, 18,* 317–348.

Lerner, J.W. (2000). *Children with learning disabilities: Theories, diagnosis, teaching strategies* (8th ed.). Boston, MA: Houghton Mifflin.

Lonigan, C.J., Anthony, J.L., Bloomfield, B.G., Dyer, S.M., & Samuel, C.S. (1999). Effects of two shared-reading interventions on emergent literacy skills of at-risk preschoolers. *Journal of Early Intervention, 22,* 306–322.

MacArthur, C.A. (2009). Reflections on research on writing and technology for struggling writers. *Learning Disabilities Research and Practice, 24*(2), 93–103.

Mäki, H.S., Voetens, M.J.M., Vauras, M.M.S., & Poskiparta, E.H. (2001). Predicting writing skill development with word recognition and preschool readiness skills. *Reading and Writing: An Interdisciplinary Journal, 14,* 643–672.

Mehta, P.D., Foorman, B.R., Branum-Martin, L., & Taylor, W.P. (2005). Literacy as a unidimensional multilevel construct: Validation, sources of influence, and implications in a longitudinal study in grades 1 to 4. *Scientific Studies of Reading, 9,* 85–116.

National Center for Education Statistics (NCES). (2007). *National Assessment of Educational Progress (NAEP), 2002 and 2006 writing assessments.* Washington, DC: Institute of Education Sciences, U.S. Department of Education.

National Center for Education Statistics (NCES). (2012). *The Nation's report card: Writing 2011.* Washington, DC: Institute of Education Sciences, U.S. Department of Education.

National Institute of Child Health and Human Development (NICHD). (2000). *Report of the National Reading Panel. Teaching children to read: An evidence-based assessment of the scientific research literature on reading and its implications for reading instruction: Reports of the subgroups.* (NIH Publication No. 00-4754.) Washington, DC: U.S. Government Printing Office.

Rogers, L.A., & Graham, S. (2008). A meta-analysis of single subject design writing intervention research. *Journal of Educational Psychology, 100,* 879–906.

Shanahan, T. (2006). Relations among oral language, reading, and writing development. In C. MacArthur, S. Graham, & J. Fitzgerald (Eds.), *Handbook of writing research* (pp. 171–186). New York, NY: Guilford.

Troia, G., & Graham, S. (2002). The effectiveness of a highly explicit, teacher-directed strategy instruction routine: Changing the writing performance of students with learning disabilities. *Journal of Learning Disabilities, 35,* 290–305.

Vanderberg, R., & Swanson, H.L. (2007). Which components of working memory are important in the writing process? *Reading and Writing, 20,* 721–752.

4

Integrating Reading and Writing Instruction

Karen R. Harris and Steve Graham

The National Commission on Writing in America's Schools and Colleges reported nearly a decade ago that, of the three *R*s, writing had become the most neglected in classrooms (National Commission on Writing in America's Schools and Colleges, 2003). Writing development and instruction have long taken a backseat to reading, and more recently to science, technology, engineering, and mathematics (STEM) in terms of a host of interrelated and important factors, including research funding, time allocated in schools, curriculum development, educational reform, and national attention (Harris, Graham, Brindle, & Sandmel, 2009). Further adding to this picture, research indicates the majority of teachers report inadequate pre- and in-service preparation in writing instruction, and often do not implement evidence-based interventions or instruction (Applebee & Langer, 2011; Cutler & Graham, 2008; Gilbert & Graham, 2010).

This neglect of writing is surprising, given its importance. Students who struggle significantly with writing face a terrible disadvantage in today's world. By the upper elementary grades, writing becomes a critical tool both for learning and for showing what a student knows. Writing is vital to gathering, refining, extending, preserving, and transmitting information and understandings; making ideas readily available for consideration, evaluation, and future discourse; fostering the examination of unexamined assumptions; creating cognitive disequilibrium that spurs learning; and promoting personal development (Harris et al., 2009; Prior, 2006). When writing abilities are not well developed, students cannot draw on the power of writing to support and extend learning and development, and adults with inadequate writing skills can face significant barriers in further education and employment.

The class of 2012 obtained an average score of 488 on the writing portion of the Scholastic Aptitude Test (SAT), leading the College Board (2012) to conclude that 43% of those who took the SAT are not ready for college-level work. In fact, a large majority of colleges and universities today have determined that they must offer remedial writing support to incoming students (Harris et al., 2009), and $2 billion is spent each year on remedial courses for postsecondary students, which includes courses on writing (Fulton, 2010). What about those not taking the SAT and applying for college? Data from the National Assessment of Educational Progress (NAEP) tells a similar story (National Center for Education

Statistics, 2012). In 2011, only 27% of 8th- and 12th-grade students scored at or above the "proficient" level on the writing test, whereas 20% of 8th graders and 21% of 12th graders scored "below basic" (not meeting the minimum standard for their grade level). Clearly, far too many of our students are not adequately prepared for work or continuing education in the new "knowledge economy" (Business Roundtable, 2009; Conference Board, 2006; IRA/NICHD, 2012). Businesses spend $3.1 billion annually on writing remediation alone (National Commission on Writing, 2004).

Today, due to the efforts of many (including those referenced here) and the growing recognition of the importance of writing, writing is joining center stage with reading and math. In this chapter, we focus on one critical impetus for the current attention to writing: the growing evidence that learning to read and learning to write are connected to each other in important ways and that each can be leveraged to the benefit of the other. Writing is a foundational ability; research shows that instruction and competence in writing can boost comprehension and achievement across subject areas and that direct writing instruction and frequent practice can improve overall reading proficiency (Bangert-Downs, Hurley, & Wilkinson, 2004; Graham & Perin, 2007).

We are not, however, arguing that reading and writing should only, or even mostly, be taught together. Research clearly indicates that each requires significant, separate, and focused instruction (IRA/NICHD, 2012). It is not reasonable to assume that, if we just teach writing, students will become good readers, or vice versa. However, time also needs to be dedicated to teaching writing and reading together; it is important to remember that these are not mutually exclusive practices.

Much of the current interest in reading and writing connections is driven by the advent of the Common Core State Standards (CCSS). The CCSS represent an effort led by the National Governors Association Center for Best Practices and the Council of Chief State Schools Officers (NGA/CCSSO, 2010). The goal of this effort is to transform the process of schooling by providing teachers and schools with a blueprint of what students need to master to become college and career ready. A central component of the CCSS is a set of language arts standards for becoming proficient and skilled readers and writers. These standards go beyond simply learning how to read and write, emphasizing using reading and writing to support each other and using both to support learning more broadly (see Morrow, Wixson, & Shanahan, 2013). For example, in grade 6, it is expected that students will be able to gather and assess the relevance of information from multiple print and digital sources as they develop ideas for their written text; use writing to trace, dissect, and evaluate specific arguments and claims presented in text; and apply reading and writing as tools to support learning in science, social studies, and other technical subjects. In other words, it is now expected that students will use reading to facilitate writing, writing to facilitate reading, and both to facilitate the learning of content materials.

To date, 45 states have adopted the CCSS; these states include approximately 87% of all public school students in the United States. These standards push many teachers and schools into new territory. This is easily illustrated by considering just one part of the equation: how writing is taught. Before the advent of the CCSS, teachers spent very little time teaching students how to write after third grade, students did very little writing in school at any grade, and writing was rarely used as a tool for helping students think about the text they were reading or the content they were learning in subject matter classes (Applebee & Langer, 2011; Cutler & Graham, 2008; Gilbert & Graham, 2010; Kiuhara, Graham, & Hawken, 2009). If students are to meet the writing objectives in the CCSS, this must change or many students will acquire neither the skills nor the disposition to write well or to use writing to support reading and learning.

The tension that the CCSS are placing on schools was captured in a recent issue of *Education Week* (Sawchuk, 2012). David Saba, the chief executive officer of Laying the Foundation and a partner with the Partnership for the Assessment of Readiness for College and Careers (PARCC, a CCSS assessment consortium), was quoted as saying, "Common core is causing serious angst in your states, your districts, and your schools" (p. 6). A teacher quoted in the same article declared of teachers, "It will really change how they teach . . . It will be outside their comfort zone" (p. 6). This is especially true as teachers look to implement new methods and approaches where reading and writing are used to support each other. Although it is beyond the scope of this chapter to discuss every possible avenue for supporting the reading and writing connection, we offer several examples of how this can be done in the classroom.

WRITE TO SUPPORT READING

One way to connect writing and reading is to use writing as a tool for thinking about text that is read. Graham and Hebert (2011) found that students' comprehension of text read was enhanced on both norm-referenced and researcher-designed measures when they wrote about it. Examples of writing activities that improved students' understanding of text are presented in Box 4.1.

The writing activities presented in Box 4.1 vary in how they facilitate thinking about text and ultimately the comprehension of it. For example, writing answers to text questions focuses students' attention on important information and can support remembering the information. It also makes it easier to think about spoken information, as written answers are available for review, reevaluation, and reconstruction.

The act of taking written notes about text material enhances comprehension, as this activity involves sifting through text to determine what is most relevant, transforming and reducing the substance of these ideas into written phrases or key words. Intentionally or unintentionally, note takers organize the abstracted material in some way, connecting one idea to another while blending new information with their own knowledge.

Likewise, writing a summary of text requires making decisions about what information is most important as well as deciding what information to cull, combine, and transform. The act of creating a summary further requires the writer to think about how ideas in text are related one to another.

> **Box 4.1.** Research-supported practices for writing about text (from Graham and Hebert, 2011)
>
> - Answer questions about text in writing or create and answer written questions about text.
> - Write notes about text read.
> - Summarize in writing material read.
> - Respond to text read by writing a personal reaction to it or by analyzing and interpreting it (e.g., defending a point of view related to information presented in text or describing how the information in text can be applied to a real life problem).

Putting these ideas into one's own words makes the writer think about what the ideas mean, and transforming these ideas into text requires additional thought about the essence of the material read. This results in a written summary that can be readily critiqued and reworked.

Newer and better understandings of text also occur when students write about text in more extended ways involving analysis, interpretation, or personalization. For instance, writing an essay to defend or refute a particular point of view presented in text requires thinking about the material read in complex ways; focusing on major issues; examining, critiquing, and determining how text content supports or refutes the selected point of view; and considering this information in light of existing knowledge, beliefs, and biases. Similarly, a writing assignment that involves drawing a parallel between text and a personal experience requires thinking more carefully about the material read as well as considering how it is relevant.

In some of the studies reviewed by Graham and Hebert (2011), writing about text had a positive effect on reading comprehension even when students were not taught how to apply such activities. There was some evidence, however, that the impact of writing about text was enhanced when instruction on how to apply these writing activities was provided, at least for older students. This may be because the writing activities older students were asked to apply were more sophisticated, and as a result, these students required more assistance to make them work. In any event, we think it is prudent for teachers to model how to apply any writing-to-reading activity they expect students to use as well as to provide them with assistance applying the writing activity until they can do so independently. Evidence also indicates that many students will profit from explicit strategy instruction for these writing–reading activities (cf. Mason, Snyder, Sukhram, & Kedem, 2006).

READ TO SUPPORT WRITING

Just as writing can enhance comprehension of text, reading can help students think productively about the text they are writing. A basic element of writing involves authors critically rereading their text to determine if it is compelling, complete, coherent, and correct (Hayes, 1996). Through meta-analysis, Graham, Harris, and Hebert (2011) identified two successful reading strategies that students can apply to help them improve the quality of their writing. In one, students can be asked to reread text they have written and evaluate it using specific criteria. Successful self-evaluation procedures ranged from teaching students to use a rubric to assess the merits of specific features of their writing (e.g., ideation, organization, voice, vocabulary, sentence formation, conventions) to teaching specific strategies for evaluating a first draft of a paper for substantive (e.g., clarity) or mechanical (e.g., misspelled words) problems in their text (see Box 4.2 for an example of a self-evaluation strategy).

The basic logic underlying reading and evaluating one's own writing using specific criteria is that this helps students acquire declarative and procedural knowledge that they then can use to regulate their future writing. It is also possible that such knowledge can be obtained by evaluating the writing of others; Graham and colleagues

> **Box 4.2.** Example of a Self-Evaluation Strategy (Andrade, Wang, Du, & Akawi, 2009)
>
> Students were asked to read and discuss a model essay, consider its strengths and weaknesses, and develop a list of the qualities of a good essay. Next, the teacher presented a rubric for scoring essays and described and demonstrated how to use it. The rubric assessed the following attributes: ideas and content, organization, voice, word choice, sentence fluency, and conventions. The score for each attribute ranged from 0 to 3, and students were provided with example text for each score. Students used the rubric to score their first drafts of papers prior to revising them.

(2011) found that the quality of a student's own writing can be improved by asking him or her to read text produced by peers and provide feedback using specific criteria. For example, MacArthur, Schwartz, and Graham (1991) reported that students' first drafts of their compositions began to change after they were taught a strategy where they read peers' text, evaluated it using specific criteria, and shared their evaluations with the author. The criteria focused students' attention on clarity and completeness of the material they were reading (e.g., identify text that is unclear and where more detail is needed) as well as mechanical correctness (e.g., identify misspelled words).

It must be noted that, in some studies reviewed by Graham and colleagues (2011), peer evaluation was successful in improving both the evaluator's writing and the peer's writing, even though students were not provided with instruction on how to do this. Because these data are based on group performance and not necessarily true for all students, we recommend that teachers model and explicitly teach students how to read peers' text, apply the target criteria, and provide thoughtful and considerate feedback. Strategy instruction for the peer-revising process has been successful (cf. Harris et al., 2008).

Although we strongly believe that time needs to be dedicated specifically to teaching writing as well as reading, we also believe that this instruction needs to be designed in such a way that there are benefits for both reading and writing whenever possible. As Shanahan (2006) argued, reading and writing are connected, as they draw on a common bank of knowledge, skills, and processes. Although students often apply these resources differently when they read and write, we can purposefully design instruction so that skills, strategies, or knowledge for reading and writing are taught together.

TEACH WRITING AND READING SKILLS TOGETHER

We provide an example from our research to illustrate this maxim. Graham, Harris, and Fink-Chorzempa (2002) examined whether teaching spelling had a positive impact on the spelling and reading of second-grade students. The instructional program for spelling was designed to 1) teach students how to spell words children their age typically use when writing and 2) increase their knowledge of the spelling system so that they are better able to spell words not directly taught. To accomplish these goals, Graham and colleagues designed eight units, with each unit focusing on two or more spelling patterns involving long and short vowels (e.g., the short vowel sound and /ck/ at the end of a monosyllabic word and the long vowel sound and /ke/ at the end of a monosyllabic word).

At the start of each unit, the teacher and students completed a spelling word sort to introduce the children to the target spelling patterns. The teachers started the word sort by placing two master words next to each other (e.g., back, like), saying the word while emphasizing the target feature (i.e., the sound of the vowel) and then asking students how the words were similar and different, emphasizing the sounds and letters in each word. Next, the teacher drew a card from a pack of 11 or 12 words, said the word, emphasized the target sound, and placed it under the appropriate master word. Before placing the word under the master category, the teacher modeled aloud the thinking process that led to that decision. After several words, the teacher encouraged students to help place the words, encouraging them to form and test hypotheses about the rule underlying the placement. Once all cards were placed, the teacher helped students state a rule for the target spelling patterns.

During the next 4 days of the unit, students did an activity where they practiced sound-symbol associations for consonants, blends, digraphs, and vowels. This involved a peer showing them a picture (e.g., of a sack) and asking the child to say what letter made the first, last, or middle sound. Children were able to give each other feedback, as the card had the correct answer on the back of it. During these 4 days, each child also learned how to spell eight new words (missed on a pretest administered before the start of the study) that corresponded to the target spelling patterns. They initially practiced these words using a traditional study procedure involving visualization of the word and writing it correctly from memory. Once they felt they had made enough progress in learning the words, they played games with peers that required that they spell the word correctly to make a move during the game.

Graham and colleagues (2002) purposefully built into their program two reading activities. Each day, students were encouraged and reinforced for findings words from their reading (and writing) that matched the target spelling patterns emphasized in the unit. They also completed a word-building activity, where they were provided with a rime (e.g., -ack, -ike) and 18 onsets and asked to build as many real words as they could with a peer. It was felt that the inclusion of these reading activities would not only strengthen students' spelling skills but also enhance their word recognition and word attack skills. The combination of these spelling and reading activities proved advantageous, as students evidenced improved spelling and word reading skills on norm-referenced measures.

TEACH WRITING AND READING STRATEGIES TOGETHER

The work of Olson and her colleagues (Olson et al., 2012) provides another example of how instruction can be purposefully designed so that similar or complementary aspects of writing and reading are taught together. They argued that students draw on a common pool of processes as they read and write text, including strategies for clarifying, monitoring, visualizing, making connections, summarizing, evaluating, planning, goal-setting, questioning, and tapping prior knowledge. Their work has repeatedly demonstrated that these strategies can be taught together to help students think productively about the text they read as well as the text they produce.

A good example of the deliberate and integrative approach taken by Olson and colleagues is illustrated in a recent study with middle and high school students (Olson, Land, Anselmi, & AuBuchon, 2010). These students were asked to write essays about novels read in class and develop a theme about each novel and interpret them in terms of setting, plot, character, and symbolism. This proved to be a very difficult task for most of the students in this study, so Olson and her colleagues worked with teachers to scaffold students' reading and writing about such novels. This involved a 2-week unit that focused on teaching students to apply the types of strategies listed in the previous paragraph (e.g., planning, goal-setting, tapping prior knowledge, visualizing, evaluating) as they read a new novel and was followed by applying these same strategies to analyze and revise an essay written about a novel they had read previously.

Instruction can further be designed so that students are taught different writing and reading strategies but learn to apply them together to meet specific literacy goals. This is illustrated in the work of Mason, Snyder, Sukhram, and Kedem (2006). They took a previously validated reading strategy designed to help students *T*hink before reading, think *W*hile reading, and think *A*fter reading (TWA) and combined it with a previously validated writing strategy (PLANS: *P*ick goals, *L*ist ways to meet goals, *A*nd make *N*otes, *S*equence notes) designed to help students write better text. With TWA, students think about the author's purpose, what they already know about the topic, what they want to learn, appropriate speed of reading, linking knowledge while reading, rereading as needed, identifying the main idea, summarizing text, and deciding what they learned. With PLANS, students pick goals for what their composition will accomplish, identify ways to meet the goals, generate ideas for their paper, and sequence them. Using the self-regulated strategy development model of strategy instruction (Harris, Graham, Mason, & Friedlander, 2008), Mason and colleagues taught elementary-age students to think about material they were reading using TWA and then to extend their thinking about this reading material by writing an expository retelling of it using the PLANS strategy. This had a positive impact on students' oral and written recall of material read. Mason, Reid, and Hagaman (2012) provide additional validated strategies for reading and writing for adolescents.

CONCLUSION

Writing stands poised to join reading and STEM in terms of research funding, time allocated in schools, curriculum development, educational reform, and national attention. Although this is exciting, it also poses numerous challenges to teachers, administrators, and school systems. There is a research base regarding both writing and reading–writing connections, but the historical lack of focus on writing has resulted in far less research on both writing and reading–writing connections than on reading. As schools work to address the CCSS, they must also seek to understand and apply the evidence base on writing and reading–writing connections while at the same time recognizing the limitations of that evidence base.

Today, a much higher level of literacy abilities is required for success in both work and continuing education than was required just 10 or 20 years ago, and evidence suggests that this trend is accelerating (Business Roundtable, 2009). The educational community must face this challenge together, bridging the research-to-practice gap and at the same time supporting research needed to take us further down this road. How successful the movement toward CCSS will be as part of facing this challenge remains to be seen. Similar to so many important and well-intentioned unfunded (or underfunded) mandates before it, the CCSS face a host of challenges. Recent surveys have found differing results regarding how well teachers feel prepared to teach the new standards (Gewertz, 2013). Many teachers report insufficient knowledge of the CCSS, inadequate professional development, concerns about the alignment of the CCSS with their current curriculum materials and textbooks, and inadequate preparation to teach CCSS to students with disabilities and English language learners (Editorial Projects in Education Research Center, 2013).

To further complicate matters, although the majority of states and districts are moving toward full implementation of CCSS, opponents of the CCSS are actively pushing states to reconsider or abandon the CCSS and/or the consortia developing tests aligned with the Common Core, and they are increasing legislative pressure and public relations efforts against CCSS (Ujifusa, 2013). Concerns include the possible intention to lay groundwork for a national curriculum, inappropriate use of taxpayer dollars, and the level of emphasis on student testing.

On the other hand, many positive aspects of the CCSS movement have been cited as well. Some believe that the assessments being developed for CCSS are likely to assess deeper levels of learning than previous approaches and thus have a great impact on learning (Gewertz, 2013). Others have noted that the anti-CCSS movement is clearly a minority view and that benefits outweigh these concerns. Support from the private sector and higher education has been clear (Ujifusa, 2013), whereas others note the need for CCSS due to a highly mobile population and the potential to create a marketplace for much-needed innovative, educational technology. Michael Petrilli (a vice president of the Washington-based

Thomas B. Fordham Institute) has criticized aspects of the financial ties between CCSS and federal grants for states yet argued that dropping the CCSS would be like "reverting to rotary phones" (Ujifusa, 2013).

In spite of the concerns raised and the uncertain future of the CCSS, we remain optimistic about both the CCSS and the future of writing instruction. We recently overheard an enthusiastic administrator explaining the CCSS to the person sitting next to her on our plane. The person sitting next to her asked an excellent question, wondering how much preparation teachers in this district had been given to prepare for this change. The administrator answered honestly that it had not been enough, but then voiced her opinion that in the long run, this movement would be good for our children and good for schools. We agree. Based on more than 30 years of work with committed, motivated teachers and administrators (who have made up the large majority of those with whom we have worked) facing some of the most challenging jobs out there, we believe that these largely unsung heroes will continue to make a difference and that CCSS will help make that possible.

REFERENCES

Andrade, H.L., Wang, X., Du, Y., Akawi, R.L. (2009). Rubric-referenced self-assessment and self-efficacy for writing. *The Journal of Education Research, 102*, 287–301.

Applebee, A., & Langer, J. (2011). A snapshot of writing instruction in middle and high schools. *English Journal, 100*, 14–27.

Bangert-Drowns, R.L., Hurley, M.M., & Wilkinson, B. (2004). The effects of school-based Writing-to-Learn interventions on academic achievement: A meta-analysis. *Review of Educational Research, 74*, 29–58.

Business Roundtable. (2009). *Getting ahead—staying ahead: Helping America's workforce succeed in the 21st century.* Retrieved from http://businessroundtable.org/studies-and-reports/the-springboard-project-releases-final-recommendations-to-strengthen-a

College Board (2012). *Report on college and career readiness 2012.* Retrieved from http://research.college board.org/programs/sat/data/cb-seniors-2012

Conference Board. (2006). *Are they really ready to work? Employers' perspectives on the basic knowledge and applied skills of new entrants to the 21st-century workforce.* Prepared with the Partnership for 21st-Century Skills, Corporate Voices for Working Families, and the Society for Human Resources Management. Retrieved from http://www.p21.org/index.php?option=com_content&task=view&id=250&Itemid=64

Cutler, L., & Graham, S. (2008). Primary grade writing instruction: A national survey. *Journal of Educational Psychology, 100*, 907–919.

Editorial Projects in Education Research Center. (2013). *Teacher perspectives on the Common Core.* Bethesda, MD: Editorial Projects in Education Research Center.

Fulton, M. (2010). *State reports on the cost of remedial education.* Denver, CO: Education Commission of the States. Retrieved from http://www.gettingpastgo.org/docs/CostofRemedialEducation-StateReports.pdf

Gewertz, C. (2013). Teachers say they are unprepared for Common Core. *Education Week, 32*(22), 1, 12.

Gilbert, J., & Graham, S. (2010). Teaching writing to elementary students in grades 4 to 6: A national survey. *Elementary School Journal, 110*, 494–518.

Graham, S., Harris, K.R., & Fink-Chorzempa, B. (2002). Contributions of spelling instruction to the spelling, writing, and reading of poor spellers. *Journal of Educational Psychology, 94*, 669–686.

Graham, S., Harris, K.R., & Hebert, M. (2011). *Informing writing: The benefits of formative assessment.* Washington, DC: Alliance for Excellence in Education.

Graham, S., & Hebert, M. (2011). Writing to read: A meta-analysis of the impact of writing and writing instruction on reading. *Harvard Educational Review, 81*(4), 710–744.

Graham, S., & Perin, D. (2007). *Writing next: Effective strategies to improve writing of adolescents in middle and high schools* [A report from the Carnegie Corporation of New York]. Washington, DC: Alliance for Excellent Education.

Harris, K.R., Graham, S., Brindle, M., & Sandmel, K. (2009). Metacognition and children's writing. In D. Hacker, J. Dunlosky, & A. Graesser (Eds.), *Handbook of metacognition in education* (pp. 131–153). Mahwah, NJ: Erlbaum.

Harris, K.R., Graham, S., Mason, L., & Friedlander, B. (2008). *Powerful writing strategies for all students.* Baltimore, MD: Paul H. Brookes Publishing Co.

Hayes, J. (1996). A new framework for understanding cognition and affect in writing. In M. Levy & S. Ransdell (Eds.), *The science of writing: Theories, methods, individual differences, and applications* (pp. 1–27). Mahwah, NJ: Erlbaum.

International Reading Association & the *Eunice Kennedy Shriver* National Institute of Child Health and Human Development (IRA/NICHD). (2012). *The reading-writing connection.* Retrieved from http://www.reading.org/Libraries/resources/reading-writingconnection_final.pdf

Kiuhara, S., Graham, S., & Hawken, L. (2009). Teaching writing to high school students: A national survey. *Journal of Educational Psychology, 101,* 136–160.

MacArthur, C., Schwartz, S., & Graham, S. (1991). Effects of a reciprocal peer revision strategy in special education classrooms. *Learning Disabilities Research and Practice, 6,* 201–210.

Mason, L., Reid, R., Hagaman, J. (2012). *Building comprehension in adolescents: Powerful strategies for improving reading and writing in content areas.* Baltimore, MD: Paul H. Brookes Publishing Co.

Mason, L., Snyder, K., Sukhram, D., & Kedem, Y. (2006). TWA + PLANS strategies for expository reading and writing: Effects for nine fourth-grade students. *Exceptional Children, 73,* 69–89.

Morrow, L., Wixson, K., & Shanahan, T. (Eds.). (2013). *Teaching with the common core standards for English language arts: Grades 3–5.* New York, NY: Guilford Press.

National Center for Education Statistics. (2012). *The Nation's report card: Writing 2011.* Washington, DC: Institute of Education Sciences, U.S. Department of Education. Retrieved from http://nationsreportcard.gov/writing_2011/summary.asp

National Commission on Writing in America's Schools and Colleges. (2003). The neglected "R": The need for a writing revolution. Retrieved from http://www.collegeboard.com/prod_downloads/writingcom/neglectedr.pdf

National Commission on Writing in America's Schools and Colleges. (2004). *Writing: A ticket to work . . . or a ticket out.* New York, NY: College Board.

National Governors Association Center for Best Practices & Council of Chief State School Officers (NGA/CCSSO). (2010). *Common Core State Standards: English language arts standards.* Washington, DC: Authors.

Olson, C., Kim, J., Scarcella, R., Kramer, J., Pearson, M., van Dyk, D., . . . Land, R. (2012). Enhancing the interpretative reading and analytic writing of mainstreamed English learners in secondary school: Results from a randomized field trial using a cognitive strategies approach. *American Educational Research Journal, 49,* 323–355.

Olson, C., Land, R., Anselmi, T., & AuBuchon, C. (2010). Teaching secondary English learners to understand, analyze, and write interpretive essays about theme. *Journal of Adolescent and Adult Literacy, 54,* 245–256.

Prior, P. (2006). A sociocultural theory of writing. In C. MacArthur, S. Graham, & J. Fitzgerald (Eds.), *Handbook of writing research* (pp. 54–66). New York, NY: Guilford Press.

Sawchuk, S. (2012, August 29). Educator cadres formed to support common tests. *Education Week, 32,* 6.

Shanahan, T. (2006). Relations among oral language, reading, and writing development. In C. MacArthur, S. Graham, & J. Fitzgerald (Eds.), *Handbook of writing research* (pp. 171–183). New York, NY: Guilford Press.

Ujifusa, A. (2013). Pressure mounts in some states against Common Core. *Education Week, 32*(20), 1, 26.

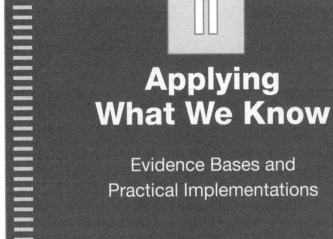

II

Applying
What We Know

Evidence Bases and
Practical Implementations

5

What Is an Evidence Base and When Can It Be Implemented?

Peggy McCardle and Brett Miller

For at least two decades, the education community has been moving toward adoption of evidence-based practices in schools to improve education practice and student learning outcomes. This requires not only that researchers produce such evidence but also that it be provided in a useable form for practical implementation. It also requires us to think about what constitutes sufficient evidence that can be informative and useful in education practice, how that information can best be conveyed to those who would implement it to help ensure fidelity, and what supports are necessary to implement and sustain change in practice.

Of the many topics that educators must consider, reading has one of the longest research histories, has arguably the most solid research base, and is the topic for which the most effort has been expended to bring that research base to practical attention. Others have considered the issue of what that evidence is, where it comes from, and how it should inform policy or practice, and their discussions have informed the thinking brought forward in this chapter. These sources consist of both specific publications (e.g., Davies, 1999; Hargreaves, 1996; McCardle, Chhabra, & Kapinus, 2008; McCardle & Miller, 2009; National Research Council, 2002; 2012d; Nutley, Davies, & Tilley, 2000; Pasquinelli, 2011; Thomas & Pring, 2004; U.S. Department of Education, 2003) and the work of organizations that exist to conduct syntheses and meta-analyses to inform decision making and practice (e.g., the Campbell Collaboration, http://www.campbellcollaboration.org; the Evidence for Policy and Practice Information and Coordinating Centre [EPPI-Centre], http://eppi.ioe.ac.uk/cms).

Given the amount of available research on reading—and the growing amount of research on writing—these two areas provide an example of many facets of the evidence issues: how to decide what evidence is needed (i.e., what informs the decision of what research topics to investigate and the types of data appropriate to build an evidence base on the topic); how the evidence has been or should be compiled (e.g., Are meta-analyses possible? Have systematic syntheses been done? What were the criteria for the compilation of evidence and the conclusions drawn from the data?); and how to utilize the existing evidence base to inform decisions. In addition, educators face challenges in identifying and sorting through that evidence, determining what in fact constitutes evidence, and then deciding if and how it can be useful in their own schools and classrooms, and whether the evidence is sufficient to motivate a change in practice.

WHERE DID THE PHRASE *EVIDENCE-BASED PRACTICE IN EDUCATION* COME FROM?

Legislation has played a major role in promoting the notion of *evidence-based practice in education*. The term became a popular phrase in the 1990s in both the United States and the United Kingdom (e.g., Hargreaves, 1996) as both countries sought to improve educational outcomes. In the United States, the National Assessment of Educational Progress (NAEP) helped bring to light the stark need for improvement in education outcomes for U.S. students. The NAEP is a snapshot of how U.S. students are performing and allows general comparisons over time. Planned with funding through a grant from the Carnegie Corporation in 1964, the NAEP was congressionally mandated in 1969 and conducted the first national assessment in that year.[1] It was reauthorized most recently in 2002 (NAEP, PL 107-279) and has allowed the United States to monitor student performance in various content areas, including reading. In the 1990s, NAEP data indicated a serious problem in the proportions of children in grades 4, 8, and 12 not succeeding in reading (e.g., U.S. Department of Education, 1993, 1996; for more recent data, see National Center for Education Statistics, 2011). President Clinton cited NAEP data in his 1996 State of the Union address (The White House, 1996), after which the House Committee on Education and the Workforce[2] held hearings and decided that what teachers needed was to learn about and apply the most recent research—and the move toward evidence-based practice in education began. The Reading Excellence Act (REA) of 1998 (PL 105-277) was passed with broad bipartisan support, providing funds from formula grants for teacher professional development in scientifically based reading research (SBRR) through a specific application and review process. Efforts were made to compile that research, based on the continued accrual of NAEP data and on summaries of research data in national reports (discussed later in this chapter). In 2001, with encouragement from President Bush, Congress passed the Reading First (RF) and Early Reading First legislation, implemented through the No Child Left Behind Act (2002; PL 107-110); this legislation used the REA definitions of reading as well as SBRR and incorporated the instructional principles shown to be effective in the report of the National Reading Panel (National Institute of Child Health and Human Development, 2000).

At the same time that the RF legislation was being developed, the U.S. Department of Education (ED) commissioned a National Research Council report, *Scientific Research in Education* (National Research Council, 2002), which called for more rigorous research in education and the development of a "scientific culture" within education research in order to continue to provide reliable, high-quality research as a basis for education practice. In response, in the 2002 reauthorization of the research component of ED (then the Office of Education Research and Improvement), Congress replaced the existing office with the new Institute of Education Sciences (IES). (For a more detailed account of the history of these laws, see Sweet, 2004; for more information on further legislation and reports that had an impact on special education, see McCardle & Miller, 2009.) Clearly the idea of evidence-based practice had come to education, and there was attention given to the quality of the evidence.

---

[1]A detailed history of the planning and implementation of NAEP is available at http://nces.ed.gov/nations reportcard/about/naephistory.asp.

[2]The House Committee on Education and the Workforce is the Congressional authorizing committee for the U.S. Departments of Education, Health and Human Services, and Labor.

WHERE HAS THE EVIDENCE COME FROM?

Evidence comes from research, which usually is published in peer-reviewed scientific journals typically written by and for researchers. Bringing the various sources of evidence together and systematically synthesizing the results has and continues to be a limiting challenge for both researchers and other interested parties (e.g., practitioners) attempting to access research findings directly and to act on them. Some efforts to bring the evidence together in some summary form to make it more accessible and useful do exist (noted as *companion documents* later in this section). In addition to some helpful published volumes on evidence-based practice (e.g., Thomas & Pring, 2004) and how to approach systematic reviews (e.g., Gough, Oliver, & Thomas, 2012), there are two major online sources of information about how to produce evidence syntheses and that offer the results of syntheses to users.

As noted earlier, the Campbell Collaboration offers a potential source of evidence. It is a dynamic international research network that produces systematic reviews of the effects of social—including education—interventions. They offer guidelines for conducting a systematic review, including explicit predefined procedures to allow for replication, transparency, and minimization of bias. They offer assistance with planning and conducting reviews, methodological support, and sometimes financial assistance for the conduct of reviews. As noted on their web site, "The Campbell Library provides free online access to the full text of our systematic reviews in the areas of education, criminal justice and social welfare. The library is a peer-reviewed source of reliable evidence of the effects of interventions" (Campbell Collaboration, 2013). Although few education reviews exist, the Collaboration has an education coordinating group, and there appears to be much interest in assisting in and promoting systematic reviews and meta-analyses. Similarly, the Evidence for Policy and Practice Information and Coordinating Centre (EPPI-Centre) of the social science research unit at the Institute of Education, University of London, also carries out systematic reviews. The center is "dedicated to making reliable research findings accessible to the people who need them, whether they are making policy, practice or personal decisions" (EPPI-Centre, 2013), and, similar to the Campbell Collaboration, offers assistance in the conduct of systematic reviews. The center provides a methods document, "EPPI-Centre Methods for Conducting Systematic Reviews," and an evidence library online.

Within the United States, there have been some government-supported efforts to bring relevant, education-related research evidence together into larger, summary documents. The goals of these reports were to compile information clarifying the extent to which the research on certain topics converged, and based on the compilation of evidence and its convergence, to make recommendations about how to better support instruction in the areas in question. In reading, there are four major examples of these types of documents, comprising both consensus panel reports and research review and synthesis reports, which provide a convergence of evidence from a variety of types of studies and from which recommendations were drawn for application of the findings to classroom practice: *Preventing Reading Difficulties in Young Children* (Snow, Burns, & Griffin, 1998), a report of the National Research Council; *Teaching Children to Read: The Report of the National Reading Panel* (National Institute of Child Health and Human Development [NICHD][3], 2000), a report requested by the U.S. Congress and supported by the NICHD of the National Institutes of Health; *Reading for Understanding* (Snow, 2002), a report commissioned by the U.S. Department of

---

[3]Note that the Institute was renamed in 2008 to be the *Eunice Kennedy Shriver* National Institute of Child Health and Human Development, although the acronym remains NICHD. This publication and support for the National Reading Panel predated that renaming.

Education and produced by the RAND Corporation; and *Improving Adult Literacy Instruction: Options for Practice and Research*, a report sponsored by the U.S. Department of Education (National Research Council, 2012b). McCardle and Miller (2009) described the value of these reports this way:

> Although it is important that teachers and students benefit from research findings, it is equally important that confidence in those findings not be overturned by the next study to be published, considering the precious financial resources expended on changes in practice and the time and energy of the teachers invested in learning, preparing, and implementing new practices. Convergent evidence can take various forms. Replication of studies in slightly different groups of students, under slightly different conditions, with the same essential finding is one such form. Another is multiple studies performed with differing designs and different populations, measures, or conditions, that result in the same or highly similar findings. These sorts of evidence give confidence that changing practice based on them will be a worthwhile and productive effort. (p. 25)

In fact, these reports do bring together information that gave confidence to many that changing practice based on them would be worthwhile and productive. The issue then became how to translate that information for classroom implementation. The first two and the final of these reports also had companion documents meant to do that. The National Academies, publishers of *Preventing Reading Difficulties in Young Children*, produced a companion document for parents, teachers, and child care providers (Burns, Griffin, & Snow, 1999); (in the case of the *Improving Adult Literacy Instruction* report, they also produced companion documents for instructor and professional development instructors). The National Reading Panel report (NICHD, 2000) was the basis of companion documents for teachers and parents developed by the National Institute for Literacy (Partnership for Reading, 2001a; 2001b). Based on the *Improving Adult Literacy Instruction* report, the National Research Council released two documents to supplement the research recommendations focused on supporting learning and motivation and the development of reading and writing skills in late adolescent and adult learners (National Research Council, 2012a; 2012c). Researchers themselves have also produced meta-analyses and syntheses. As more of these research summaries and syntheses have been completed, there have been increasing efforts to provide renditions that are more accessible and to include writing—generally acknowledged to be part of literacy but much neglected in terms of research reports. Some key examples of other research summaries written for educators are a series of adolescent literacy reports supported by the Carnegie Foundation of New York and published by the Alliance for Excellent Education—for example, *Reading Next* (Biancarosa & Snow, 2004), *Writing Next* (Graham & Perin, 2007), and *Writing to Read* (Graham & Hebert, 2011). A book was also written that summarized the findings in the national reading reports listed earlier and others summaries, including some that address writing; this volume also addresses moving the findings to practice, with classroom scenarios to provide implementation examples (McCardle, Chhabra, & Kapinus, 2008).

Now almost two decades after those seminal focused efforts, the gap between research evidence and practical implementation—although narrowed somewhat—remains, and the need for translation of research-based evidence to practical implementation will only increase with the widespread adoption of the Common Core State Standards (CCSS; National Governors Association Center for Best Practices & Council of Chief State School Officers, 2010). As noted in the chapters by Strickland (Chapter 10) and by Urbani and colleagues (Chapter 9), these standards are giving rise to curriculum development and targeted practices for implementation. The CCSS also heighten the need and push the timetable for making existing findings more readily available and for continuing to conduct research on how best to reduce the achievement gaps that continue to exist. The translation of research findings, though, is fraught with challenges for the practitioner; in short, educators need to evaluate the merits of research practices for possible implementation in the classroom, and this is not as simple as the phrase might indicate. The understanding of what constitutes evidence, and when "evidence" can and should be used in practice, is not as straightforward as one would wish (e.g., Davies, 1999). Many speak of levels of evidence or the accumulation of sufficient convergent evidence to merit changes in practice. How does one judge the adequacy of evidence for a practice or program? What should guide instruction in the classroom when sufficient solid evidence does not exist?

JUDGING EVIDENCE

Addressing the question of what constitutes evidence, the U.S. Department of Education lays out specific standards for trustworthy evidence (Institute of Education Sciences, 2013), with well-implemented randomized controlled trials (RCTs) considered to constitute strong evidence, and quasi-experimental studies as meeting their evidentiary standards—but with reservations. Recent reports describe evidence standards developed for regression discontinuity and single case study designs (Kratochwill et al., 2010; Schochet et al., 2010). To alleviate the need for educators and the public to have to determine the details of whether a study meets these criteria, IES recruits and trains reviewers to evaluate the research and offers a series of reports—practice guides with recommendations for classroom instruction, intervention reports, single case study reviews, and quick reviews of recent research. Of these, the practice guides and intervention reports summarize studies and are therefore—among the various reports provided—likely to be of the broadest usefulness to educators.

As noted earlier, we would not advocate adoption of the results of a single study as a basis for dramatic changes in practice, although if a single study were to demonstrate success in a particular instructional technique that had been used in a similar setting with a group of students similar to those a teacher would work with, trying out such a technique to try to move the class or some individual students forward is certainly a viable option. In fact, this example serves to highlight what educators at various levels might need to consider when judging what evidence to trust or to try out. A district superintendent, for example, would not likely recommend a district- or school-wide change in instruction based on a single study found in a research journal or a single case study, even on a federal agency web site; she or he might, however, entertain such changes based on these conditions: 1) a major synthesis showed that multiple studies agreed on findings that a particular approach or program worked, and 2) the studies in that synthesis included sufficient student population diversity to give confidence that students in his or her own district should benefit from adoption of that approach.

Even then, the road is neither smooth nor easy. Who implemented the approach or program? Were they researchers or research associates who received specialized training on the implementation? Was it also implemented by actual classroom teachers, and if so, was it as effective? How much training and ongoing professional development was needed to maintain the gains that were found? Was there classroom support for the implementation, and is that support sustainable when research is not being conducted? Is it cost-effective? Can it be implemented within the classroom, either with the entire class or in small groups, in a way that the teacher can implement efficiently and effectively?

WHERE WILL ADDITIONAL EVIDENCE THAT CAN BE USEFUL IN CLASSROOMS COME FROM?

Many states are in the process of developing statewide education databases that will enable them to track things such as graduation rates and student progress over time and across different schools and districts; the Statewide Longitudinal Data Systems program is supported by the IES (National Center for Education Statistics, 2012). This is wise, given that we are a mobile society, and students moving from district to district or school to school can "get lost" in the system. Even as states are providing schools with data about classrooms, schools, and districts so that schools can track progress, such data systems could also determine whether the adoption of a new program of instruction or professional development or a new curriculum is working. To do this, schools are hiring individuals trained in research and large data sets; yet it is unlikely that these individuals will have the time, resources, or team needed to conduct research with the data. Increasingly, university researchers are seeking to partner with schools. To conduct research on what works in schools, researchers need access to schools and classrooms. There is mutuality in this need—schools need programs and approaches that will result in better student outcomes, and researchers need teachers and students to try out new approaches and programs so that the effectiveness of those approaches and programs can be tested. Where there is mutual need, mutual benefit is possible.

The coinciding development of state databases and the implementation of the CCSS—where expectations for student accomplishments are delineated—provide a golden opportunity for a partnership of research and practice that can decrease the chasm between research and practice as well as between evidence production and implementation. Researchers are trained to solve puzzles, and the problems and issues that teachers face can be cast as puzzles for researchers to help solve. Teachers could develop their ideas for innovative practices together with researchers and have them tested as they try to implement them; researchers could present their ideas, and teachers could help them troubleshoot the practicalities of putting them in place and testing them in classrooms. The scale of these efforts would vary depending on what evidence already existed to address the issues in question or the "risks" involved. By the time these ideas have been successfully demonstrated and are ready to take to scale, databases should be in place; the databases have the potential to enable teachers to see progress in their individual students while researchers get the bigger picture of how well techniques are succeeding on the school and district levels,[4] with comparison groups already in place. If the databases can be efficiently populated, such a scenario could enable researchers, teachers, and education administrators to track the lasting effects of an instructional change over time, because students would be less likely to be lost to follow-up with the new state databases. And when such interventions or instructional changes have been successfully implemented, we would urge that researchers publish the results in peer-reviewed journals to document them; we would then advocate for systematic reviews of such studies, as these publications accrue, to continue the cycle of building the evidence base, even as we move existing evidence to practice.

---

[4]These large-scale databases, though, are often not currently optimized to provide teachers with formative data that provides sufficient specificity and frequency of measurement to allow for dynamic instructional changes but, rather, function to see from a summative lens, how interventions—whether at the classroom, school, or district level—have an impact on study achievement. In addition, the data may not currently be available in sufficient time to inform instruction; however, these are not inherent limitations of these databases and corresponding analytic tools.

None of this will be easy to do and will depend on factors such as efficient management and quality control of the data itself to ensure accuracy, researchers' timely access to databases, cooperation and clear communication between researchers and teachers, funding to support the entire endeavor, and stability; if the principal or the district or state superintendent who approved the project leaves, teams of researchers and teachers may find themselves without access to students or data midproject. The nation is pushing evidence-based practice, the CCSS are a reality, and databases are under development. Teachers and researchers are committed to improved student outcomes and to solving the puzzles of why some students struggle with specific aspects of reading, writing, and the interface of the two. Using all this to advantage seems a wise path to follow. Many working teams of researchers and teachers are already in place, as some of the chapters in this volume demonstrate. Even so, more are needed. We acknowledge that there are many challenges, but both the research and the implementation of the evidence it produces are possible.

REFERENCES

Biancarosa, G., & Snow, C.E. (2004.) *Reading next: A vision for action and research in middle and high school literacy* [A report from the Carnegie Corporation of New York]. Washington, DC: Alliance for Excellent Education.

Burns, M.S., Griffin, P., & Snow, C.E. (1999). *Starting out right: A guide to promoting children's reading success.* Washington, DC: National Academy Press.

Campbell Collaboration. (2013). *Producing a review.* Retrieved from http://www.campbellcollaboration.org/systematic_reviews/index.php?page=1

Davies, P. (1999). What is evidence-based education? *British Journal of Educational Studies, 47*(2), 108–121.

Evidence for Policy and Practice Information and Coordinating Centre (EPPI-Centre). (2012). *About the EPPI-Centre.* Retrieved from http://eppi.ioe.ac.uk/cms/Default.aspx?tabid=53

Gough, D., Oliver, S., & Thomas, J. (2012). *An introduction to systematic reviews.* Thousand Oaks, CA: Sage.

Graham, S., & Hebert, H. (2010). *Writing to read: Evidence for how writing can improve reading* [A report from the Carnegie Corporation of New York]. Washington, DC: Alliance for Excellent Education.

Graham, S., & Perin, D. (2007). *Writing next: Effective strategies to improve writing of adolescents in middle and high schools* [A report from the Carnegie Corporation of New York]. Washington, DC: Alliance for Excellent Education.

Hargreaves, D. (1996). Teaching as a research-based profession: Possibilities and Prospects. *Teacher Training Association Annual Lecture 1996.* Retrieved from http://eppi.ioe.ac.uk/cms/Portals/0/PDF reviews and summaries/TTA Hargreaves lecture.pdf

Institute of Education Sciences. (2013). Procedures and Standards Handbook. *What Works Clearinghouse.* Retrieved from http://ies.ed.gov/ncee/wwc/documentsum.aspx?sid=19

Kratochwill, T.R., Hitchcock, J., Horner, R.H., Levin, J.R., Odom, S.L., Rindskopf, D.M., & Shadish, W.R. (2010). Single-case designs technical documentation. Retrieved from http://ies.ed.gov/ncee/wwc/pdf/wwc_scd.pdf

McCardle, P., Chhabra, V., & Kapinus, B. (2008). *Reading research in action: A teacher's guide for student success.* Baltimore, MD: Paul H. Brookes Publishing Co.

McCardle, P., & Miller, B. (2009). Why we need evidence-based practice in reading and where to find that evidence. In S. Rosenfield & V. Berninger (Eds.), *Translating science-supported instruction into evidence-based practices: Understanding and applying the implementation process* (pp. 19–48). Oxford, UK: Oxford University Press.

National Assessment of Education Progress, PL 107-279, 116 Stat. 1983, 20 U.S.C. § 9622.

National Center for Education Statistics. (2011). *The nation's report card: Reading 2011.* Washington, DC: Institute of Education Sciences, U.S. Department of Education. Retrieved from http://nces.ed.gov/nationsreportcard/pdf/main2011/2012457.pdf

National Center for Education Statistics. (2012). *Statewide longitudinal data systems grant program.* Retrieved from http://nces.ed.gov/programs/slds/index.asp

National Governors Association Center for Best Practices & Council of Chief State School Officers (NGA/CCSSO). (2010). *Common Core State Standards: English language arts standards.* Washington, DC: Authors.

National Institute of Child Health and Human Development (NICHD). (2000). *Teaching children to read: An evidence-based assessment of the scientific research literature on reading and its implications for reading instruction.* (NIH Publication No. 00-4754). Washington, DC: U.S. Government Printing Office.

No Child Left Behind. (2002). Act of 2001, PL 107-110, 115 Stat. 1452, 20 U.S.C. §§ 6301 *et. seq.*

National Research Council. (2002). *Scientific research in education.* Committee on Scientific Principles for Education Research, R.J. Shavelson, & L. Towne (Eds.). Division of Behavioral and Social Sciences and Education. Washington, DC: National Academy Press.

National Research Council. (2012a). *Improving adult literacy instruction: Developing reading and writing.* Committee on Learning Sciences: Foundations and Applications to Adolescent and Adult Literacy, A.M. Lesgold, & M. Welch-Ross (Eds.). Division of Behavioral and Social Sciences and Education. Washington, DC: The National Academies Press.

National Research Council. (2012b). *Improving adult literacy instruction: Options for practice and research.* Committee on Learning Sciences: Foundations and Applications to Adolescent and Adult Literacy, A.M. Lesgold, & M. Welch-Ross (Eds.). Division of Behavioral and Social Sciences and Education. Washington, DC: The National Academies Press.

National Research Council. (2012c). *Improving adult literacy instruction: Supporting learning and motivation.* Committee on Learning Sciences: Foundations and Applications to Adolescent and Adult Literacy, A.M. Lesgold, & M. Welch-Ross (Eds.). Division of Behavioral and Social Sciences and Education. Washington, DC: The National Academies Press.

National Research Council. (2012d). *Using science as evidence in public policy.* Committee on the Use of Social Science Knowledge in Public Policy, K. Prewitt, T.A. Schwandt, & M.L. Straf (Eds.). Division of Behavioral and Social Sciences and Education. Washington, DC: The National Academies Press.

Nutley, S., Davies, H., & Tilley, N. (2000). Viewpoints: Editorial: Getting research into practice. *Practice, Public Money, and Management, 20*(4), 3–6.

Partnership for Reading. (2001a). *Put reading first: Helping your child learn to read. A parent guide. Preschool through grade 3.* Washington, DC: National Institute for Literacy, National Institute of Child Health and Human Development, U.S. Department of Education.

Partnership for Reading. (2001b). *Put reading first: The research building blocks for teaching children to read. Kindergarten through grade 3.* Washington, DC: National Institute for Literacy, National Institute of Child Health and Human Development, U.S. Department of Education.

Pasquinelli, E. (2011). Knowledge- and evidence-based education: Reasons, trends, and contents. *Mind, Brain, and Education, 5,* 186–195.

Reading Excellence Act. (1998). PL 105-277, 112 Stat. 2681–337, 2681–393, 20 U.S.C. § 6661a *et. seq.*

Schochet, P., Cook, T., Deke, J., Imbens, G., Lockwood, J.R., Porter, J., & Smith, J. (2010). Standards for regression discontinuity designs. Retrieved from http://ies.ed.gov/ncee/wwc/pdf/wwc_rd.pdf

Snow, C. (2002). *Reading for understanding: Toward an R&D program in reading comprehension.* Arlington, VA: RAND.

Snow, C., Burns, S., & Griffin, P. (Eds.). (1998). *Preventing reading difficulties in young children.* Washington, DC: National Academies Press.

Sweet, R. (2004). The big picture: Where we are nationally on the reading front and how we got here. In P. McCardle & V. Chhabra (Eds.), *The voice of evidence in reading research* (pp. 13–44). Baltimore, MD: Paul H. Brookes Publishing Co.

Thomas, G., & Pring, R. (2004). *Evidence-based practice in education.* Berkshire, UK: Open University Press.

U.S. Department of Education. (1993). *NAEP 1992 reading report card for the nation and the states.* Washington, DC: Office of Educational Research and Improvement, National Center for Education Statistics.

U.S. Department of Education (1996). *NAEP 1994 reading report card for the nation and the states: Findings from the national assessment of educational progress and trial state assessments.* Washington, DC: Office of Educational Research and Improvement, National Center for Education Statistics. Retrieved from http://nces.ed.gov/nationsreportcard/pdf/main1994/96045.pdf

U.S. Department of Education. (2003). *Identifying and implementing educational practices supported by rigorous evidence: A user friendly guide.* Washington, DC: Institute of Education Sciences, National Center for Education Evaluation and Regional Assistance.

6

Teacher Education for the Reading–Writing Connection

Devon Brenner

As the other chapters have demonstrated, teaching the reading–writing connection is complex, and it is important. Those of us involved in teacher education are charged with creating preservice and in-service programs that support teachers' acquisition of the knowledge of reading and writing, along with the curriculum materials and pedagogy they will need to support the reading–writing connection in their classrooms. The strongest teachers for the reading–writing connection create safe, inclusive, and engaging learning environments where students can take risks; they use a variety of formal and informal assessments to guide and plan instruction and to give students feedback; they engage students in copious amounts of meaningful reading of a wide variety of genres and types of texts and facilitate responses to those texts; they create opportunities for students to use a process for writing a wide variety of texts for multiple purposes and audiences; and although they teach reading and writing separately on occasion, they generally try to integrate reading and writing (along with other language arts) to support learning in literacy (National Board for Professional Teaching Standards, 2012). In other words, they create the kinds of instruction described in this volume's other chapters.

Some attempt has been made to delineate a knowledge base for teachers of reading, as in the Snow, Griffin, and Burns (2005) volume, *Knowledge to Support the Teaching of Reading*. When we layer in writing and the reading–writing connection, the list grows, and with the advent of the Common Core State Standards (CCSS; National Governors Association Center for Best Practices & Council of Chief State School Officers [NGA/CCSSO], 2010) and the changing literacy demands of the 21st century, the answer to the question "What do teachers need to know to teach the reading-writing connection?" becomes monumental. Though there may be varying opinions about which issues are most important or need the most emphasis, the teacher who is prepared to teach the reading–writing connection—in all its complexity—should know, at a minimum, the following: how language, both oral and written, works (phonics, phonemic awareness, syntax and grammar, text structures, etc.); how reading and writing are used in context and across disciplines; state and national standards; pedagogies, curricula, and strategies for teaching reading on its own, writing on its own, and the two in conjunction (and the evidence base supporting these); how students develop and how that development can vary;

how to interpret assessments and ways to support students with different levels of accomplishment; how people learn in general and in literacy classrooms; sociopolitical aspects of literacy learning, including the complex relationship between learning school-based literacy practices and students' identities; metacognition and the role of strategy instruction; technology, including the technology people (including students) use out of school to read and write as well as technology for teaching; and information literacies (Hall, Johnson, Juzwik, Wortham, & Mosley, 2010; Malm, 2009; Pardo, 2006; Schnellert, Butler, & Higginson, 2008; Scott & Mouza, 2007; Shanahan & Shanahan, 2008; Snow et al., 2005; Torres & Mercado, 2006; Williams & Coles, 2007).

Whether reading–writing teachers know all they need, and whether they are able to put that knowledge into practice in the classroom, is important. We know that teachers matter—students learn more in classrooms with high-quality teachers (Darling-Hammond, 2000; Nye, Konstantopoulos, & Hedges, 2004; Rice, 2003). Teacher quality is particularly important in the literacy classroom (Flippo, 2001; Foorman, Francis, Fletcher, & Schatschneider, 1998; National Institute of Child Health and Human Development [NICHD], 2000). Students achieve more in classrooms where teachers create opportunities for reading and writing in a variety of genres and forms for a variety of purposes (Freedman & Carver, 2007). The most effective literacy teachers are those who teach processes of reading and writing, separately and together, in ways that meet individual students' needs and move entire classes of students to greater achievement.

CONCERNS ABOUT TEACHER KNOWLEDGE AND EFFECTIVENESS

Teacher education programs spend a lot of time and energy preparing teachers to teach literacy. In general, preservice elementary teachers are required to take more courses focusing on literacy pedagogy than pedagogy courses in other content areas. Many states set minimum standards for credit hours in reading or in content-area literacy for all teachers, pre-K–12. Unfortunately, these may not be sufficient to ensure that all teachers are able to teach the reading–writing connection. Concerns about teacher preparation to teach literacy can be seen throughout academic and popular literature. For example, the last decade saw many calls to increase content-area teachers' understanding of literacy pedagogy (Carnegie Council on Advancing Adolescent Literacy, 2010; Council of Chief State School Officers, 2010; National Education Association, 2000). These reports suggest that students learn better when content-area teachers understand how to integrate reading and writing in meaningful ways, provide students with opportunities to read a variety of content-area texts, and are prepared to teach students to write in the discipline-specific formats and genres—and that teachers are not well prepared to do these things.

Additional concerns have been raised about whether teachers, especially elementary and special education teachers, are prepared with sufficient knowledge of the linguistic system (Binks-Cantrell, Washburn, Joshi, & Hougen, 2012; Moats, 2009), knowledge of pedagogy (Manzo, 2006), or engagement and experience as readers (Applegate & Applegate, 2004; Daisey, 2009; Powell-Brown, 2003). Applegate and Applegate (2004) described teachers' lack of knowledge and experience with literacy as *the Peter effect*, equating teachers with the Apostle Peter, who told a beggar that he could not give what he did not have; teachers cannot teach what they do not know and cannot create engaged readers if they themselves do not read.

Many of these warnings and reports have focused on teacher preparation to teach reading. Whether we adequately prepare teachers to teach writing or the reading–writing connection is a concern that has received less attention, largely because writing simply has not received the attention in our field and in the policy realm that reading has received (Pardo, 2006). The No Child Left Behind act focused on reading and math (and not writing). Panels have been formed to study "teacher education in reading" such as the International Reading Association's survey of preservice preparation in reading (Hoffman, Roller, & National Commission on Excellence in Elementary Teacher Preparation for Reading Instruction, 2001), the report of the National Reading Panel (NICHD, 2000), and *Preventing Reading Difficulties,* a report of the National Research Council (Snow, Burns, & Griffin, 1998). Such reports are less prevalent in writing.

The focus on reading to the exclusion of writing or the reading–writing connection can be seen in teacher education programs nationwide. Assuming the titles of our courses reflect our commitments, teacher preparation focuses on reading more than on writing. An examination of the titles of undergraduate courses in three states, as listed in their online catalogs, reveals 61 course titles that refer only to reading, such as "Reading Fundamentals" and "Content-Area Reading." Only 5 courses had only "writing" in the title, including "Writing across the Curriculum" and "Writing Process and Assessment K–8"; the other 75 course titles refer to both reading and writing (e.g., "Reading and Writing in the Middle Grades"), to language arts (e.g., "Secondary Language Arts Education"), or to literacy (e.g., "Early Literacy Instruction"). Half of these courses, however, have a reading (RDG) prefix, reflecting a long-standing institutional commitment to reading instruction, and several mention reading in addition to literacy or language arts (e.g., "Developmental Approaches to Reading and Literacy").

As these titles reflect, the teachers in our classrooms have been more prepared to teach reading than writing or the reading–writing connection, a finding also noted by Graves (2002). We can presume that most reading pedagogy courses include at least some attention to instruction that involves writing, such as using writing to respond to reading or to write about the meanings of vocabulary words. Still, an emphasis on reading to the exclusion of writing in teacher education is cause for concern, as increasingly greater emphasis is placed on writing instruction and the reading–writing connection in the classroom.

Of course, even teachers who are well prepared for literacy teaching may struggle to implement what they have learned in the classroom. Poor leadership, mandated curricula, state and national policies, and other classroom contexts can make teaching the reading–writing connection challenging (Achinstein & Ogawa, 2006; Crocco & Costigan, 2007; MacGillivray, Ardell, Curwen, & Palma, 2004). The increasing number of teachers entering the classroom through alternate routes that may or may not be required to meet the same standards for literacy teacher preparation exacerbates concerns about teacher preparation for the reading–writing connection. As states transition to the CCSS and as policy places increasing emphasis on teaching writing in the pre-K–12 classroom, teacher education programs will need to respond.

TEACHER EDUCATION FOR THE READING–WRITING CONNECTION

We know that teacher preparation has generally prepared teachers to teach reading more than writing. We also know that well-designed and -implemented teacher education programs make a difference. For example, the International Reading Association (IRA) Commission on Excellence in Elementary Teacher Preparation (Hoffman et al., 2001) found that graduates of strong literacy teacher preparation programs that are built around a cohesive vision for literacy teacher preparation and are provided with the resources and autonomy needed to create programs that meet their students' needs are able to create qualitatively different and more literacy-rich classrooms as compared to graduates of other programs.

Although there is still much to learn about teacher preparation for the reading–writing connection, and studies that follow teachers into classrooms or connect teacher preparation directly to student outcomes are rare, a number of review articles offer a consensus around the characteristics of effective literacy teacher education programs (Darling-Hammond, 2000; Hoffman & Pearson, 2000; Hoffman et al., 2005; Pearson, 2001; Risko et al., 2008). Although multiple approaches exist (4-year, 5-year, site-based, post-BA, etc.), the strongest teacher education programs share many characteristics. The best teacher education programs are organized around a coherent vision and work within their higher education and state and local contexts to carry out that vision. They provide students with a strong knowledge base that includes both content (e.g., language systems, reading, and writing) and knowledge of theory and pedagogy. Effective programs provide teacher candidates with opportunities to observe models of desired teaching practices through meaningful and extensive field experiences, to practice those ways of teaching themselves, and to work with strong teachers who are seen as members of the teacher education community. These field and practicum experiences are most effective when they are connected to coursework and when teacher candidates are supported in making connections between coursework and fieldwork and in reflecting on what they see and do in the field. In addition to sharing these characteristics, effective teacher education programs often engage preservice teachers in experiences that mirror the instruction we hope they will provide to students in the classroom (Cantrell, 2002; Freedman & Carver, 2007; Pytash, 2012). This kind of modeling may be especially important for writing, in part because so few new teachers have participated in writing instruction.

Some intriguing new practices are also emerging that can support teacher education for the reading–writing connection. We are just beginning to understand the potential of technology for teacher preparation. New technologies and media are changing the ways that we read and write at home and in the workplace. Social media, tablet computers, smart phones, and online course management systems are among the many innovations that can and should have an impact on teacher preparation. These are becoming a crucial part of the content of teacher preparation, as teachers must increasingly understand the communication technologies and modes of reading and writing students already use and will use outside of school (Alvermann, 2004). These tools are also changing how teacher education in literacy can be structured and delivered. For example, online video classes can bring preservice teachers into the classrooms of accomplished reading–writing teachers when such models may not be available in local schools (Wang & Hartley, 2003). Asynchronous discussion boards are one feature of course management systems that may allow preservice teachers to engage in deeper reflection and more engaged learning than traditional methods (Ajayi, 2009). (See also Atwill and Blanchard's chapter [Chapter 12] for more on use of technology in education.)

Another innovation in teacher education for the reading–writing connection is an increasing focus on collaboration with academic libraries and librarians. In part because of the CCSS, teachers are being asked to engage students in information literacy—to use the Internet and other tools to locate and evaluate sources and to use writing and multimedia tools to communicate about their learning. Librarians and media specialists are beginning to partner with teacher educators to prepare teachers for their roles as teachers of information literacy (Emmons et al., 2009; Williams & Coles, 2007).

Finally, those of us engaged in teacher preparation for the reading–writing connection should take a careful look at our courses, syllabi, and curricula. Although the titles and course descriptions may belie a richer commitment to the reading–writing connection than is obvious from the surface, and simply changing the prefixes of our courses from RDG (reading) to R-W (reading–writing) or LIT (literacy) will not ensure that new teachers are prepared to teach writing and the reading–writing connection, careful reflection on our teacher education programs in their entirety may prompt us to consider how teacher preparation is organized. We all must align our programs with the requirements of multiple state and national standards and of our accrediting bodies and the needs of our local school districts. This must be done within the constraints of our institutional contexts during the few short months we have while students are enrolled in our teacher education programs. At the same time, we also have a commitment to ensure that our teacher preparation programs, both formally in our catalogs and in practice in our classrooms, reflect the reading–writing connection.

PROFESSIONAL DEVELOPMENT FOR THE READING–WRITING CONNECTION

Well-designed teacher preparation programs are extremely important. However, even if teacher education programs were perfect and all new teachers actively took part in them, teacher preparation coursework could never be sufficient for developing the level of expertise and practice necessary to integrate reading and writing in the ways described in the other chapters. Teachers need ongoing professional development across the span of their careers—in the beginning, to help them transfer learning in teacher preparation into their classroom, and over time, to help them refine and improve practice. Professional development also provides opportunities for teachers to learn about new developments in research and pedagogy and to learn about emerging technologies and practices. Effective professional development is especially important right now, as our expectations for students' reading and writing are changing and becoming more complex and because so many teachers in our schools are not prepared to teach writing or the reading–writing connection (Hoffman et al., 2005; Pardo, 2006). Many efforts to reform learning pre-K–12 by changing teaching practices have not been as successful as reformers have hoped. Nichols, Young, and Rickelman (2007) suggest, "When change does not occur, teacher resistance is frequently blamed. However, research suggests that rather than teacher resistance, it is the lack of quality staff development that is the more likely culprit" (p. 112).

In spite of the importance of providing teachers with meaningful professional development to support accomplished practice, good professional development is rare. Too many teachers are required to participate in professional development that does little or nothing to support teaching. The most common model for professional development continues to be the isolated, one-session workshop—a model we know does not work (Borko, 2004; Scott & Mouza, 2007). Borko (2004) describes the wasted expenditure of federal dollars on in-service programs that are "fragmented, intellectually superficial, and do not take into account what we know about how teachers learn" (p. 3).

CHARACTERISTICS OF EFFECTIVE PROFESSIONAL DEVELOPMENT

We can do better. Although there is still much to learn, research on teacher learning has reached consensus about some of the key characteristics of successful professional development. These characteristics include 1) a focus on developing teachers' knowledge of subject

matter and the pedagogical content knowledge to support student learning; 2) content that
is relevant to the teachers' day-to-day needs and connected to their own students and contexts; 3) a design of sufficient duration, including ongoing opportunities for learning, follow-up, and support; 4) active learning experiences, including opportunities for teachers to
engage in the pedagogy they are being asked to implement; 5) opportunities to learn with
school, grade-level, and/or content-area colleagues; and 6) the involvement of administrators who understand and value the content and develop policies that support the practices
being recommended (Borko, 2004; Cochran-Smith & Lytle, 2001; Garet, Porter, Desimone, Birman, & Yoon, 2001; Guskey, 2003).

One particularly strong model for professional development is the development of a
community of practice (Schnellert et al., 2008). Similar practices include peer-coaching study
teams (e.g., Baker & Smith, 1999; Showers & Bruce, 1996) and professional learning communities (Vescio, Ross, & Adams, 2008). When these models are the structure of professional
development, groups of teachers come together regularly to study teaching and learning.
Teachers in a community of practice might read and discuss research studies, reports, or
other professional literature; work together to share and evaluate student work samples; analyze school-, classroom-, or individual-level data and plan instruction based on that data; or
share drafts of instructional plans and give one another feedback. Teachers might also use
these meetings as sites for inquiry, asking questions about their own teaching and learning
and using classroom-based data to answer those questions (Córdova & Matthiesen, 2010).

As a model for teacher professional development, communities of practice may provide a structure or mechanism to support the development of practices for teaching the
reading–writing connection; however, the structure of regular teacher meetings, in and of
itself, may not be sufficient to support teacher learning. Communities of practice are more
successful when teachers have a strong sense of collegiality and shared purpose. Simply
mandating that teachers meet once a week does not ensure that teachers will learn from
one another. In addition, many of the teaching practices that support the reading–writing
connection require knowledge of and experience with practice that members may not pos-
sess. The expertise of others who are not members of the faculty may be necessary for communities of practice or teachers on a faculty to change teaching practice. Nonetheless, this
model does have the potential to support teacher learning.

Another promising practice in professional development involves recordings of classroom practice. This can happen on two levels. Teachers might record their own teaching
and reflect on what the videos reveal about their own practices. Viewing and then discussing their own or their colleagues' teaching with peers helps teachers to interpret and reflect
on what they see and on their own teaching, enabling them to remember more and engage
in deeper reflection than teachers who rely only on memory (Rosaen, Lundeberg, Cooper,
Fritzen, & Terpstra, 2008). Video technology also enables teachers to observe, reflect on,
and learn from teaching beyond their classrooms. Video cases of exemplary teaching and
of specific teaching practices are increasingly available online and in a variety of platforms and formats. Viewing and discussing these video cases has been shown to support
changes in teachers' practices (Córdova & Matthiesen, 2010; Pea, 2006). Of course, there
are many authors of video cases with many perspectives on accomplished practice, and it
is important to know who selected and edited the cases being presented and whether or not
evidence supports the practices being highlighted. In addition, whether teachers view their
own teaching practices or video cases of other classrooms, the expertise and skill of those
helping them to reflect and to consider the video's implications for their own practice can
shape what teachers learn from watching examples of teaching practice.

As with preservice teacher education, new technologies are also opening up new formats for in-service teacher learning and professional development. Online platforms, which can range from short workshops to massive open online courses (MOOCs) to for-credit college courses, all allow teachers to learn from anywhere and can overcome the challenges of expense, geography, and scheduling (Russell, Dash, O'Dwyer, de Kramer, & Masters, 2010). Online professional development is just beginning to be studied, but these formats have a great deal of potential. As with any other professional development opportunity, teachers and schools must be wise consumers of online learning opportunities. It is important, for example, to determine the experience, expertise, reliability, and point of view or agenda of the authors, teachers, and developers of online learning experiences and whether or not research and theory support the practices being promulgated. It is also important to remember that even the most expert of online teachers must be able to design opportunities that support teacher learning. The best online professional development (including online courses) is structured to build active learning experiences, to foster engagement and a sense of community, and to support teachers in building relevant knowledge of pedagogy and practice (Borko, Whitcomb, & Liston, 2009; Sobel, Sands, & Dunlap, 2009). When these are achieved, the many interactive and multimodal features of online learning have the potential to promote teacher learning for the reading–writing connection.

Some teachers are increasingly joining online communities of educators who share resources through social media. Often referred to as *personal learning networks* (PLNs),[1] these systems take advantage of a variety of technological tools (e.g., iPads/tablets, smart phones, computers) to connect teachers to support their learning. As they create their PLNs, teachers join into groups with their colleagues near and far using Twitter, Tumblr, Pinterest, Ning!, and other social media platforms to ask one another questions, share resources, and provide support. PLNs are very new and not yet well researched; however, they hold potential for helping teachers overcome the isolation of the classroom, connect with colleagues around the nation and the world, and reflect on their own practice. Of course, the quality of PLNs depends on the colleagues with whom teachers connect, and teachers must be aware of and vigilant about issues of privacy when sharing about their own classrooms. Nonetheless, PLNs have interesting potential. They may be especially valuable for teachers in rural schools, where size and geography mean that teachers do not have access to colleagues to join with as members of learning communities or access to resources available in other settings.

Whether professional development takes place in weekly study teams and learning communities, online in MOOCs or e-learning workshops, or in any of several other formats that allow for long-term and intensive study, active learning, and teacher collaboration, research suggests some particular areas of focus for professional development for instruction in the reading–writing connection. Writing may need to be a special focus of professional development for the foreseeable future, because (as noted earlier) teacher education may not have prepared teachers for teaching writing or the reading–writing connection as thoroughly as is needed. Effective professional development to strengthen writing instruction often involves teachers in engaging in writing tasks and processes such as reading and analyzing model texts, planning and drafting writing in various genres, getting and giving feedback and revising texts, and sharing their work with multiple audiences; all these support the development of writing instruction (National Writing Project & Nagin, 2006). As they engage in this sort of writing, teachers also reflect on the contexts

---

[1] See, for example, http://www.schrockguide.net/creating-your-pln.html

that support them as writers; the thought processes they use to plan, draft, and revise; and the learning community required for teachers to take risks as writers. Reflection on their own writing process is intended to help teachers think about how to arrange writing instruction in their own classrooms and may be supported by reading research and the professional literature in the context of writing and learning about writing instruction in a learning community (Lieberman & Wood, 2002).

Teacher professional development that focuses on student assessment data can also have a strong impact (Langer, Colton, & Goff, 2003; Schnellert et al., 2008). Teachers might share examples of student work samples, use study time to talk about how to use a rubric or other assessment tool to score student work and develop a shared understanding of the characteristics of well-written texts, or look across multiple student work samples to note patterns—including strengths and weaknesses. From there, teachers can support one another in developing teaching approaches to address areas of weakness (Harris et al., 2012; Schnellert et al., 2008). These are among the many potential topics for professional learning that can support the reading–writing connection.

CONCLUSION

This chapter just begins to scrape the surface and outline some of the key features of teacher education and professional development that can support the reading–writing connection.

Although we know that there are many teachers who are well prepared and who are continuing to learn throughout their careers, we also know that there is room for improvement and that many teachers do not have these learning opportunities.

Teacher preparation must respond to our advancing understanding of the reading–writing connection. In particular, teacher preparation programs should examine the ways teachers are prepared to teach writing—on its own and in conjunction with reading. Teacher educators may need to work with colleagues across campuses and in schools to support new teachers' learning of information literacy, content-area literacy, and digital tools—among many other areas—before graduates take over in their own classrooms.

Increasing emphasis on the reading–writing connection also means that professional development is more important than ever before. The increasing demands of CCSS and the changes in out-of-school literacy practices will require new teaching practices. Alternate routes to teacher preparation and increasing teacher shortages may mean increasing variation in the preservice experiences for many of our nation's teachers. These and other contexts demand an increasing emphasis on teacher support through professional development.

The practices described in this chapter are a good place to start. Teacher preparation that focuses on the reading–writing connection, that builds teachers' knowledge base and provides them with field experiences and other models of accomplished practice, and that encourages reflection and receives institutional support will better prepare teachers to teach reading and writing. Ongoing professional development that is intensive, relevant, and engaging can support teacher learning across teachers' entire careers. When professional development focuses on teachers' school and classroom contexts and provides them with opportunities to build expertise with colleagues, teaching can change.

But we also have so much to learn. Even though we know many of the key characteristics of effective teacher education, preservice, and in-service, continued research is needed. Research can help us identify how best to prepare teachers for the reading–writing connection. Longitudinal studies that follow graduates into the classroom and examine the impact of teacher education practices on long-term outcomes such as student achievement and teacher retention can help us refine our programs. We know the characteristics of effective professional development but have less knowledge of how to bring those models to scale in a systematic way to support teachers across the nation. There are also many promising practices for both teacher preparation and professional development that we are just beginning to understand. We know, for example, that online platforms and social media can support preservice and practicing teachers' learning, but we also know that these formats are not always well designed. Research is needed to evaluate emerging practices for teacher education and to understand both their affordances and their limits. Finally, we have very little research that studies the preparation of teacher educators. As we learn more about how to prepare teachers for the reading–writing connection, research that examines how the instructors, professors, and providers of professional development learn and improve their craft could have long-term benefits for teachers and their students.

REFERENCES

Achinstein, B., & Ogawa, R.T. (2006). (In)fidelity: What the resistance of new teachers reveals about professional principles and prescriptive educational policies. *Harvard Educational Review, 76*(1), 30–63.

Ajayi, L. (2009). An exploration of preservice teachers' perceptions of learning to teach while using asynchronous discussion board. *Journal of Educational Technology and Society, 12*(2), 86–100.

Alvermann, D.E. (2004). Media, information communication technologies, and youth literacies: A cultural studies perspective. *American Behavioral Scientist, 48*(1), 78–83. doi:10.1177/0002764204267271

Applegate, A.J., & Applegate, M.D. (2004). The Peter effect: Reading habits and attitudes of preservice teachers. *Reading Teacher, 57*(6), 554–563.

Baker, S., & Smith, S. (1999). Starting off on the right foot: The influences of four principles of professional development in improving literacy instruction in two kindergarten programs. *Learning Disabilities Research and Practice, 14*(4), 239–253.

Binks-Cantrell, E., Washburn, E.K., Joshi, R.M., & Hougen, M. (2012). Peter effect in the preparation of reading teachers. *Scientific Studies of Reading, 16*(6), 526–536. doi:10.1080/10888438.2011.601434

Borko, H. (2004). Professional development and teacher learning: Mapping the terrain. *Educational Researcher, 33*(8), 3–15.

Borko, H., Whitcomb, J., & Liston, D. (2009). Wicked problems and other thoughts on issues of technology and teacher learning. *Journal of Teacher Education, 60*(3), 3–7. doi:10.1177/0022487108328488

Cantrell, S.C. (2002). Promoting talk: A framework for reading discussions in teacher education courses. *Journal of Adolescent and Adult Literacy, 45*(7), 642.

Carnegie Council on Advancing Adolescent Literacy. (2010). *Time to act: An agenda for advancing adolescent literacy for college and career success.* New York: Carnegie Corporation of New York.

Cochran-Smith, M., & Lytle, S.L. (2001). Beyond certainty: Taking an inquiry stance on practice. In A. Lieberman & L. Miller (Eds.), *Teachers caught in the action: Professional development that matters* (pp. 45–58). New York, NY: Teachers College Press.

Córdova, R.A., & Matthiesen, A.L. (2010). Reading, writing, and mapping our worlds into being: Shared teacher inquiries into whose literacies count. *The Reading Teacher, 63*(6), 452–463. doi:10.1598/rt.63.6.2

Council of Chief State School Officers. (2010). *Adolescent literacy toolkit.* Washington, DC: Authors.

Crocco, M.S., & Costigan, A.T. (2007). The narrowing of curriculum and pedagogy in the age of accountability: Urban educators speak out. *Urban Education, 42*(6), 512–535.

Daisey, P. (2009). The reading experiences and beliefs of secondary preservice teachers. *Reading Horizons, 49*(2), 167–190.

Darling-Hammond, L. (2000). Teacher quality and student achievement: A review of state policy evidence. *Education Policy Analysis Archives, 8*(1), 1–44.

Emmons, M., Keefe, E.B., Moore, V.M., Sanchez, R.M., Mals, M.M., & Neely, T.Y. (2009). Teaching information literacy skills to prepare teachers who can bridge the research-to-practice gap. *Reference and User Services Quarterly, 49*(2), 140–150.

Flippo, R.F. (2001). Point of agreement: A display of professional unity in our field. In R.F. Flippo (Ed.), *Reading researcher in search of common ground* (pp. 7–21). Newark, DE: International Reading Association.

Foorman, B.R., Francis, D.J., Fletcher, J.M., & Schatschneider, C. (1998). The role of instruction in learning to read: Preventing reading failure in at-risk children. *Journal of Educational Psychology, 90*(1), 37–55.

Freedman, L., & Carver, C. (2007). Preservice teacher understandings of adolescent literacy development: Naïve wonder to dawning realization to intellectual rigor. *Journal of Adolescent and Adult Literacy, 50*(8), 654–665.

Garet, M.S., Porter, A.C., Desimone, L.M., Birman, B.F., & Yoon, K.S. (2001). What makes professional development effective? Results from a national sample of teachers. *American Educational Research Journal, 38*(4), 915–945.

Graves, D.H. (2002). *Testing is not teaching: What should count in education.* Portsmouth, NH: Heinemann.

Guskey, T.R. (2003). Analyzing lists of the characteristics of effective professional development to promote visionary leadership. *NASSP Bulletin, 87*(637), 4–20. doi:10.1177/019263650308763702

Hall, L.A., Johnson, A.S., Juzwik, M.M., Wortham, S.E.F., & Mosley, M. (2010). Teacher identity in the context of literacy teaching: Three explorations of classroom positioning and interaction in secondary schools. *Teaching and Teacher Education, 26*(2), 234–243. doi:10.1016/j.tate.2009.04.009

Harris, K.R., Lane, K.L., Graham, S., Driscoll, S.A., Sandmel, K., Brindle, M., & Schatschneider, C. (2012). Practice-based professional development for self-regulated strategies development in writing: A randomized controlled study. *Journal of Teacher Education, 63*(2), 103–119. doi:10.1177/0022487111429005

Hoffman, J.V., & Pearson, P.D. (2000). Reading teacher education in the next millennium: What your grandmother's teacher didn't know that your granddaughter's teacher should. *Reading Research Quarterly, 35*(1), 28–44.

Hoffman, J.V., Roller, C., Maloch, B., Sailors, M., Duffy, G., & Beretvas, S.N. (2005). Teachers' preparation to teach reading and their experiences and practices in the first three years of teaching. *Elementary School Journal, 105*(3), 267–287.

Hoffman, J.V., Roller, C., & National Commission on Excellence in Elementary Teacher Preparation for Reading Instruction. (2001). The IRA excellence in reading teacher preparation commission's report: Current practices in reading teacher education at the undergraduate level in the United States. In C. Roller (Ed.), *Learning to teach reading: Setting the research agenda* (pp. 32–79). Newark, DE: International Reading Association.

Langer, G., Colton, A., & Goff, L. (2003). *Collaborative analysis of student work: Improving teaching and learning.* Alexandria, VA: Association for the Supervision of Curriculum Development.

Lieberman, A., & Wood, D.R. (2002). The National Writing Project. *Educational Leadership, 59*(6), 40.

MacGillivray, L., Ardell, A.L., Curwen, M.S., & Palma, J. (2004). Colonized teachers: Examining the implementation of a scripted reading program. *Teaching Education, 15*(2), 131–144.

Malm, B. (2009). Towards a new professionalism: Enhancing personal and professional development in teacher education. *Journal of Education for Teaching, 35*(1), 77–91. doi:10.1080/02607470802587160

Manzo, K.K. (2006). Teacher ed. faulted on reading preparation. *Education Week, 25*(39), 14.

Moats, L. (2009). Still wanted: Teachers with knowledge of language. *Journal of Learning Disabilities, 42*(5), 387–391.

National Board for Professional Teaching Standards. (2012). Literacy: Reading–language arts standards (2nd ed.). Arlington, VA: Authors.

National Education Association. (2000). Should all teachers be trained in the teaching of reading? *NEA Today, 18*(5), 11.

National Governors Association Center for Best Practices & Council of Chief State School Officers (NGS/CCSSO). (2010). *Common Core State Standards: English language arts standards.* Washington, DC: Authors.

National Institute of Child Health and Human Development (NICHD). (2000). *Teaching children to read: An evidence-based assessment of the scientific research literature on reading and its implications for reading instruction.* (NIH Publication No. 00-4769). Washington, DC: U.S. Government Printing Office.

National Writing Project, & Nagin, C. (2006). *Because writing matters: Improving student writing in our schools.* San Francisco, CA: Jossey Bass.

Nichols, W.D., Young, C.A., & Rickelman, R.J. (2007). Improving middle school professional development by examining middle school teachers' application of literacy strategies and instructional design. *Reading Psychology, 28*(1), 97–130. doi:10.1080/02702710601115497

Nye, B., Konstantopoulos, S., & Hedges, L. (2004). How large are teacher effects? *Educational Evaluation and Policy Analysis, 26*(3), 237–257.

Pardo, L.S. (2006). The role of context in learning to teach writing. *Journal of Teacher Education, 57*(4), 378–394.

Pea, R.D. (2006). Video-as-data and digital video manipulation techniques for transforming learning sciences research, education, and other cultural practices. In J. Weiss (Ed.), *International handbook of virtual learning environments* (pp. 1321–1393). Dordrecht, The Netherlands: Springer.

Pearson, P.D. (2001). Learning to teach reading: The status of the knowledge base. In C. Roller (Ed.), *Learning to teach reading: Setting the research agenda* (pp. 4–19). Newark, DE: International Reading Association.

Powell-Brown, A. (2003). Can you be a teacher of literacy if you don't love to read? *Journal of Adolescent and Adult Literacy, 47*(4), 284–288.

Pytash, K. (2012). Engaging preservice teachers in disciplinary literacy learning through writing. *Journal of Adolescent and Adult Literacy, 55*(6), 527–538. doi:10.1002/jaal.00062

Rice, J.K. (2003). *Teacher quality: Understanding the effectiveness of teacher attributes.* Washington, DC: Economic Policy Institute.

Risko, V.J., Roller, C.M., Cummins, C., Bean, R.M., Block, C.C., Anders, P.L., & Flood, J. (2008). A critical analysis of research on reading teacher education. *Reading Research Quarterly, 43*(3), 252–288.

Rosaen, C.L., Lundeberg, M., Cooper, M., Fritzen, A., & Terpstra, M. (2008). Noticing noticing: How does investigation of video records change how teachers reflect on their experiences? *Journal of Teacher Education, 59*(4), 347–360.

Russell, M., Dash, S., O'Dwyer, L.M., de Kramer, R.M., & Masters, J. (2010). The effects of online professional development on fourth grade English language arts teachers' knowledge and instructional practices. *Journal of Educational Computing Research, 43*(3), 355–375. doi:10.2190/EC.43.3.e

Schnellert, L.M., Butler, D.L., & Higginson, S.K. (2008). Co-constructors of data, co-constructors of meaning: Teacher professional development in an age of accountability. *Teaching and Teacher Education, 24*(3), 725–750. doi:10.1016/j.tate.2007.04.001

Scott, P., & Mouza, C. (2007). The impact of professional development on teacher learning, practice and leadership skills: A study on the integration of technology in the teaching of writing. *Journal of Educational Computing Research, 37*(3), 229–266. doi:10.2190/EC.37.3.b

Shanahan, T., & Shanahan, C. (2008). Teaching disciplinary literacy to adolescents: Rethinking content-area literacy. *Harvard Educational Review, 78*(1), 40–59.

Showers, B., & Bruce, J. (1996). The evolution of peer coaching. *Educational Leadership, 53*(6), 12–17.

Snow, C.E., Burns, M.S., & Griffin, P. (Eds.). (1998). *Preventing reading difficulties in young children.* Washington, DC: National Academies Press.

Snow, C.E., Griffin, P., & Burns, M.S. (2005). *Knowledge to support the teaching of reading: Preparing teachers for a changing world.* San Francisco, CA: John Wiley & Sons.

Sobel, D.M., Sands, D.I., & Dunlap, J.C. (2009). Teaching intricate content online: It can be done and done well. *Action in Teacher Education, 30*(4), 28–44.

Torres, M., & Mercado, M. (2006). The need for critical media literacy in teacher education core curricula. *Educational Studies, 39*(3), 260–282. doi:10.1207/s15326993es3903_5

Vescio, V., Ross, D., & Adams, A. (2008). A review of research on the impact of professional learning communities on teaching practice and student learning. *Teaching and Teacher Education, 24*(1), 80–91. doi:http://dx.doi.org/10.1016/j.tate.2007.01.004

Wang, J., & Hartley, K. (2003). Video technology as a support for teacher education reform. *Journal of Technology and Teacher Education, 11*(1), 105–138.

Williams, D., & Coles, L. (2007). Teachers' approaches to finding and using research evidence: An information literacy perspective. *Educational Research, 49*(2), 185–206. doi:10.1080/00131880701369719

7

The Role of Linguistic Differences in Reading and Writing Instruction

Julie A. Washington, Megan C. Brown, and Katherine T. Rhodes

U.S. schools serve students from diverse language backgrounds, including recent immigrants and students whose families have been U.S. residents for many generations. Students with language variations present unique challenges for our educational system. In particular, the proportion of children who are English language learners (ELL), or who speak English dialects that have a negative impact on literacy attainment, affects the nature of reading and writing instruction and levels of achievement overall (Lesaux, Kieffer, Faller, & Kelley, 2010).

The federal definition of an ELL student (also often referred to as limited English proficient [LEP] or dual language learner) has four primary elements. Specifically, the ELL designation includes students 1) between 3 and 21 years of age; 2) enrolled in primary or secondary school; 3) from a country outside of the United States or from an environment in which a language other than English is used, which has a significant impact on the development of English language proficiency; and 4) whose difficulties in reading, writing, or speaking English affect performance on state testing and interfere with achievement in classrooms where the language of instruction is English (No Child Left Behind [NCLB], PL 107-110).

A *dialect* is best understood as any specific variety of a language, including the standard variety (Wolfram & Schilling-Estes, 2006). Mainstream American English (MAE; also called Standard American English [SAE]) dialect is generally recognized as the dialect of instruction within classrooms, although most native English speakers within the United States speak some form of dialect (e.g., African American English [AAE] dialect, Appalachian English dialect, Cajun English dialect). Similar to ELL students, speakers of these dialects should also be considered linguistic minorities, particularly as it relates to educational achievement. These students experience significant difficulty with literacy tasks—particularly reading and writing—which has been linked both directly and indirectly to their linguistic differences. Similar to ELLs, dialect speakers who have not mastered Mainstream Classroom English (MCE) will experience significant difficulty accessing the curriculum and succeeding in school. Currently, there is little official or unofficial acknowledgement of the impact that significant variations *within* English have on the development of reading and writing skills, despite mounting evidence that such relationships exist. On the contrary, the reading difficulties experienced by these children are more likely to be attributed to sociodemographic factors (e.g., poverty or cultural differences) than to language variation, as heavy dialect users are also frequently from working-class or impoverished communities.

This chapter will use two groups of students as examples of how language variation affects reading and writing achievement. African American children who speak AAE will be referenced to discuss within-language variation; AAE is the most studied dialect of English (Wolfram & Thomas, 2002), and a growing body of literature on reading and writing focuses on these children. Second, this chapter will reference ELL students whose first language is Spanish to discuss the effects of language variation; an estimated 80% of students classified as ELLs in the United States speak Spanish as a first language (Kinder, 2002). These two groups, AAE speakers and Spanish-speaking ELLs, provide well-documented, illustrative examples of the educational challenges facing speakers of various dialects and languages. Accordingly, this chapter will focus on achievement disparities and present the current knowledge base in both reading and writing for these two student populations.

ACHIEVEMENT DISPARITIES

Both Hispanic and African American children underperform in literacy activities relative to their White, non-Hispanic peers. The National Assessment of Educational Progress (NAEP), whose data are reported in *The Nation's Report Card* (National Center for Education Statistics [NCES], 2012a), consistently reports achievement disparities for Hispanic and African American children in reading and writing relative to White and Asian American children. Although the NAEP data may not be ideal, this assessment continues to provide the most consistent and reliable national data on student performance. Hispanic[1] and African American students' NAEP reading and writing performance are discussed later.

Reading

There are long-standing disparities in reading achievement between students with language variation and other students. African American students have had poor overall academic performance since the first race-based performance reporting occurred in the early 1970s (Beaton et al., 2011; Nettles & Diehl, 2010). Called the "Black-White achievement gap," the disparity between African American children and their White peers has received considerable attention. Between the early 1970s and the late 1980s, the achievement gap narrowed significantly (Nettles & Diehl, 2010). In the 1990s, this progress came to a halt, and the reading achievement gap has not decreased measurably since. As it stands, an average of 15% of African American students in the fourth and eighth grades read at proficient or advanced levels (NCES, 2012a). Hispanic students have also fared poorly: An average of 18% of students in the fourth and eighth grades read at proficient or advanced levels (NCES, 2012a). For comparison, an average of 44% of White students and 48% of Asian American students in the fourth and eighth grades read at proficient or advanced levels on the same assessment (NCES, 2012a). For both groups, African Americans and Hispanics, these assessment outcomes are only the latest in a long pattern of poor performance compared to that of their White and Asian American peers.

In addition to linguistic variables that will be discussed in this chapter, socioeconomic status also plays a hand in maintaining the achievement gap. Wilde (2010) compared the

---

[1]Although Hispanic and ELL do not always coincide, as there are certainly Hispanic students whose first language is English, this is the only indicator that can serve as a proxy for ELL achievement nationwide. Similarly, not all African American children speak AAE, but again this is the best currently available proxy.

performance of ELLs, former ELLs, and English Proficient students on the reading tests of the NAEP Long-Term Trend Assessment. When ELLs are subdivided by socioeconomic status, ELLs in poverty scored significantly lower than all students (including ELLs) who were not impoverished. Perhaps most interesting, the English reading performance of ELLs *not* growing up in poverty was nearly identical to the scores of non-ELLs who *were* impoverished. This latter finding mirrors one widely cited for African American students. That is, the reading skills of middle-income African American children are comparable to the reading skills of their low-income White peers (Singham, 1998; Gosa & Alexander, 2007).

National reading achievement disparities have persisted despite advances in reading research. Continuing efforts to provide ELLs access to direct English instruction in school settings and significantly improved instruction for African American students have had only a slight impact on these outcomes. Future efforts will have to account for the role of sociodemographic context, including socioeconomic and cultural differences on student performance and the instructional and curricular changes that may be required to achieve effective reading and writing instruction in the face of these differences.

Writing

The NAEP began assessing writing achievement in 1998. Not surprisingly, similar poor performance and achievement gaps are evident in the writing performance of Hispanic and African American students as have been reported for reading performance. When assessed in the fourth grade, only 8% of Hispanic students and 13% of African American students wrote at or above grade-level proficiency (NCES, 2012b). The writing assessment changed a great deal for 8th and 12th graders, and students of both language variations continued to fare poorly in these upper grades. Specifically, when completing the NAEP's revised computer-based, purpose-driven, audience-specific writing task, an average of 10% of African American students and 13% of Hispanic students in the 8th and 12th grades scored at proficient or advanced levels (NCES, 2012b). For comparison, an average of 34% of White students and 42% of Asian American students in the 8th and 12th grades wrote at proficient or advanced levels on the same assessment (NCES, 2012b). Researchers suggest that African American students experienced a "plateau" for writing achievement across grades and testing years, beginning with the first NAEP writing assessment in 1998 (Nettles & Diehl, 2010); it appears a similar phenomenon may occur for Hispanic students. The complexity of writing and how writing relies on oral language, reading ability, and a student's ability to produce well-organized, meaningful text may produce a lower ceiling on this writing assessment for students struggling with any of these subskills.

These long-standing disparities in reading and writing achievement are worrisome for educators and researchers concerned with the social and educational well-being of Hispanic and African American children. Explanations for the presence and persistence of these achievement disparities are widely varied. In the sections that follow, one major variable that has been implicated will be explored for ELL and for African American students: cultural-linguistic differences.

READING, WRITING, AND CULTURAL-LINGUISTIC DIFFERENCES
English Language Learners and Reading

There is ample evidence from research focused on ELLs that many of the foundational skills that support reading development in a child's first language (L1) also support reading development in the second language (L2). These skills include vocabulary knowledge, alphabet knowledge, phonological awareness, and rapid naming abilities (August & Shanahan, 2006; National Early Literacy Panel [NELP], 2009; Vaughn et al., 2006). Phonological awareness in particular is a known predictor of success in L1 reading (NELP, 2009) and an important influence on L2 reading fluency (Bernhardt, 1991) for students who are learning to read in alphabetic orthographies such as English. ELLs who are learning to read in L2 orthographic systems that more closely resemble their L1 (e.g., Spanish to English) experience beneficial transfer between writing systems during L2 reading acquisition. Importantly, many studies have found that ELLs perform similarly to monolinguals on measures of phonological processing and word reading accuracy, both of which are often connected with decoding ability (Aarts & Verhoeven, 1999; Carlisle & Beeman, 2000; Lesaux, 2006; Lesaux, Crosson, Kieffer, & Pierce, 2011; Lesaux & Siegel, 2003). For example, Knell and colleagues (2007) confirmed that L2 letter identification and phonological awareness supported word identification for ELLs, similar to the support provided for monolingual language development.

The foundations that support successful L1 reading are formed early—long before reading instruction begins (Snow, Burns, & Griffin, 1998). Among young developing readers in particular, strong oral language skills in either L1 or L2 provide a critical foundation upon which reading skills ultimately will be developed. Students who are introduced to English in the school setting frequently arrive at school with far less oral language knowledge in both Spanish and English than do their monolingual peers (Manis, Lindsey, & Bailey, 2004; Swanson, Rosston, Gerber, & Solari, 2008). This difference in oral language proficiency for both L1 and L2 may affect how easily ELLs will learn to read. When studied in monolingual, English-only (EO) students, oral language proficiency is a weak predictor of reading ability. It has been theorized that L1 oral language proficiency likely supports L2 reading for ELLs and thus has a greater overall impact on the acquisition of reading skills for these children than it does for EO children (Gutierrez, Zepeda, & Castro, 2010; Orellana & D'warte, 2010). However, most ELL children have an imbalance in their oral language skills, such that their skills in L1 are typically stronger and more flexible than skills in L2 (Grosjean, 1998; Grosjean & Miller, 1994). Indeed, ELLs develop stronger syntactic, morphological, and phonological skills in their L1, as they are provided many more opportunities to use these skills in a broad range of contexts (Bialystok, Luk, & Kwan, 2005; Grosjean & Miller, 1994). In many cases, it is this linguistic imbalance that has an adverse effect on the development of literacy (Bialystok, 2007).

When considering reading acquisition, L2 *vocabulary knowledge* has been identified repeatedly as an oral language skill that is likely to be weak for ELLs; vocabulary knowledge is a critical foundation for the development of fluency and comprehension for all children, regardless of their initial language. It is important to note as well that for ELL children, having a robust vocabulary in L1 will enable greater depth and breadth of L2 vocabulary as they learn L2, as it provides a firm language foundation in general. Importantly, empirical investigations have established that school-age ELLs struggle with vocabulary more than their EO peers (August, Carlo, Dressler, & Snow, 2005; Cheng, Klinger, & Zheng, 2007; Hutchinson, Whiteley, Smith, & Connors, 2003; Lervåg & Aukrust, 2010; Lesaux et al., 2010; Lesaux et al., 2011; Mancilla-Martinez & Lesaux, 2010; Nakamoto, Lindsey, & Manis, 2007). Within ELLs, variation in L2 vocabulary knowledge predicts later L2 reading achievement (Cunningham & Stanovich, 1997; Duursma et al., 2007; Mancilla-Martinez & Lesaux, 2010; Reese, Garnier, Gallimore, & Goldenberg, 2000). In fact, for many ELLs, one's L2 vocabulary size is an established obstacle for L2 reading growth in the early years of reading instruction (Kieffer, 2012). As students enter upper elementary and secondary schools, limited L2 vocabulary breadth combines with lack of knowledge of vocabulary depth to hamper reading comprehension (Kieffer & Lesaux, 2012).

The differences between early elementary, upper elementary, and secondary school performance have received increased attention. There is strong evidence that ELLs in schools fall behind their peers as reading curricula shift to emphasize reading comprehension (De George, 1988; de Jong, 2004; Gándara, Rumberger, Maxwell-Jolly, & Callahan, 2003). ELL students appear to be proficient readers when their reading levels are assessed by word-reading ability and phonological awareness skills (Geva, Yaghoub-Zadeh, & Schuster, 2000). ELLs in the fourth and fifth grades appear less proficient as reading measures begin to rely on comprehension abilities (Kieffer, 2011).

This relationship between vocabulary and reading comprehension is thought to be reciprocal. That is, possessing a large vocabulary facilitates successful reading comprehension, and strong reading comprehension skills lead to greater opportunities to develop a vocabulary that is sufficient to support reading (Freebody & Anderson, 1983; Stanovich, 1986). Accordingly, many attempts to improve ELL reading ability beyond single-word reading have focused on improving L2 vocabulary breadth and depth. Though not easy to accomplish, this work has demonstrated that L2 vocabulary can be improved with appropriate instruction and that focusing on vocabulary can result in significant improvement of a wide range of reading skills (August et al., 2005; Carlo et al., 2004; Kieffer & Lesaux, 2012; Ko, Wang, & Kim, 2011; Vaughn et al., 2006; Vaughn, Mathes, Linan-Thompson, & Francis, 2005). For example, Carlo and colleagues (2004) developed an intensive 15-week intervention designed to tackle both breadth and depth of word knowledge in an effort to improve reading comprehension for a sample of 254 bilingual fifth graders. Results of the intervention revealed significant overall improvement on measures of vocabulary and comprehension, including generating sentences that conveyed multiple meanings of polysemous words; completing cloze passages; and improving knowledge of word meanings, word associations, and word morphology. They also identified three important methods for developing L2 vocabulary: 1) using language cognates to capitalize on L1 knowledge to build connections between L1 and L2; 2) teaching labels of basic words that EO students likely already know (e.g., baby, clock); and 3) building in consistent review and practice of target vocabulary.

One challenge for designing vocabulary interventions for ELLs involves identifying which words to target and how many different words to teach. Lesaux and colleagues (2010) recommended choosing words that are high utility in academic contexts (e.g., *analyze* or *compare*) and teaching a small number of words with deep understanding. Academic language knowledge has been identified as a particularly critical skill for the academic success of ELLs who may not know a lot of English words but who also do not have thorough knowledge of the English words that they recognize (August & Hakuta, 1997; August & Shanahan, 2006). Accordingly, teaching of a small number of high-utility words focuses on the semantics and morphology of targeted vocabulary across varied contexts (Stahl & Nagy, 2006), thereby improving vocabulary depth rather than increasing breadth by teaching a large number of words that may or may not be useful in educational settings.

Finally, it is largely agreed that vocabulary interventions should focus equally on teaching strategies that facilitate learning new words and on teaching specific vocabulary words. Focusing on development of morphological awareness (MA)—improving a student's understanding of the structure of words (e.g., prefixes, suffixes, and word roots)—is widely supported and shows great promise for improving ELLs' vocabulary. MA interventions focus on teaching students to analyze these elements within words and to make connections between known words and unknown words. Kieffer and Lesaux (2012) found that, even when the influence of word-reading skills (i.e., phonological awareness and vocabulary breadth) is controlled, MA contributes independently to the reading comprehension skills of fifth-grade ELLs. Further, they determined that the magnitude of the relationship between MA and reading comprehension increases between fourth and fifth grade, suggesting that this skill becomes more important as students move to higher grades.

African American English and Reading

Like all children who come from communities that use different linguistic systems at the time that they enter school, African American children use the dialect of their community—AAE (Craig & Washington, 2002; Washington & Craig; 1994, 2002). AAE has an impact on the morphosyntax and phonology of English in predictable ways and is evident in the speech of African American children across the United States (see Craig & Washington, 2004; Washington & Craig, 1994; 2002 for a list of these features). Variability in the use of AAE is influenced by sociodemographic factors such as gender and socioeconomic status (SES); boys use nearly twice as much AAE as girls (Connor & Craig, 2006; Craig & Washington, 2002; Washington & Craig, 1998), and low-income African American children typically use more AAE than their middle-income peers (Washington & Craig, 1998). In addition, the features of AAE that are most commonly encountered can vary from one region of the country to another, and this is particularly true when a prominent regional dialect intersects with AAE, as has been found in the southern United States (Oetting & Pruitt, 2005). However, *zero copula and auxiliary forms of the verb "to be"* ("Where the brush?") and *subject-verb agreement* ("Now she need some shoes") are the most frequent morphosyntactic AAE forms regardless of the speaker's age or geographic locale (Craig & Washington, 1994; 2004; Washington & Craig, 2002).

The limited research focused on the developmental trajectory of AAE phonology reveals significant differences from SAE. In particular, consonants that appear in the final position of words develop more slowly for AAE-speaking children than for their SAE-speaking counterparts (Pearson, Velleman, Bryant, & Charko, 2009). Deletion of final consonants is a prevalent feature of AAE and has been used to explain differences in development for African American children. That is, because final consonants are variably included in AAE, it has been hypothesized that it takes longer for African American children to acquire and to recognize sounds in the final position of words.

These developmental differences suggest that dialect-influenced phonological features (e.g., final consonant deletion) may be poor choices for assessing phonological awareness in African American children acquiring reading skills (Pearson et al., 2009; Seymour, Bland-Stewart, & Green, 1996). Thomas-Tate, Washington, and Edwards (2004) found that low-income, African American first graders scored significantly below the mean on the early elementary version of the Test of Phonological Awareness (TOPA; Torgesen & Bryant, 1994), which assesses awareness of final consonants. In contrast, the same children scored within normal limits on the kindergarten version, which assesses awareness of initial consonants. AAE does not have an impact on initial consonants, making them a good choice for determining phonological awareness abilities of African American children.

Overall researchers have observed statistically significant associations between AAE production and reading performance, though they do not always agree on the nature or explanations for these associations. Historically, speech-to-print mismatches have been implicated, such that children who do not make the switch from AAE to the classroom language do not fare well when learning to read (Charity, Scarborough, & Griffin, 2004;

Craig, Zhang, Hensel, & Quinn, 2009; Labov & Baker, 2010; Terry, Connor, Petscher, & Conlin, 2012; Terry, Connor, Thomas-Tate, & Love, 2010; Terry & Scarborough, 2011). Of note are three recent longitudinal studies that showed children who begin kindergarten or first grade using significant levels of AAE performed worse on tasks of word-reading and reading comprehension compared to African American children who enter school using less AAE (Conlin, 2009; Terry et al., 2010; 2012). By the end of first and second grade, the reading trajectory for these children significantly decelerated, putting them behind their peers who were reading at grade level.

In contrast to these investigations are those that have identified strong language and literacy skills among children who use AAE. Fewer of these studies exist, but they suggest that there may be some advantages to being a good dialect speaker. For example, in an early investigation, Craig and Washington (1994) found that impoverished African American preschoolers who spoke AAE exhibited strong syntax skills and that these syntactic strengths were positively correlated with reading achievement in first through third grade (Craig, Connor, & Washington, 2003). This finding is consistent with studies of ELLs that have demonstrated that children who are proficient speakers of their community language at the time of school entry typically have stronger language skills overall (Bialystok, 2007). Unfortunately, the existing literature often does not focus on the advantages of language and dialect variation and instead highlights the deficits associated with the use of AAE.

It is important to note further that the differences between AAE and SAE will not have an impact on all aspects of reading acquisition. For example, Labov and Baker (2010) found that many of the oral reading errors made by their African American subjects were unrelated to dialect differences. Further, they determined that when dialect-based differences were apparent, these differences did not have an impact on reading comprehension. Similarly, Terry and Scarborough (2011) found that their participants who spoke AAE had precise lexical knowledge of SAE phonology, a skill that has been hypothesized to be required for successful word reading (Elbro, Borstrøm, & Peterson, 1998; Fowler & Swainson, 2004; Metsala & Walley, 1998; Perfetti, 2007).

Taken together, evidence from recent investigations has demonstrated that use of AAE is significantly related to literacy achievement in school-age African American children; however, not all children who use AAE have difficulty reading. In fact, children who can be characterized as low to moderate users often have little difficulty acquiring reading, whereas those who are high dialect users struggle with acquisition of reading skills. Although this relationship between high dialect use and struggling reading has been confirmed in several investigations (Conlin, 2009; Terry et al., 2010; 2012), it is important to note that African American children who are high dialect users are also more likely to be poor. For many of these children, it appears that the combination of language difficulties associated with poverty (e.g., decreased vocabulary knowledge) and the use of AAE dialect may create a "perfect storm" that increases the cognitive load to an extent that reading acquisition is slowed so significantly that children are unable to rebound without effective and explicit reading interventions. Although more intervention research is needed, early attempts to improve reading trajectories in this population of impoverished, AAE-speaking children have shown positive outcomes (see Connor et al., this volume).

Similar to the issues researchers face with ELL students, the question of where to start and what skills to target are important to consider with AAE-speaking children growing up in poverty, who often have multiple deficits in the development of oral language skills that complicate attempts to teach reading. Terry and colleagues (Terry et al., 2010; 2012) have suggested that reading difficulties experienced by these children can be improved simply by focusing on general language abilities such as vocabulary and morphological skills. In this view, AAE is not conceptualized as a risk factor but simply as one of many language areas that need to be addressed with this population. In contrast, others have advocated addressing AAE directly in order to improve both reading and writing performance (see Connor et al., this volume). In this view, contrastive analysis techniques, used to teach children the difference between their home language and school language, are viewed as essential to development of Standard Classroom English (SCE), which is, in turn, viewed as essential to development of grade-level reading skills. The debate is far from over, and it will take additional empirical research to determine what intervention is appropriate for which African American children at what point in their development of both language and reading skills.

Writing

Good writing is dependent on a student's existing language and reading skills. It is a more complex skill than reading due to the additional motor, cognitive, communicative, and organizational skills necessary to be successful at the task (Zamel, 1987). Writing instruction has taken on heightened importance for educators, as both the NAEP and state-mandated, standards-based tests have begun to include sections on writing (Aguirre-Muñoz & Boscardin, 2008). Of importance, standardized assessments show similar race-based achievement gaps for writing as they do for reading (Horkay et al., 2006; Jerry, Ballator, & Rogers, 1999).

Empirical studies of writing for both ELLs and AAE-speaking students are less plentiful than reading studies, and this is particularly true for very young children in the emergent writing stage. For both populations of students, evaluating writing may be challenging, as students with language variation typically write like they speak. For example, whereas AAE is an oral dialect, AAE features appear in the compositions of AAE speakers (Cronnell, 1985; Smitherman, 1993; Terrebonne & Terrebonne, 1976; Whiteman, 1981; Wolfram & Whiteman, 1971). Evaluation of writing skills often counts features of AAE that appear in writing as incorrect or too informal for the writing situation. Similarly for ELLs learning to write, use of syntax and morphology that is appropriate for L1 can be considered ungrammatical in L2 writing.

Research is beginning to explain how ELLs' literacy skills transfer between L1 and L2 to support writing practice and achievement. In a meta-analysis of 56 studies focused on multilingual writing in school settings, Fitzgerald (2006) reported transfer of higher-level cognitive processes and skills from L1 to L2 in the writing of ELL students. Students in the primary grades are able to transfer skills in phonological processing, spelling, and concepts of print between languages. Secondary students are able to use spelling skills, strategies for making meaning, and text-composition abilities in both their first and second languages. Researchers have identified high-level skills that they claim are evidence of cross-linguistic abilities: quality of content, organization, writing style, and the use of cohesive devices (Liu & Braine, 2005; Olateju, 2006; Purves, 1992; Tillema, Van den Bergh, Rijlaarsdam, & Sanders, 2012). However, scoring these qualities can be quite difficult—there will be variations in scorers from different cultures and languages as well as variations between students' abilities to write successfully in diverse genres (Hinkel, 2002; Van den Bergh et al., 2009). Even though cross-linguistic transfer happens, educators should not assume that L1 writing skills would transfer to L2 without instruction (Carson, 1992). Much of the work on L1 transfer has been completed with adolescent and adult language learners; this work suggests that instruction in skill transfer may help younger ELLs become better writers earlier.

In a similar vein, there are differences in dialect features that appear in writing and in speech over the course of writing development. Initially, features of AAE that appear in writing are phonological and morphological changes. Features of AAE that are highly stigmatized are the first to be eliminated from writing, possibly through instruction (Whiteman, 1981; Wolfram & Schilling-Estes, 1998). As texts become more complex and require logical arguments, higher order (and less often studied) aspects of AAE continue to be present, such as rhetorical style and voice. Ivy and Masterson (2011) suggested that the writing of child AAE speakers may be influenced not only by oral dialect use but also by the development of understanding of inflectional morphology. Indeed Connor and colleagues (in this volume) found that contrasting SAE morphology with AAE morphology in writing was effective for improving both writing and reading comprehension skills in school-age African American children. Further, Ivy and Masterson (2011) found third graders used six AAE features equally often in speaking and writing; however, in the eighth grade, African American students used features far more often in speech than in writing. This study suggests that the dialect shift in writing occurs much later than the dialect shifts in either oral language or oral reading. Decreases in dialect use in oral language and reading that coincide with the start of school and the introduction of reading instruction (Craig, Thompson, Washington, & Potter, 2003; Craig & Washington, 2004) also have a significant impact. AAE feature use in writing is far less frequent than in oral language and is more closely related to reading proficiency than are dialect density outcomes (Craig et al., 2009).

One point where dialect and ELL writing concerns clearly diverge is the order of writing skills development. ELLs develop L2 writing skills in a different order than L1 writing skills (Weigle, 2002). However, the process of L2 writing skill development is not well specified due to unmeasured individual differences between bilinguals and limitations in our ability to assess the writing of ELLs. In order to accurately describe individual variation for ELLs, researchers must account for many of the same factors that affect L1 writing acquisition: socioeconomic status; access to educational resources in L1 and L2 (Capps et al., 2005; Cohen, Deterding, & Clewell, 2005; Gándara et al., 2003; Grabe & Kaplan, 1996); measures of L1 and L2 oral, reading, and writing proficiency (Bernhardt, 2000); and age range of L1 and L2 acquisition (Johnson & Newport, 1989; Stevens, 2006). Furthermore, there are large differences between L2 writing instruction and assessment. When writing is taught well, educators often use a process approach in which a student's writing is evaluated by its improvement over the course of a project. In contrast, when writing is assessed, a product approach is often used in which L2 writing proficiency is evaluated using brief, static assessments of short writing tasks (East, 2008; Raimes, 1990). Students who speak another dialect or language may benefit from process-based approaches, as they can scaffold writing between L1 and L2 or between AAE and SAE using a variety of learned skills (e.g., contrastive analysis) and instructional technologies (e.g., digital or analog dictionaries, word recognition software).

As should be expected, high-quality writing instruction leads to better writing outcomes for at-risk students whether or not they are ELLs or dialect speakers (Moats, Foorman, & Taylor, 2006). Many of the most successful methods are geared toward teaching AAE speakers to be bidialectal rather than encouraging students to replace their AAE use with MAE use (Connor et al., this volume; Delpit, 2006; Ladson-Billings, 1992). Most methods of instruction aim to teach code switching using the revision of writing. In many of these approaches, contrastive analysis is used to help students improve academic writing skills (Aguirre-Muñoz & Boscardin, 2008; Wheeler, Cartwright, & Swords, 2012; Wheeler & Swords, 2006). Contrastive analysis appears to be successful for development of the metacognitive and metalinguistic skills students need in order to switch from the use of their community language to the language of the classroom.

CONCLUSIONS AND FUTURE DIRECTIONS

Although the discussion about how dialect variation affects writing acquisition and instruction is speculative at best, students who speak a nonmainstream dialect may benefit from some of the same interventions as ELLs. In particular, vocabulary knowledge and poor morphological awareness have been identified as barriers to reading acquisition for both groups. Vocabulary learned in natural contexts is accomplished incidentally over time through repeated exposure to words. However, there is mounting evidence that children with language variation, especially those growing up in poverty, are not successfully acquiring vocabulary using these methods. Instead, these students appear to need word analysis skills taught through tasks focused on morphological awareness in order to learn the meanings and structure of words. Morphological awareness seems important to pursue for both groups, as it has the potential to provide students with the kind of "vocabulary attack" skills that phonological awareness provides them in the form of "word attack" skills. In particular, MA provides critical instruction on the structure of words, teaching students—whose language systems include significant variability—the obligatory rules for word construction and meaning needed to facilitate development of strong reading comprehension skills.

It is also important to evaluate where appropriate instruction for ELL students and AAE speakers may diverge. For example, difficulty with morphology clearly develops for very different reasons in these populations of students despite the apparent similarity in skill deficits. For ELLs, lack of knowledge of English words, phonology, and inflectional morphology creates poor English word knowledge. For African American children who are native English speakers, variable inclusion and exclusion of morphemes that are permitted in AAE complicate the task of learning obligatory rules for inclusion of SAE morphology in both reading and writing. These differences in the nature and origins of linguistic differences for Hispanic and African American children may have an impact on *how* morphological skills are taught, but the inconsistencies documented for development of morphology in both groups clearly support the need to target these skills. Further, in both populations, disproportionate poverty has an impact on the development of *world knowledge,* which has an impact on the development of vocabulary knowledge as well; vocabulary deficits of low-income children, regardless of language origins or racial and ethnic backgrounds, are well documented. Although focusing on these vocabulary deficits is not sufficient to eliminate the gap in achievement, this focus is important for increasing access to the curriculum for AAE-speaking and ELL students. Future research addressing the amount and strength of oral language skills required to facilitate literacy and at what developmental periods, as well as important language skills in addition to vocabulary and morphological awareness, would help educators make research-based decisions about language of instruction for literacy as well as when and how to move students from community language use to use of SCE necessary to be good readers.

REFERENCES

Aarts, R., & Verhoeven, L. (1999). Literacy attainment in a second language submersion context. *Applied Psycholinguistics, 20*(3), 377–393.

Aguirre-Muñoz, Z., & Boscardin, C.K. (2008). Opportunity to learn and English learner achievement: Is increased content exposure beneficial? *Journal of Latinos and Education, 7*(3), 186–205.

August, D., Carlo, M., Dressler, C., & Snow, C. (2005). The critical role of vocabulary development for English language learners. *Learning Disabilities Research and Practice, 20*(1), 50–57. doi:10.1111/j.1540-5826.2005.00120.x

August, D., & Hakuta, K. (1997). *Improving schooling for language-minority children: A research agenda.* Washington, DC: National Academies Press.

August, D., & Shanahan, T. (2006). *Developing literacy in second-language learners: Report of the National Literacy Panel on language minority children and youth.* Mahwah, NJ: Lawrence Erlbaum.

Beaton, A.E., Rogers, A.M., Gonzalez, E., Hanly, M.B., Kolstad, A., Rust, E., . . . Jia, Y. (2011). *The NAEP primer* (NCES Publication 2011-463). Washington, DC: National Center for Education Statistics.

Bernhardt, E.B. (1991). *Reading development in a second language: Theoretical, empirical, and classroom perspectives.* Norwood, NJ: Ablex.

Bernhardt, E.B. (2000). Second-language reading as a case study of reading scholarship in the 20th century. In P.D. Pearson, R. Barr, & M.L. Kamil (Eds.), *Handbook of reading research* (Vol. 3; pp. 793–811). New York, NY: Routledge.

Bialystok, E., Luk, G., & Kwan, E. (2005). Bilingualism, biliteracy, and learning to read: Interactions among languages and writing systems. *Scientific Studies of Reading, 9*(1), 43–61. doi:10.1207/s1532799xssr0901_4

Capps, R., Fix, M., Murray, J., Ost, J., Passel, J.S., & Herwantoro, S. (2005). *The new demography of America's schools: Immigration and the No Child Left Behind Act.* Washington, DC: The Urban Institute.

Carlisle, J.F., & Beeman, M.M. (2000). The effects of language of instruction on the reading and writing achievement of first-grade Hispanic children. *Scientific Studies of Reading, 4*(4), 331–353.

Carlo, M.S., August, D., McLaughlin, B., Snow, C.E., Dressler, C., Lippman, D.N., . . . White, C.E. (2004). Closing the gap: Addressing the vocabulary needs of English language learners in bilingual and mainstream classrooms. *Reading Research Quarterly, 39*(2), 188–215.

Carson, J.G. (1992). Becoming biliterate: First language influences. *Journal of Second Language Writing, 1*(1), 37–60.

Charity, A.H., Scarborough, H.S., & Griffin, D.M. (2004). Familiarity with school English in African American children and its relation to early reading achievement. *Child Development, 75*(5), 1340–1356. doi:10.1111/j.1467-8624.2004.00744.x

Cheng, L., Klinger, D.A., & Zheng, Y. (2007). The challenges of the Ontario Secondary School Literacy Test for second language students. *Language Testing, 24*(2), 185–208. doi:10.1177/0265532207076363

Conlin, C.R. (2009). Non-mainstream American English and first-grade children's language and reading skills growth. *Electronic Theses, Treatises and Dissertations, Paper 3479.* Tallahassee, FL: The Florida State University. Retrieved from http://diginole.lib.fsu.edu/etd/3479/

Connor, C.M., & Craig, H.K. (2006). African American preschoolers' language, emergent literacy skills, and use of African American English: A complex relation. *Hearing Research, 49*(August), 771–793.

Craig, H., Connor, C.M., & Washington, J.A. (2003). Early positive predictors of later reading comprehension for African American students: A preliminary investigation. *Language, Speech, and Hearing Services in Schools, 34,* 31–43. Retrieved from http://lshss.asha.org/cgi/content/abstract/34/1/31

Craig, H.K., Thompson, C.A., Washington, J.A., & Potter, S.L. (2003). Phonological features of child African American English. *Journal of Speech, Language, and Hearing Research, 46*(3), 623–635.

Craig, H.K., & Washington, J.A. (1994). The complex syntax skills of poor, urban, African-American preschoolers at school entry. *Language, Speech, and Hearing Services in Schools, 25,* 181–190.

Craig, H.K., & Washington, J.A. (2002). Oral language expectations for African American preschoolers and kindergartners. *American Journal of Speech-Language Pathology, 11*(1), 59–70. doi:10.1044/1058-0360(2002/007)

Craig, H.K., & Washington, J.A. (2004). Grade-related changes in the production of African American English. *Journal of Speech, Language, and Hearing Research, 47*(2), 450–63. doi:10.1044/1092-4388(2004/036)

Craig, H.K., Zhang, L., Hensel, S.L., & Quinn, E.J. (2009). African American English-speaking students: An examination of the relationship between dialect shifting and reading outcomes. *Journal of Speech, Language, and Hearing Research, 52*(4), 839–55. doi:10.1044/1092-4388(2009/08-0056)

Cronnell, B. (1985). Language influences in the English writing of third- and sixth-grade Mexican-American students. *Journal of Educational Research, 78*(3), 168–173.

Cunningham, A.E., & Stanovich, K.E. (1997). Early reading acquisition and its relation to reading experience and ability 10 years later. *Developmental Psychology, 33*(6), 934–945. Retrieved from http://www.ncbi.nlm.nih.gov/pubmed/9383616

Cohen, C.C., Deterding, N., & Clewell, B.C. (2005). *Who's left behind? Immigrant children in high and low LEP schools.* Washington, DC: The Urban Institute.

De George, G.P. (1988). Assessment and placement of language minority students: Procedures for mainstreaming. *Equity and Excellence, 23*(4), 44–56.

de Jong, E.J. (2004). After exit: Academic achievement patterns of former English language learners. *Education Policy Analysis Archives, 12*(50), 1–18.

Delpit, L. (2006). *Other people's children: Cultural conflict in the classroom.* New York, NY: New Press.

Duursma, E., Romero-Contreras, S., Szuber, A., Proctor, P., Snow, C., August, D., & Calderón, M. (2007). The role of home literacy and language environment on bilinguals' English and Spanish vocabulary development. *Applied Psycholinguistics, 28*(1), 171–190. doi:10.1017/S0142716407070099

East, M.R. (2008). *Dictionary use in foreign language writing exams: Impact and implications.* Philadelphia, PA: John Benjamins Publishing.

Elbro, C., Borstrøm, I., & Peterson, D.K. (1998). Predicting dyslexia from kindergarten: The importance of distinctness of phonological representations of lexical items. *Reading Research Quarterly, 33*(1), 36–60.

Fitzgerald, J. (2006). Multilingual writing in preschool through 12th grade: The last 15 years. In C.A. MacArthur, S. Graham, & J. Fitzgerald (Eds.), *Handbook of Writing Research* (pp. 337–354). New York, NY: Guilford Press.

Fowler, A.E., & Swainson, B. (2004). Relationships of naming skills to reading, memory, and receptive vocabulary: Evidence for imprecise phonological representations of words by poor readers. *Annals of Dyslexia, 54*(2), 247–280.

Freebody, P., & Anderson, R.C. (1983). Effects of vocabulary difficulty, text cohesion, and schema availability on reading comprehension. *Reading Research Quarterly, 18*(3), 277–294.

Gándara, P., Rumberger, R., Maxwell-Jolly, J., & Callahan, R. (2003). English learners in California schools: Unequal resources, unequal outcomes. *Education Policy Analysis Archives, 11*(36), 1–54.

Gosa, T., & Alexander, K. (2007). Family (dis)advantage and the educational prospects of better off African American youth: How race still matters. *Teacher College Record, 109*(2), 285-321.

Geva, E., Yaghoub-Zadeh, Z., & Schuster, B. (2000). Understanding individual differences in word recognition skills of ESL children. *Annals of Dyslexia, 50*(1), 121–154.

Grabe, W., & Kaplan, R.B. (1996). *Theory and practice of writing: An applied linguistic perspective.* New York, NY: Longman.

Grosjean, F. (1998). Studying bilinguals: Methodological and conceptual issues. *Bilingualism: Language and Cognition, 1*(2), 131–149.

Grosjean, F., & Miller, J.L. (1994). Going in and out of languages: An example of bilingual flexibility. *Psychological Science, 5*(4), 201–206.

Gutierrez, K.D., Zepeda, M., & Castro, D.C. (2010). Advancing early literacy learning for all children: Implications of the NELP report for dual-language learners. *Educational Researcher, 39*(4), 334–339. doi:10.3102/0013189X10369831

Hinkel, E. (2002). *Second language writers' text: Linguistic and rhetorical features.* Mahwah, NJ: Lawrence Erlbaum Associates.

Horkay, N., Bennett, R.E., Allen, N., Kaplan, B., Yan, F., & Russell, E.M. (2006). Does it matter if I take my writing test on computer? An empirical study of mode effects in NAEP. *The Journal of Technology, Learning, and Assessment, 5*(2), 1–50.

Hutchinson, J.M., Whiteley, H.E., Smith, C.D., & Connors, L. (2003). The developmental progression of comprehension-related skills in children learning EAL. *Journal of Research in Reading, 26*(1), 19–32.

Ivy, L.J., & Masterson, J.J. (2011). A comparison of oral and written English styles in African American students at different stages of writing development. *Language, Speech, and Hearing Services in Schools, 42*, 31–40.

Jerry, L., Ballator, N., & Rogers, A. (1999). *NAEP 1998 writing.* Washington, DC: National Center for Education Statistics.

Johnson, V.E., & Newport, E.L. (1989). Critical period effects in second language learning: The influence of maturational state on the acquisition of English as a second language. *Cognitive Psychology, 21*(1), 60–99.

Kieffer, M.J. (2011). Converging trajectories: Reading growth in language minority learners and their classmates, kindergarten to grade 8. *American Educational Research Journal, 48*(5), 1187–1225.

Kieffer, M.J. (2012). Early oral language and later reading development in Spanish-speaking English language learners: Evidence from a nine-year longitudinal study. *Journal of Applied Developmental Psychology, 33*(3), 146–157.

Kieffer, M.J., & Lesaux, N.K. (2012). Knowledge of words, knowledge about words: Dimensions of vocabulary in first and second language learners in sixth grade. *Reading and Writing, 25*(2), 347–373.

Kindler, A.L. (2002). *Survey of the states' limited English proficient students and available educational programs and services: 2000–2001 summary report.* Washington, DC: Office of English Language Acquisition, Language Enhancement and Academic Achievement for Limited English Proficient Students, U.S. Department of Education.

Knell, E., Haiyan, Q., Miao, P., Yanping, C., Siegel, L.S., Lin, Z., & Wei, Z. (2007). Early English immersion and literacy in Xi'an, China. *The Modern Language Journal, 91*(3), 395–417.

Ko, I.Y., Wang, M., & Kim, S.Y. (2011). Bilingual reading of compound words. *Journal of Psycholinguistic Research, 40*(1), 49–73.

Labov, W., & Baker, B. (2010). What is a reading error? *Applied Psycholinguistics, 31*(4), 735.

Ladson-Billings, G. (1992). Liberatory consequences of literacy: A case of culturally relevant instruction for African American students. *Journal of Negro Education, 61*(3), 378–391.

Lervåg, A., & Aukrust, V.G. (2010). Vocabulary knowledge is a critical determinant of the difference in reading comprehension growth between first and second language learners. *Journal of Child Psychology and Psychiatry, and Allied Disciplines, 51*(5), 612–620. doi:10.1111/j.1469-7610.2009.02185.x

Lesaux, N.K. (2006). Building consensus: Future directions for research on English language learners at risk for learning difficulties. *Teachers College Record, 108*(11), 2406–2438. doi:10.1111/j.1467-9620.2006.00787.x

Lesaux, N.K., Crosson, A.C., Kieffer, M.J., & Pierce, M. (2011). Uneven profiles: Language minority learners' word reading, vocabulary, and reading comprehension skills. *Journal of Applied Developmental Psychology, 31*(6), 475–483. doi:10.1016/j.appdev.2010.09.004

Lesaux, N.K., Kieffer, M.J., Faller, S.E., & Kelley, J.G. (2010). The effectiveness and ease of implementation of an academic vocabulary intervention for linguistically diverse students in urban middle schools. *Reading Research Quarterly, 45*(2), 196–228.

Lesaux, N.K., & Siegel, L.S. (2003). The development of reading in children who speak English as a second language. *Developmental Psychology, 39*(6), 1005–1019. doi:10.1037/0012-1649.39.6.1005

Liu, M., & Braine, G. (2005). Cohesive features in argumentative writing produced by Chinese undergraduates. *System, 33*(4), 623–636.

Mancilla-Martinez, J., & Lesaux, N.K. (2010). Predictors of reading comprehension for struggling readers: The case of Spanish-speaking language minority learners. *Journal of Educational Psychology, 102*(3), 701–711. doi:10.1037/a0019135

Manis, F.R., Lindsey, K.A., & Bailey, C.E. (2004). Development of reading in grades K–2 in Spanish-speaking English language learners. *Learning Disabilities Research and Practice, 19*(4), 214–224.

Metsala, J.L., & Walley, A.C. (1998). Spoken vocabulary growth and the segmental restructuring of lexical representations: Precursors to phonemic awareness and early reading ability. In J.L. Metsala & L.C. Ehri (Eds.), *Word recognition in beginning literacy* (pp. 89–120). Hillsdale, NJ: Erlbaum.

Moats, L., Foorman, B., & Taylor, P. (2006). How quality of writing instruction impacts high-risk fourth graders' writing. *Reading and Writing, 19*(4), 363–391.

Nakamoto, J., Lindsey, K.A., & Manis, F.R. (2007). A longitudinal analysis of English language learners' word decoding and reading comprehension. *Reading and Writing, 20*(7), 691–719.

National Center for Education Statistics (NCES). (2012a). *The nation's report card: Reading 2011.* Washington, DC: Author.

National Center for Education Statistics (NCES). (2012b). *The nation's report card: Writing 2011.* Washington, DC: Author.

National Early Literacy Panel (NELP). (2009). *Developing early literacy: Report of the National Early Literacy Panel.* Jessup, MD: National Institute for Literacy.

Nettles, D.H., & Diehl, H. (2010). *Strategies for powerful comprehension instruction: It takes more than mentioning!* Huntington Beach, CA: Shell Education.

No Child Left Behind Act of 2001, PL 107-110, 115 Stat. 1452, 20 U.S.C. §§ 6301 *et. seq.*

Oetting, J.B., & Pruitt, S. (2005). Southern African-American English use across groups. *Journal of Multilingual Communication Disorders, 3*(2), 136–144. doi:10.1080/14769670400027324

Olateju, M.A. (2006). Cohesion in ESL classroom-written texts. *Nordic Journal of African Studies, 15*(3), 314–331.

Orellana, M.F., & D'warte, J. (2010). Recognizing different kinds of "Head Starts." *Educational Researcher, 39*(4), 295–300. doi:10.3102/0013189X10369829

Pearson, B.Z., Velleman, S.L., Bryant, T.J., & Charko, T. (2009). Phonological milestones for African American English-speaking children learning mainstream American English as a second dialect. *Language, Speech, and Hearing Services in Schools, 40*(3), 229.

Perfetti, C. (2007). Reading ability: Lexical quality to comprehension. *Scientific Studies of Reading, 11*(4), 357–383.

Purves, A.C. (1992). Reflections on research and assessment in written composition. *Research in the Teaching of English, 26*(1), 108–122.

Raimes, A. (1990). The TOEFL test of written English: Causes for concern. *TESOL Quarterly, 24*(3), 427.

Reese, L., Garnier, H., Gallimore, R., & Goldenberg, C. (2000). Longitudinal analysis of the antecedents of emergent Spanish literacy and middle-school English reading achievement of Spanish-speaking students. *American Educational Research Journal, 37*(3), 633–662.

Seymour, H.N., Bland-Stewart, L., & Green, L.J. (1996). Difference versus deficit in child African American English. *Language, Speech and Hearing Services in Schools, 29*(1), 96–109.

Singham, M. (1998). The canary in the mine: The achievement gap between black and white students. *Phi Delta Kappan, 80*(1), 8-15.

Smitherman, G. (1993). *"The blacker the berry, the sweeter the juice": African American student writers and the National Assessment of Educational Progress.* Paper presented at the annual conference of the National Council of Teachers of English, Pittsburgh, PA, November 17–22.

Snow, C.E., Burns, M.S., & Griffin, P. (Eds.). (1998). *Preventing reading difficulties in young children.* Washington, DC: National Academies Press.

Stahl, S.A., & Nagy, W.E. (2006). *Teaching word meanings.* Mahwah, NJ: Lawrence Erlbaum Associates.

Stanovich, K.E. (1986). Matthew Effects in reading: Some consequences of individual differences in the acquisition of literacy. *Reading Research Quarterly, 21*(4), 360–407.

Stevens, G. (2006). The age-length-onset problem in research on second language acquisition among immigrants. *Language Learning, 56*(4), 671–692.

Swanson, H.L., Rosston, K., Gerber, M., & Solari, E. (2008). Influence of oral language and phonological awareness on children's bilingual reading. *Journal of School Psychology, 46*(4), 413–429.

Terrebonne, N.G., & Terrebonne, R.A. (1976). *The patterning of language variation in writing.* Paper presented at the annual meeting of the Midwest Modern Language Association, St. Louis, MO, November 4–6.

Terry, N.P., Connor, C.M., Petscher, Y., & Conlin, C.R. (2012). Dialect variation and reading: Is change in nonmainstream American English use related to reading achievement in first and second grades? *Journal of Speech, Language, and Hearing Research, 55*(February), 55–69. doi:10.1044/1092-4388(2011/09-0257)

Terry, N.P., Connor, C.M., Thomas-Tate, S., & Love, M. (2010). Examining relationships among dialect variation, literacy skills, and school context in first grade. *Journal of Speech, Language, and Hearing Research, 53*(1), 126–145. Retrieved from http://jslhr.highwire.org/cgi/content/abstract/53/1/126

Terry, N.P., & Scarborough, H.S. (2011). The phonological hypothesis as a valuable framework for studying the relation of dialect variation to early reading skills. In S.A. Brady, D. Braze, & C.A. Fowler (Eds.), *Explaining individual differences in reading: Theory and evidence* (pp. 97–117). New York, NY: Psychology Press.

Thomas-Tate, S., Washington, J.A., & Edwards, J. (2004). Standardized assessment of phonological awareness skills in low-income African American first graders. *American Journal of Speech-Language Pathology, 13*(2), 143–149.

Tillema, M., Van den Bergh, H., Rijlaarsdam, G., & Sanders, T. (2012). Quantifying the quality difference between L1 and L2 essays: A rating procedure with bilingual raters and L1 and L2 benchmark essays. *Language Testing, 30*(1), 71–97. doi:10.1177/0265532212442647

Torgesen, J.K., & Bryant, B.R. (1994). *Test of phonological awareness.* Austin, TX: Pro Ed.

Van den Bergh, H., Rijlaarsdam, G., Janssen, T., Braaksma, M., Van Weijen, D., & Tillema, M. (2009). Process execution of writing and reading: Considering text quality, learner and task characteristics. In M.C. Shelley II, L.D. Yore, & B. Hand (Eds.), *Quality research in literacy and science education* (pp. 399–425). New York, NY: Springer.

Vaughn, S., Mathes, P., Linan-Thompson, S., Cirino, P., Carlson, C., Pollard-Durodola, S., . . . Francis, D.J. (2006). Effectiveness of an English intervention for first-grade English language learners at risk for reading problems. *The Elementary School Journal, 107*, 153–180.

Vaughn, S., Mathes, P.G., Linan-Thompson, S., & Francis, D.J. (2005). Teaching English language learners at risk for reading disabilities to read: Putting research into practice. *Learning Disabilities Research and Practice, 20*(1), 58–67.

Washington, J.A., & Craig, H.K. (1994). Dialectal forms during discourse of poor, urban, African American preschoolers. *Journal of Speech, Language, and Hearing Research, 37*(4), 816–823.

Washington, J.A., & Craig, H.K. (1998). Socioeconomic status and gender influences on children's dialectal variations. *Journal of Speech, Language, and Hearing Research, 41*(3), 618–626. Retrieved from http://jslhr.highwire.org/cgi/content/abstract/41/3/618

Washington, J.A., & Craig, H.K. (2002). Morphosyntactic forms of African American English used by young children and their caregivers. *Applied Psycholinguistics, 23*(2), 209–231. doi:10.1017/S0142716402002035

Weigle, C. (2002). *Assessing writing.* Bremen, Germany: Ernst Klett Sprachen.

Wheeler, R., Cartwright, K.B., & Swords, R. (2012). Factoring AAVE into reading assessment and instruction. *The Reading Teacher, 65*(6), 416–425.

Wheeler, R., & Swords, R. (2006). *Code-switching: Teaching standard English in urban classrooms.* Urbana, IL: National Council of Teachers of English.

Whiteman, M.F. (1981). Dialect influence in writing. In M.F. Whiteman & C.H. Frederick (Eds.), *Variation in writing: Functional and linguistic cultural differences* (Vol. 1; pp. 153–166). New York, NY: Routledge.

Wilde, J. (2010). *Comparing results of the NAEP long-term trend assessment: ELLs, former ELLs, and English-proficient students.* Paper presented at the annual meeting of the American Educational Research Association, Denver, CO.

Wolfram, W., & Schilling-Estes, N. (1998). *American English: Dialects and variation.* Malden, MA: Blackwell.

Wolfram, W., & Schilling-Estes, N. (2006). *American English: Dialects and variation* (2nd ed.; Language and Society, Vol. 25). Cambridge: Basil Blackwell.

Wolfram, W., & Thomas, E.R. (2002). *The development of African American English.* Malden, MA: Blackwell.

Wolfram, W., & Whiteman, M.F. (1971). The role of dialect interference in composition. *Florida FL Reporter, 9*(1), 34–38.

Zamel, V. (1987). Recent research on writing pedagogy. *TESOL Quarterly, 2*(4), 697–715.

8

Discussion as a Means of Learning to Reason, Read, and Write Analytically

Joanne F. Carlisle, Julie Dwyer, and Julie E. Learned

he Common Core State Standards (CCSS) provide a new emphasis on the development of upper elementary and middle school students' reasoning and argumentation in oral and written language contexts. The standards explicitly identify competencies in critical thinking that contribute to advanced capabilities in reading and writing. In fact, the development of reasoning and argumentation is important for students' educational attainment in all content areas. Although many will view the emphasis on reasoning and argumentation in CCSS as a welcome change, the standards are likely to present new challenges for teachers. With the goal of providing support for teachers, we offer a review of research and guidelines for practitioners on using oral discussions of written texts as a basis for learning to reason and develop effective arguments, which in turn contribute to students' reading comprehension and argumentation in written compositions.

To frame our discussion, we start by reviewing several CCSS for late elementary and middle school students that highlight the roles that reasoning and argumentation play in both speaking and listening (Table 8.1) and in literacy (Table 8.2). In Table 8.1, we note the emphasis on using critical thinking skills in collaborative discussion—a format for learning to express one's ideas, formulate arguments, sequence ideas logically, and reflect on others'

Table 8.1. Selected Common Core State Standards reflecting reasoning and argumentation in oral contexts

---

Gr. 4, anchor standards. English language arts (ELA) Literacy. College and Career Readiness Anchor (CCRA). Speaking and Listening (SL) 3: Evaluate a speaker's point of view, reasoning, and use of evidence and rhetoric.

Gr. 4, anchor standards. ELA Literacy, CCRA. SL 4: Present information, findings, and supporting evidence such that listeners can follow the line of reasoning and so the organization, development, and style are appropriate to task, purpose, and audience.

Gr. 6, speaking and listening. ELA Literacy. SL 6.1: Engage effectively in a range of collaborative discussions (one-to-one, in groups, and teacher-led) with diverse partners on grade 6 topics, texts, and issues, building on others' ideas and expressing their own clearly.

Gr. 6, speaking and listening. ELA Literacy. SL 6.3: Delineate a speaker's argument and specific claims, distinguishing claims that are supported by reasons and evidence from claims that are not.

Gr. 6, speaking and listening. ELA Literacy. SL 6.4: Present claims and findings, sequencing ideas logically and using pertinent descriptions, facts, and details to accentuate main ideas or themes.

Source: National Governors Association Center for Best Practices, Council of Chief State School Officers (2010).

Table 8.2. Selected CCSS for reading and writing

Gr. 4, reading, Information Texts. ELA Literacy. R 1.4.8: Explain how an author uses reasons and evidence to support particular points in a text.

Gr. 6, reading. ELA Literacy. R 1.6.8: Trace and evaluate the argument and specific claims in a text, distinguishing claims that are supported by reasons and evidence from claims that are not.

Gr. 4, writing. ELA Literacy. W 4.1: Write opinion pieces on topics or texts, supporting a point of view with reasons and information. (One subpart: Provide reasons that are supported by facts and details; link opinion and reasons using words and phrases.)

Gr. 6, writing. ELA Literacy. W 6.1: Write arguments to support claims with clear reasons and relevant evidence.

Gr. 6, writing. ELA Literacy. Writing in History/Social Studies, Science, and Technical Subjects (WHST) 6.8.1: Write arguments focused on discipline-specific content.

Source: National Governors Association Center for Best Practices, Council of Chief State School Officers (2010).

thinking. We should not be surprised that there are similarities in the standards for reading and writing because here, too, reasoning and argumentation are integral parts of a communication process. Some examples are shown in Table 8.2. We note the emphasis placed on building an argument by presenting reasons and providing evidence to support these reasons. The standards also specify aspects of argumentation expected of sixth graders (e.g., distinguishing a claim from a counterclaim).

From the focus in CCSS on analytic reasoning in oral and written contexts, we might infer that there are good reasons to link instruction in oral discussion, argumentation, and high-level literacy competencies. Small group discussion of written texts coupled with instruction and guidance in argumentation serve to prepare students for presentation of written arguments—and in some cases, there is evidence that oral discussion contributes to students' gains in both reading comprehension and writing (Applebee, Langer, Nystrand, & Gamoran, 2003; Murphy, Wilkinson, Soter, Hennessey, & Alexander, 2009; Reznitskaya, Anderson, & Kuo, 2007; Voss & Means, 1991).

Though teachers are likely to see the value of linking oral and written reasoning, we expect that they might have more difficulty seeing how to adjust their instructional routines to accommodate the new standards. For example, we wondered if teachers are familiar with recommended procedures for conducting discussions that foster children's competence in language and literacy. We also wondered whether teachers know how to facilitate the development of effective argumentation. This chapter was written with such issues in mind. Our central goal is to show how oral discussion of written texts can be used as a means of developing oral and written language capabilities of upper elementary and middle school students and, in particular, the quality of their reasoning and argumentation.

DEVELOPMENT OF REASONING AND ARGUMENTATION

Long before they reach the late elementary grades, students are quite capable of using basic elements of reasoning and argumentation in familiar contexts (Mercier, 2011). They can draw conclusions from observations or facts (i.e., inductive reasoning). For example, students pick up signs of the mood of their classroom teacher (e.g., staring out the window, glowering at the first person who asks a question) and realize (i.e., conclude) that this is not a day to instigate trouble during class. They can also apply a generalization to a particular situation (i.e., deductive reasoning) to evaluate its truth. For example, a student might say, "Disney movies are really boring, and [name of movie] is a Disney movie, so I am sure it will be boring, and I don't want to go see it."

Reasoning develops in social contexts and serves as the foundation on which argumentation is built. The underlying mechanisms through which students learn to mount and evaluate arguments are social and cognitive. Argumentation is a process of thinking and social interaction that is best developed in a social context (Nussbaum, 2011). As Mercier (2011) has said, "Reasoning should be at its best in argumentative contexts. Such contexts naturally arise when a group willing to work together disagrees" (p. 183). In upper elementary and middle school classrooms, this typically entails small group discussion in which participants have a chance to mount a position, explain or support it, and respond critically to each other's arguments.

Discussion groups serve as a format or organizational structure usually involving a small group of students; teachers often but not always are members of the discussion groups in their classroom, especially in the elementary years. The goals are varied. Certainly, one goal of discussion is to help students develop good communication practices, and another is to engage students in analysis of written texts. However, not all small group discussion formats have the purpose of developing effective argumentation. When they do, certain conditions should be in place for group discussion to be effective. The issues or topics for discussion should be of interest to students, and there should be ample opportunity for all participants to share their ideas. More generally, the teacher needs to create a classroom culture that honors diverse backgrounds and perspectives among the students. With experience and support in the processes of discussion and reasoning, students come to appreciate differences in perspective and the value of listening to others' arguments. Over time, oral discussion and argumentation can contribute to students' abilities to formulate and present ideas that are substantive and convincing (Nystrand, Wu, Gamoran, Zeiser, & Long, 2003).

Although upper elementary and middle school students may have had lots of experience with argumentation in familiar situations (e.g., arguing for a later bedtime or a larger allowance), scholars believe that students need both instruction and experience to learn how to develop an argument and present it effectively for discussion (e.g., Mercier, 2011; Reznitskaya et al., 2001). They need help understanding participation structures and elements of effective argumentation (Reznitskaya et al., 2001). The teacher plays a critical role in this process.

CHARACTERISTICS OF DISCUSSION THAT SUPPORT THE DEVELOPMENT OF LITERACY

The nature of the communication process between writer and reader is such that the writer presents ideas and information to others who are not present. Issues of content, genre, language, culture, philosophical stances—all these require readers to strive to understand what the writer intended. The writer needs to learn how to provide clear, defensible, and well-organized arguments that readers can follow. Through group discussion, students come to understand the roles and responsibilities of readers and writers, and the opportunity for students to work together to understand and evaluate written texts fosters the development of language, reading, and writing (Beck & McKeown, 2006). Murphy and colleagues (2009) argued that "articulate student talk supports inquiry, collaborative learning, high-level thinking, and making knowledge personally meaningful" (p. 142).

To support the development of "articulate student talk," teachers are advised to assist students in learning how to learn from discussions about texts (Beck & McKeown, 2006; Wilkinson, Soter, & Murphy, 2010). Some system or guidance needs to be in place to encourage students to express ideas and interpretations about a text, to support their ideas by close examination of the text, and to engage in exchanges of different perspectives (Beck & McKeown, 2006; Goldenberg, 1992; Reznitskaya et al., 2007). Established group discussion programs vary somewhat in the procedures they recommend to teachers (e.g., Murphy et al., 2009). However, scholars have identified general characteristics of group discussions and teachers' instructional actions that facilitate the development (and interrelations) of language, reasoning, reading, and writing. The three characteristics we have chosen to focus on are active participation, extended talk, and cognitive challenge. Each of these is discussed in turn.

Active Participation in Discussion of Texts

A necessary feature of discussion is that participants need to see themselves as members of a discourse community (Nystrand et al., 2003). As such, students must be encouraged or taught to play an active role in the discussion of texts and evaluation of arguments focused on interpretation of texts. The role of the teacher is more of a guide than a dictator. Students must understand that their views are valued and that they share the responsibility of thinking about and talking about the text. Wilkinson and his colleagues (2010) have suggested that *shared control* is an important concept associated with quality talk. The teacher has control over the topic and the text that is chosen for discussion, whereas the students have interpretive authority and control of turns (i.e., who gets the floor).

Some instructional actions (i.e., teacher behaviors) that are used to bring about active participation among the students are these (e.g., Goldenberg, 1992):

- Encourage students to express their ideas.

- Accept students' contributions to the discussion.

- Praise students for trying to answer difficult questions.

Among conditions associated with quality talk, Wilkinson and colleagues (2010) spoke about supporting both knowledge-driven and affective comments. The latter is important to engage students personally and emotionally.

Sustained and Extended Discussion

One challenge teachers face is finding ways to foster sustained discussion. Sustained conversations are necessary for students to develop the ability to formulate and articulate their views, adjust their thinking through reflecting on each other's ideas, and reach some kind of closure. Extended discussion as dialogic and effective communication is a cooperative endeavor. In contrast, brief exchanges (particularly those made up of teacher questions and brief student responses) are not likely to contribute to students' development of skills of argumentation.

The choice of reading or discussion topics may affect students' interest or willingness to engage in sustained discussion (Almasi, O'Flahavan, & Arya, 2001). Students will be more likely to share their ideas when the topic is familiar or relevant to their personal experiences than when it is not familiar or interesting. Further, the classroom teacher can provide important scaffolds that augment and foster children's communicative competence; for example, the teacher's actions might include directing, organizing, simplifying, defining, and reminding (Lloyd, 1990). The discourse actions that teachers use to facilitate extended discussion may be particularly necessary for younger students and for those with less well-developed communication capabilities (e.g., students who are English language learners or who have language learning disabilities; Boyd & Rubin, 2006).

Some discourse practices that teachers can use to support extended talk (e.g., Boyd & Rubin, 2006; O'Connor & Michaels, 1993) include the following:

- "Revoice" a student's contribution (i.e., clarify the student's idea for others to understand and respond to).

- Use open-ended questions (i.e., those for which there is no single right answer).

- Engage in contingent responding (i.e., the teacher requests a student to expand on or clarify a comment or idea).

Contingently responsive teachers facilitate the development of discussion skills by creating opportunities for students to practice initiating topics, elaborating on their own responses, and responding to questions from members of the group—including the teacher (Boyd & Rubin, 2006). One effect of techniques such as contingent questioning is that there is an underlying coherence in the sharing of information. In contrast, close-ended or display questions (typically where the teacher knows the answers) tend not to be related to one another and tend not to build on students' responses; therefore, close-ended questions are not conducive to sharing the process of constructing meaning of a text. The teacher's goal is to promote coherence by "building on the voices of others and establishing intertextual links among speakers" (Nystrand et al., 2003, p. 146).

Cognitive Challenge

The quality of classroom talk is dependent, in part, on the extent to which the content, activities, and group discussion are challenging and therefore stimulating to students (Wolf, Crosson, & Resnick, 2005). Wolf and her colleagues (2005) studied characteristics of learning environments and teachers' practices that enable students to achieve high academic standards. Even though teachers in this study were given guidelines for rigorous instruction, there was marked variation in the quality of their discourse moves. For example, although teachers were asked to hold students accountable for accurate knowledge, some did so by focusing on facts (e.g., "Does anyone remember the dog's name?"), whereas others asked questions that demanded reasoning and reflection (e.g., "How did you know that?" or "What were you thinking?"). Rigorous academic content, formats for learning, activities, and engaging discourse contributed to students' interest and participation.

One important aspect of cognitive challenge is instruction in effective argumentation. This might involve teaching students to provide evidence to support their ideas, to consider the quality of such evidence, to evaluate counterclaims, and to strive to reach consensus where possible. Instruction is largely dependent on the guidance teachers provide during discussions. Examples of instructional actions teachers might use include the following:

- Asking follow-up questions such as, "How did you know that . . . ?" and "Why do you think . . . ?"

- Directing students to use text to provide evidence to support their reasoning

- Initiating students' uses of or references to the text with prompts such as, "Where in the text did you find that?"

According to Reznitskaya and colleagues (2007), cognitively challenging argumentation in dialogic settings can lead students to develop an argument schema that "incorporates both logical and psychological aspects of argumentation" (p. 451). This can be seen through their ability to present reasoned arguments and counterarguments, recognize logical connections, and draw warranted conclusions (i.e., conclusions well supported by evidence; Chinn, Anderson, & Waggoner, 2001; Clark et al., 2003; Michaels, O'Connor, & Resnick, 2008). Further, coupling oral discussion with follow-up writing assignments provides opportunities for students to formulate an argument on their own. Oral discussion can give students the opportunity to try out an argument that they then incorporate in a written composition. In sum, appropriate cognitive challenge is likely to contribute to higher-level thinking and effective argumentation in oral and written contexts.

APPROACHES AND ESTABLISHED PROGRAMS

There are a number of established programs for discussion group formats that teachers might want to explore. Teachers (and schools) face the challenge of choosing a program that shows promise for effective development of students' literacy and argumentation and that might contribute to their attainment of the CCSS. Because established programs vary in stance or purpose and in the procedures for planning and implementing discussions, we suggest that teachers study a meta-analysis carried out by Murphy and colleagues (2009) that describes characteristics and analyzes benefits of a number of different discussion programs. These researchers examined evidence of the effects of classroom discussion on measures of teacher and student talk and on students' comprehension and critical thinking. Results showed that some discussion approaches produced increases in the amount of student talk with concomitant reductions in teacher talk; in some there were also noticeable improvements in text comprehension. In addition, Wilkinson and his colleagues (2010) have written a synthesis of different approaches and offer a model called Quality Talk. Both are valuable resources.

Of the nine programs or approaches discussed in Murphy and colleagues' meta-analysis, we have chosen to provide an overview of three effective approaches. We focus primarily on *collaborative reasoning* (e.g., Clark et al., 2003) because of the extensive research that has been carried out to study this program, but we also provide brief descriptions of two other programs: *instructional conversations* (Goldenberg, 1992; Saunders & Goldenberg, 1999) and *questioning the author* (Beck & McKeown, 2006).

Collaborative Reasoning

Researchers have studied collaborative reasoning (CR) as a method for expanding the ways children talk and think (Chinn et al., 2001; Clark et al., 2003). Researchers have listed the seven steps in carrying out CR discussions, shown in Box 8.1. Further, they have described teaching behaviors that CR encourages: clarifying, asking for evidence, challenging students to reason, and summarizing/synthesizing. CR ultimately aims to transfer responsibility for the discussion to students with minimal teacher support. They offer concrete suggestions concerning how to facilitate and scaffold discussion and how to transfer responsibility gradually to the students.

Researchers have also explained the roles and responsibilities of teachers and students. Teachers facilitate but do not lead the discussion; they promote students' independent thinking and self-management of turn-taking through modeling, prompting, clarifying, summarizing, and encouraging. They may challenge students' reasons, ask for clarification, or request evidence to support an idea. Students listen to each other and think out loud about the text. They offer arguments and present evidence to support these, but they also analyze the strength of others' arguments. They may try to persuade others, but they need to be willing to change their minds when presented with alternative points of view.

Results of a study of CR show benefits of this program for the quality of group discussion (Chinn et al., 2001). These researchers examined the effects of CR on patterns of

Box 8.1: Steps in implementing a lesson using collaborative reasoning (Clark et al., 2003)

1. After the class reads the day's story, a small group forms for discussion. A teacher reads rules for contributing productively to discussions.

2. The teacher poses a central question concerning a dilemma faced by a character in the story.

3. Students freely explain their positions on the central question.

4. They expand on their ideas, adding reasons and supporting evidence from the story and everyday experience.

5. They challenge each other's thinking and ways of reasoning.

6. At the end of the discussion, a final poll is taken to see where everyone stands.

7. The teacher and students review the discussion and make suggestions on how to improve future discussions.

Source: Clark et al. (2003).

fourth graders' discourse as compared to the discourse of fourth graders who participated in comprehension lessons that involved recitation. They found that the CR students were more engaged and made more use of higher-level cognitive processes in talking about the texts. These processes included providing elaboration, making predictions, providing evidence to support an argument, and addressing alternative perspectives.

Instructional Conversations

This approach has been used predominantly in classrooms with high proportions of English language learners (Goldenberg, 1992; Saunders & Goldenberg, 1999). Goldenberg (1992) has suggested that the goals of instructional conversations include promotion of more complex language and expression; reasoning to support an argument or position; and extended, connected discourse. Goldenberg (1992) argued that a discussion group format in which the teacher listens to, builds on, and folds in student responses serves to recognize the importance of individual contributions. Studies of this program suggest that it is particularly effective in helping struggling readers understand narrative texts. In addition to using instructional conversations to foster comprehension of text, Goldenberg suggested using the format to prepare students for writing well-argued compositions. Further, he proposed using the approach in content areas such as social studies, not just language arts.

Questioning the Author

This program was developed to support comprehension through focusing on elements that present problems of interpretation and meaning-making (Beck & McKeown, 2006; Beck, McKeown, Sandora, Kucan, & Worthy, 1996). The teacher plays a central role, assisting the students through the use of queries (i.e., questions designed to help students focus on the meanings of words and passages). The discussion examines the intent of the author, but program procedures also offer ways to make discussions of texts cognitively challenging for the students. For example, students are directed to find evidence in the text to support their views about the motives of characters, causes of events, and the like.

WRITTEN ARGUMENTATION

More attention has been paid to the development of reasoning in analysis of written texts than in the composition of written arguments. However, both theory and evidence suggest that participation in discussion groups contributes to the development of students' written argumentation (e.g., Michaels et al., 2007; Reznitskaya et al., 2001; Wolf et al., 2005). Teachers can begin by helping students understand that writing is a conversation with the reader. That is, written arguments, like oral arguments, are dialogic in nature.

Reznitskaya and her colleagues (2001) have argued that written argumentation is effectively developed through discussions in supportive contexts. They compared the persuasive essays of students who did or did not participate in CR discussions for a 5-week period. The essays of the students in the CR condition were better formed in a number of respects (e.g., greater number of arguments and counterarguments; better use of information). Linking argumentative writing activities to group discussion provides a way for students to acquire the experience and knowledge they need to be effective in both their oral and written reasoning. If students are unable to present and discuss ideas orally, it is unlikely that they will be able to do so in writing.

Research to date suggests several issues that teachers need to consider. One issue is the kind and amount of instruction and guidance their students need in order to become competent at developing arguments in written contexts (e.g., Nussbaum & Schraw, 2007). Explicitly linking oral and written activities may help students see the value in trying out an argument through discussion with their peers before attempting to put it down in writing. Explicit instruction is important for students to help them make the transition from orally crafting arguments to composing written arguments. This is because written language places additional demands on students (e.g., use of appropriate academic language, punctuation, and grammar). In many ways, written arguments are more complex than oral arguments.

A second issue is determination of the aspects of reasoning and argumentation that students can use effectively in writing. Even when students become skilled at participating in oral argumentation, they might still have trouble presenting and defending a position in writing in the same way. Without their peers (and teacher) to serve as a sounding board, they are left to their own devices in preparing and writing an argument. Activities with built-in guidance may help. For example, students' written arguments might improve when they are given a goal structure to assist them in planning (e.g., Chambliss & Murphy, 2002; Ferretti, MacArthur, & Dowdy, 2000). Ferretti and colleagues (2000) found that students with learning disabilities benefited from assistance developing subgoals; specifically, they were directed to include 1) a statement of their belief, 2) two or three reasons for their belief, 3) examples or supporting information for each reason, 4) two or three reasons others might disagree, and 5) why those reasons were wrong. Although support for written arguments is helpful, we know little about appropriate expectations for mastery of forms of argumentation. There is a clear need for research to guide teachers in selecting the particular elements of effective arguments that their students can learn.

A third issue is that written argumentation is, to some extent, dependent on students' basic capabilities as writers. Teaching features of effective written arguments might be considered one of many goals for development of writing. The National Association of Educational Progress's writing report card of 2011 indicated that 54% of the eighth graders performed at the basic level in writing; this level refers to partial mastery of the prerequisite knowledge and skills that are fundamental for proficient writing. Both experience and guidance from teachers may contribute to the development (and quality) of written arguments.

PUTTING NEW STANDARDS INTO PRACTICE

Oral discussion is one way (and may be the best way) for students to learn to analyze and reflect on the meaning of written texts, construct arguments about interpretations of texts, and present them in writing. Our overview of theory and research suggests that the late elementary and early middle school years are an appropriate time for teachers to use group discussion as a way to develop students' understanding of effective argumentation. The extent to which group discussion contributes to their reading comprehension and written argumentation may depend on the nature and quality of teachers' instructional procedures and forms of guidance. However, there is much we have yet to learn about the effects of quality talk on higher levels of literacy (e.g., Wilkinson et al., 2010). A major priority is development of methods for assisting teachers in implementing group discussion. It is teachers' knowledge and skills that will determine whether their students meet the standards for argumentation and high-level comprehension and writing skills set by the CCSS.

REFERENCES

Almasi, J.F., O'Flahavan, J.F., & Arya, P. (2001). A comparative analysis of student and teacher development in more and less proficient discussions of literature. *Reading Research Quarterly, 36*, 96–120.

Applebee, A.N., Langer, J.A., Nystrand, M., & Gamoran, A. (2003). Discussion-based approaches to developing understanding: Classroom instruction and student performance in middle and high school English. *American Educational Research Journal, 40*, 685–730.

Beck, I.L., & McKeown, M.G. (2006). *Questioning the author: A fresh and expanded view of a powerful approach.* New York, NY: Scholastic.

Beck, I.L., McKeown, M.G., Sandora, C., Kucan, L., & Worthy, J. (1996). Questioning the author: A yearlong classroom implementation to engage students with text. *Elementary School Journal, 96*, 385–414.

Boyd, M., & Rubin, D. (2006). How contingent questioning promotes extended student talk: A function of display questions. *Journal of Literacy Research, 38*, 141–169.

Chambliss, M.J., & Murphy, P.K. (2002). Fourth and fifth graders representing the argument structure in written texts. *Discourse Processes, 34*, 91–115.

Chinn, C., Anderson, R.C., & Waggoner, M. (2001). Patterns of discourse during two kinds of literature discussion. *Reading Research Quarterly, 36*, 378–411.

Clark, A.M., Anderson, R.C., Archodidou, A., Nguyen-Jahiel, K., Kuo, L.-J., & Kim, I. (2003). Collaborative reasoning: Expanding ways for children to talk and think in the classroom. *Educational Psychology Review, 15*, 181–198.

Ferretti, R.P., MacArthur, C.A., & Dowdy, N.S. (2000). The effects of elaborated goal on the persuasive writing of students with learning disabilities and their normally achieving peers. *Journal of Educational Psychology, 92*, 694–702.

Goldenberg, C. (1992). Instructional conversations: Promoting comprehension through discussion. *Reading Teacher, 46*(4), 316–326.

Lloyd, P. (1990). Children's communication. In R. Grieve & M. Hughes (Eds.), *Understanding children* (pp. 51–70). Cambridge, MA: Basil Blackwell.

Mercier, H. (2011). Reasoning serves argumentation in children. *Cognitive Development, 26*, 177–191.

Michaels, S., O'Connor, C., & Resnick, L. (2008). Deliberative discourse idealized and realized: Accountable talk in the classroom and in civic life. *Studies in Philosophy and Education, 27*, 283–297.

Murphy, P.K., Wilkinson, I.A.G., Soter, A.O., Hennessey, M.H., & Alexander, J.F. (2009). Examining the effects of classroom discourse on students' comprehension of text: A meta-analysis. *Journal of Educational Psychology, 101*, 746–764.

National Governors Association Center for Best Practices, Council of Chief State School Officers. (2010). *Common core state standards: English language arts standards.* Washington, DC: Author. Retrieved from ww.corestandards.org/ELA-literacy

Nussbaum, E.M. (2011). Argumentation, dialogue, theory, and probability modeling: Alternative frameworks for argumentation research in education. *Educational Psychologist, 46*, 84–106.

Nussbaum, E.M., & Schraw, G. (2007). Promoting argument-counterargument integration in students' writing. *Journal of Experimental Education, 76,* 59–92.

Nystrand, M., Wu, L.L., Gamoran, A., Zeiser, S., & Long, D.A. (2003). Questions in time: Investigating the structure and dynamics of unfolding classroom discourse. *Discourse Processes, 35,* 135–198.

O'Connor, M.C., & Michaels, S. (1993). Aligning academic task and participation status through revoicing: Analysis of a classroom discourse strategy. *Anthropology and Education Quarterly, 24,* 318–335.

Reznitskaya, A., Anderson, R.C., & Kuo, L.-J. (2007). Teaching and learning argumentation. *Elementary School Journal, 107,* 449–472.

Reznitskaya, A., Anderson, R.C., McNurden, B., Ngyuen-Jahiel, K., Archodidou, A., & Kim, S. (2001). Influence of oral discussion on written argument. *Discourse Processes, 32,* 155–175.

Saunders, W.M., & Goldenberg, C. (1999). Effects of instructional conversations and literature logs on limited and fluent English proficient students' story comprehension and thematic understanding. *Elementary School Journal, 99,* 277–301.

Voss, J.F., & Means, M.L. (1991). Learning to reason via instruction in argumentation. *Learning and Instruction, 1,* 337–350.

Wilkinson, I.A.G., Soter, A.O., & Murphy, P.K. (2010). Developing a model of quality talk about literacy text. In M. McKeown & L. Kucan (Eds.), *Bringing reading research to life* (pp. 142–169). New York, NY: Guilford Press.

Wolf, M.K., Crosson, A.C., & Resnick, L.B. (2005). Classroom talk for rigorous reading comprehension instruction. *Reading Psychology, 26,* 27–53.

9

Reading and Writing in the Service of Developing Rich Disciplinary Knowledge

Prospects in the Age of the Common Core State Standards

Jacquelyn M. Urbani, P. David Pearson, Sara Ballute, and Timothy A. Lent

The Common Core State Standards (CCSS) represent a significant change in instruction, learning, and assessment in comparison to the era of No Child Left Behind (NCLB, PL 107-110). First, instead of teaching and assessing basic learning through discrete skills and knowledge, the CCSS value higher-order skills such as critical thinking, analysis, and synthesis (National Governors Association Center for Best Practices & Council of Chief State School Officers [NGA/CCSSO], 2010). Second, the CCSS emphasize the necessity of deploying all the English language arts (ELA) skills of reading, writing, speaking, and listening in pursuit of the acquisition of rich knowledge within disciplines such as history, science, and literature. In essence, the CCSS demand a more inclusive and reciprocal learning experience in which content and language/literacy goals and activities support one another.

Our intent in this chapter is to describe the theory, research, and practices underlying the CCSS expectations of a doubly integrated curriculum. The very organization of the standards virtually mandates the application and integration of language arts within the key disciplines of literature, science, and history. In their application within the disciplines, the language arts themselves (reading, writing, and language) inform and reinforce one another—students write about their reading, read their writing, and talk extensively about both. We examine how the CCSS require active engagement of students with complex texts across the disciplines for the purposes of reading critically, developing valid arguments, and solving problems, all of which are consistent with a long tradition of project-based learning (PBL). Finally, we share the efforts—both the successes and struggles—of teachers who are implementing features of PBL in a secondary social studies classroom with the goal of developing both disciplinary literacy capacities/skills and disciplinary content knowledge, in this case history, as per the CCSS, throughout several weeks of instruction.

The Integration of Reading and Writing Instruction

Historically, reading and writing have been taught separately in American schools, with writing receiving significantly less attention and instructional time (Nelson & Calfee,

1998; see also Section 1, this volume). Even so, reading and writing have often been used to assess the other. For example, after reading text, students may be required to produce a short written piece about the topic, whereas writing must be reread by the author for the purposes of editing to produce a final product. Fitzgerald and Shanahan (2000) refer to this as the procedural approach to reading and writing, in which the "activities can be combined to accomplish external goals" (p. 39). As an alternative and preferred approach, Fitzgerald and Shanahan contend that reading and writing should be viewed as relying on shared knowledge, cognitive processes, and contexts and that instruction combining both would be more purposeful and productive. The integration of reading and writing instruction results in at least three specific benefits to students: 1) writing can enhance reading by creating an additional, specific purpose for the reading; 2) writing can enhance reading by offering students the opportunity to reflect, evaluate, and synthesize the text content with their own prior knowledge; and 3) reading enhances writing through the identification of the author's craft, specifically the use of textual features to explain, persuade, and move the story forward (Frankel, Jaeger, & Pearson, 2013; Graham & Hebert, 2010; Tierney & Shanahan, 1996; see also Harris & Graham, Chapter 4, this volume). In addition, Fitzgerald and Shanahan (2000) describe developmental stages for literacy learning across grades and ages. This developmental model is indicated within the CCSS, which detail explicit purposes and expectations for reading and writing from elementary through secondary school.

Disciplinary Literacy and Content Knowledge

The CCSS emphasize the importance of literacy within the content areas as a means of preparing students for success in college or career within a global society (NGA/CCSSO, 2010). In particular, the CCSS emphasize that reading, writing, speaking, listening, and language are vital to a full and complex understanding of the content areas. In essence, the standards are requiring teachers to integrate disciplinary and literacy instruction and to use them to support each other. Research indicates that disciplinary literacy demands higher levels of complexity and specificity than more general literacy activities, and students therefore require explicit instruction in reading comprehension strategies and in identifying the purposes and techniques for subject-specific writing (Billman & Pearson, 2013; Fang & Schleppegrell, 2010; Shanahan & Shanahan, 2008; Wineburg & Grossman, 2000). Within social studies, the area of focus for our case study, reading tasks focus on recognizing and evaluating the author's (i.e., historian's) perspective and the historical context of the text (Ravi, 2010). Active reading—in order for students to "see patterns, make sense of contradictions, and formulate reasoned interpretations" (Wineburg, Martin, & Monte-Sano, 2011, p. v)—requires engagement with the text and a more sophisticated level of critical thinking than previously taught by teachers or expected of students under NCLB.

The active reading and critical thinking emphases of the CCSS are aligned with the purposes of PBL (Halvorsen et al., 2012; Pearson, 2013; Strobel & van Bareneveld, 2009). Thomas (2000) delineates several characteristics of PBL: that projects be central to the curriculum, be focused on questions that promote constructive engagement with disciplinary content that challenges students, be student-driven, and be reality-based. With the possible exception of the last one, these characteristics map readily onto the CCSS, especially as they have been operationalized in the work that we undertook in the New Visions Schools in New York City.

CASE STUDY: PURPOSE AND CONTEXT

The Setting

In collaboration with New Visions for Public Schools[1] in New York City, we conducted a case study that examined how teacher and student practices were affected by the simultaneous learning of content and ELA within a secondary history class. Two of the authors, Pearson and Urbani, served as the documenters of the work, which emerged from an evaluation of a district-sponsored professional development for a pilot implementation of an instructional module designed to enact the CCSS. The other two authors, Ballute and Lent, were the implementers, the teachers who planned and taught the module. New Visions, currently working with approximately 80 New York City schools, aims to make academic success possible for the most underprivileged students through teacher professional development (New Visions for Public Schools, 2013). In preparation for the roll out of the CCSS, a core of New Visions teachers were invited to produce a first wave of instructional modules (2- to 6-week units) designed to develop and sharpen students' capacities to use reading and writing to enhance their learning within disciplinary (science, history, and literature) contexts.

To support teachers in implementing this newly integrated instruction, New Visions partnered with Literacy Design Collaborative (LDC)[2] with the intent of systematizing instruction and making literacy instruction foundational to core subjects (Crawford, Gali-atsos, & Lewis, 2011). In order to assist teachers, LDC created templates for developing modules and planning daily instruction. The lynchpin in each module was a culminating task, dubbed the *teaching task*, in which students would produce a substantial piece of writing, most often an essay, reflecting all they learned in the unit. This piece serves as a student's demonstration of achievement with both ELA skill development and content knowledge understanding. A combination of reading, reasoning, and writing activities support both content acquisition and literacy skill development and are designed to challenge students in ways that mimic the engagement needed in using literacy in everyday situations (Pearson, DeStefano, & Garcia, 1998).

New Visions and LDC also partnered for teacher professional development in using the module templates for planning and instruction. These professional development sessions offered teachers the opportunities to collaborate and learn from each other's successes and struggles. Ballute and Lent had participated in an ongoing teacher professional community in the summer and fall preceding the implementation of the current case and presented their work to their peers in the spring following implementation.

We studied the classroom implementation of a month-long module focused on the Industrial Revolution; the culminating assignment (the teaching task) was an argumentative essay based on close reading of primary and secondary sources that responded to the question of whether or not the Industrial Revolution was worth the costs incurred by society. On the pathway to the culminating essay, students were asked to complete a sequence of supportive activities, including 1) explaining the purpose of their writing assignment and how it would be assessed, 2) actively reading source materials, 3) developing notetaking skills, and 4) developing disciplinary vocabulary. In addition, students engaged in a number of specific writing tasks, most of which were related to the argumentative genre: 1) crafting a claim, 2) developing a line of reasoning, 3) supporting it with textual evidence,

---

[1] New Visions for Public Schools is a nonprofit organization.
[2] LDC provides guidance to schools and districts across states and is supported by the Bill & Melinda Gates Foundation.

4) addressing counterclaims, 5) editing, and 6) responding to feedback from the teacher and peers. For our research purposes, we focused on various features of this integrated instruction, including the initial planning and development of the module, teacher practices (both as planned and as enacted), associated student learning activities (i.e., content-, skill-, and strategy-based assignments), and the trail of learning from the beginning to the end of the module, which culminated in an argumentative essay.

Participants

The Teachers   This research was a case study of the work of teachers who were involved in the LDC-sponsored module development effort of New Visions. The study was conducted in Sara Ballute's tenth-grade social studies class. She had collaborated with Timothy Lent for the writing of the module and for the planning and execution of lessons. Ballute and Lent were asked to participate in the case study by New Visions because of their participation in the summer professional development, their high-quality teaching witnessed in observations, and because the topic of their module—the Industrial Revolution—was a high leverage topic in terms of the module's capacity to address content standards and serve as a model across schools.

The Students   Many of the students in the targeted classes were English language learners, among whom were a sizeable proportion of first- or second-generation immigrants who had experienced interrupted education and attendance problems. These students did not have years of U.S. history to rely on for their current learning. Because of this lack of background knowledge in history, they were not able to simply read a text and understand it; they required substantial scaffolding to build that conceptual knowledge. Several also had special learning needs.

The Researchers   Urbani and Pearson documented the unit as it was implemented and performed an initial analysis before sharing it with the teachers, Ballute and Lent, for reaction, reflection, and editing. Final versions of analyses represented consensus views of what transpired and what it meant.

Methods

We availed ourselves of a very rich data set for a study of curriculum enactment: observation notes from on-site and virtual visits to the classroom (via Skype), which focused on teacher moves in relation to student work; student work from the module introduction, designed to build content knowledge in preparation for the culminating activity; notes taken by students as they read the 23 primary and secondary sources for their essays; the special writing packet, written by Lent as part of the planning for this module and designed to scaffold skill development in preparation for the final essay; the argumentative essay itself; and transcripts of teacher interviews and meetings.

The process of analyzing student work, instructional materials, and pedagogical moves was thorough—and laborious. From Ballute's class, five focal students were identified who had all the aforementioned data sources and represented a range of scores on the culminating essay. Analysis involved the following: reading all the student materials and matching their products to instructional moves via the observation notes (taken by both Urbani and Lent); assessing the disciplinary knowledge and literacy skills demonstrated within the individual tasks throughout the module; and assessing uptake of disciplinary knowledge and literacy skills within the final essay. Throughout the analysis, there was consistent, deliberate synthesis of the multiple data sources to determine what evidence of learning surfaced in all the student work—but most specifically within the final student essays.

WHAT WE LEARNED

The fundamental question in a case study such as this one is, "What did we learn about the process of implementing rich pedagogy in preparation for challenging performance assessment tasks designed to monitor student progress in achieving the CCSS for ELA?" Implicit in this question is the context in which the assessment is set—that is, rich instructional modules in which students are asked to acquire knowledge through reading and to put that knowledge to work in writing effective argumentative essays. What we learned is best captured in our attempts to answer some guiding questions.

Student Outcomes and Qualities of Successful Tasks

What are the qualities of successful literacy tasks in support of content learning? The real answer to this question is that it all depends—on students, tasks, and we believe, teachers. Some tasks required little teacher scaffolding, whereas others challenged even the best readers in the class. Despite purposefully planning activities and choosing resources that could be accessed by students with various skill levels, Ballute and Lent recognized that some of the tasks were very difficult, such as document reading (with arcane and obscure vocabulary) and the argumentation frame (distinguishing among the elements of an argument such as claim, evidence, and reasoning.)

We identified two teaching strategies in particular that we believe led to student success and achievement: using known content to teach a new skill and providing repeated practice with the goal of the essay task, which was to determine whether or not the benefits of the Industrial Revolution outweighed the cost to society. Ballute and Lent structured literacy tasks to provide known content when a new skill was being introduced or emphasized. For example, in one observation, Ballute asked the students to work in groups of three to complete a T-chart, comparing the benefits and disadvantages of the Agrarian Revolution and determining if the benefits had been worth the cost. This is exactly the type of task students would be engaged in for the final essay. Although students were able to successfully identify the benefits and disadvantages from the offered resources, when Ballute directly asked whether the benefits outweighed the disadvantages, she was met with silence. She repeated the question and then asked if the students understood her question. Again, there was silence, followed by one quiet and quick, "No!" Sara asked the class if they understood what she meant by the question. Receiving a room full of shaking heads, she therefore instructed students to create their own T-chart, listing four benefits and disadvantages of going to high school. The students listed benefits such as meeting friends, staying out of trouble, getting educated, and being ready for college and negatives such as peer pressure, getting up early, and getting in fights. Ballute offered various synonyms for the terms of the T-chart, including positives, negatives, advantages, and costs, explaining that she would be asking students to answer the question, "Did the benefits outweigh the costs?" repeatedly throughout the unit. Next, she returned to the content question, asking students to consider and share their responses about the Agrarian Revolution in their small groups. After several minutes of small group discussion, individual students shared their thoughts with the class, demonstrating understanding by identifying the benefits and disadvantages and explaining their perspective on the guiding question (Urbani, Pearson, Ballute, & Lent,

2012). In addition to illustrating the utility of building on the known to access the new, this example also illustrates the best uses of formative assessment: The teacher's "on the spot" assessment of the students' unfamiliarity with the cost-benefit comparison led to a spontaneously developed activity to scaffold the comparative process.

The "known content to teach a new skill" strategy was incorporated numerous times in the student writing packet designed by Lent for the explicit purpose of developing the writing skills necessary for success on the essay. The writing packet offered many examples of the aspects of argument development using a specific topic: the value of fast food versus a home-cooked meal. This topic was used throughout the writing packet to serve as familiar content while students focused on new and challenging skill development. A range of steps/processes were introduced in this way: identifying the hook, background information, and claim in the introductory paragraph; locating/producing the topic sentence, evidence, analysis, summary, and citations within body paragraphs; evaluating example paragraphs to provide suggestions for improving them; identifying elements of competing arguments such as reasons and evidence for the claim; and editing sentences for convention errors such as capitalization and verb tense. Following these examples, the writing packet activities required students to engage in those skills with their own writing as they developed their essays.

In integrating content and literacy instruction, the writing tasks were especially critical for students yet challenging for teachers, as indicated by their comments:

"We're not English teachers."

"It's intimidating to teach writing."

"It gave me a complex because I don't know how to teach (literacy)." (Urbani, Pearson, Ballute, & Lent, 2012, p. 22)

With writing tasks, teachers needed to consider how to convey concepts to students but felt they lacked the specific content and pedagogical knowledge necessary to do so (see also International Reading Association & the *Eunice Kennedy Shriver* National Institute of Child Health and Human Development, 2012). In developing the writing packet, Lent described the importance of viewing the module as a whole but indicated that designing the scaffolded literacy tasks helped him "think about what needs to be done for (the students) to actually write this essay and understand" (p. 22). This type of explicit, interactive instruction has been found to be a powerful support for writing development, even for students with difficulties resulting from learning disabilities (Mason, Harris, & Graham, 2011).

While Lent developed the writing packet, it was Ballute who used it in instruction with students. She felt Lent had done an excellent job in scaffolding the learning for students. But, in particular, she thought he had scaffolded the instruction for *teachers* well. Discipline-specific teachers have little familiarity with teaching the writing process: Lent's writing packet afforded teachers step-by-step instructional moves to make their teaching more explicit.

We also identified that successful literacy tasks were structured to provide repeated practice with the guiding question of the argumentative essay. Engaging students in the task throughout the unit provided them experience with the task assignment and a deeper understanding of the content. Ballute and Lent planned multiple opportunities for students to engage with the question, beginning with the example provided previously (which was with introductory background knowledge) and including vocabulary, debates, and Cornell Notes. *Cornell Notes* were designed to be the main instructional strategy for the Industrial Revolution module; this notetaking method requires students to record main ideas of text in a column on the left of a page while adding details to the right column (Faber, Morris, & Lieberman, 2000; Pauk, 1997). Ballute and Lent adapted this format for their particular purposes: The first column was a place for students to write comments and questions, the second column was for notes and vocabulary as well as benefits and disadvantages identified from the source reading; a third column was added for students to write a summary.

The Cornell Notes strategy was intended for use with the 23 primary and secondary sources the teachers had compiled into a reading packet. Ballute and Lent were intentional in providing resources for the range of students in their classes, from struggling to striving to skilled readers. Ballute had a student at the kindergarten reading level[3] and several who could manage material beyond the tenth-grade level; she wanted to find a range to help all students feel successful and, at the same time, handle as much challenge as they could (consistent with Standard 10 on text complexity within the CCSS). The students had used Cornell Notes in previous units (on the topics of absolutism and genocide), but Ballute brought their attention to the added section for "benefits and disadvantages," which she described as the "whole purpose of the task" (Urbani, Pearson, Ballute, & Lent, 2012, p. 18).

Although the students were familiar with Cornell Notes, Ballute modeled the annotation process. In particular, she told students to "think about what you hear that's good or that could be a problem" (p. 18). After modeling the process, Ballute gave students several minutes to add to their own notes. For the next passage, she instructed the students to read silently, write notes, and then share their thoughts with a neighbor. Several students then shared their opinions on the costs and benefits with the whole class. Ballute's instruction here is an excellent example of scaffolding within a task—and within a single lesson. She moved from teacher modeling to small group work and finally to individual work, a classic example of the Gradual Release of Responsibility model at work, a framework for instruction in which teachers provide necessary supports at the beginning of lessons or units in order for students to take ownership of the learning to be independently successful (Pearson & Gallagher, 1983). She then reversed the process, encouraging students to share their thoughts again with a small group of their peers and then the whole class.

What made the literacy tasks successful was the inherent scaffolding that they provided in preparation for the culminating essay. These successful tasks required students to actively construct knowledge instead of reciting or regurgitating information. They required students to refer back to texts for evidence, whether those texts were within the reading or writing packets or from notes they took themselves. Fundamentally, successful literacy tasks were ones in which students were engaged in critical thinking and could be self-sufficient in active knowledge construction. But, as we continue to emphasize, a lot of scaffolding was required along the way.

On the whole, what is remarkable is that, despite the academic challenges experienced by the students—the majority of whom were English language learners—their engagement with and performance on the literacy tasks was quite impressive and, in modern curricular parlance, could be characterized as deeper learning (Donovan & Brandsford, 2005). In examining the individual tasks and final essays of the five focal students in the case study, there was evidence of content learning. The essays also demonstrated individual progress with writing tasks, particularly around the features of argumentative writing such as claim, evidence, and reasoning. During a calibration session in which the teachers collaborated to score the essays according to a rubric, Ballute and Lent noted that concepts Ballute had

---

[3] This struggling reader was receiving special education services. She had a paraprofessional who served as a reader and scribe in order for the student to participate in the content learning and discussion.

explicitly taught appeared in student essays. The key message here is that skills taught in class were transferring to the final essay. Even so, weaknesses in areas that had not been directly taught were still visible, even prevalent, in the essays (Urbani, Pearson, Ballute, & Lent, 2012). In effect, the literacy activities were doing their job: They were helping students be better readers and writers; however, as Lent and Ballute knew all too well, it was only a start.

Teacher Experiences

What were the teachers' experiences in developing and enacting instruction of both disciplinary content and ELA? In terms of instruction, Ballute commented that the LDC modules helped her more accurately identify her students' current levels of achievement. She explained that the structure and scaffolding inherent in the LDC modules helped her focus on more explicit teaching and modeling. In addition, the activities—specifically the Cornell Notes—offered students an active role in identifying and analyzing information instead of relying on received teacher explanations, or, as Ballute put it, "instead of me giving it to them" (Urbani, Pearson, Ballute, & Lent, 2012, p. 30).

By focusing on specific literacy tasks and scaffolding them toward the larger goal of the argumentative essay, teachers were able to identify gaps in their students' knowledge—as well as gaps in their own instruction. Ballute and Lent both commented about how scoring student essays from previous modules brought to their attention steps and processes that required explicit instruction in order to further student abilities. For example, previous essays had shown weaknesses with convention errors; therefore, Lent purposefully added activities for capitalization and verb tense to the writing packet. This is the essence of good formative assessment leading to focused teaching: Determine and respond to the needs of students through instruction.

Just as we consider the scaffolding of learning for students, we also need to consider the process of learning by teachers. Implementing the CCSS, specifically integrating literacy instruction into traditional content areas, will be a challenge for most teachers, as it requires a significant change in their practice. The LDC module format is an attempt to provide guidelines for doing so. The template appears to benefit teachers by making the larger picture more manageable; the steps toward the larger goal are made explicit, beginning with close reading to develop content knowledge and then exhibiting that knowledge through writing, including the planning, development, and editing phases. As we stated for students, using known content while they learned a new skill was a successful strategy Ballute and Lent employed. Yet, in our professional development, we often ask teachers to wrestle with both new content and instruction simultaneously! Ballute, obviously a skilled teacher, commented of the ELA emphasis: "I don't know how to teach this" (Urbani, Pearson, Ballute, & Lent, 2012, p. 32). The scaffolding to professional development provided by this approach allowed her to accomplish her teaching goals while she was still learning how to embed reading and writing within her learning goals for history.

We need to acknowledge that, as teachers begin implementing this sort of integrated reading and writing instruction within the CCSS, they will face a large cognitive load, and some aspects of their normal pedagogical repertoire may "fall off" until the instruction becomes more automatic, almost second nature. For example, Ballute struggled with using the various student materials for formative assessment during this module (although she was skilled with on-the-spot assessment of students, she had not anticipated the amount of formative data that resulted from the module materials); this may become easier once she is more comfortable with the integrated teaching and a level of automaticity appears. This learning process for teachers—and necessary scaffolds for them—would be beneficial to identify and anticipate for the profession as a whole.

Ballute and Lent not only modeled good teaching; they also modeled good learning. Despite being experienced teachers, they found the process of planning, writing, and enacting the module challenging. They relied upon each other and others within their team during the entire process, which took several months and many hours outside of their typical academic responsibilities. They were open to collaboration and feedback. They also made themselves vulnerable by asking for and receiving help—most often and most significantly from each other but also from others in the broader learning community. This willingness to learn despite difficulties will be necessary from all teachers. Establishing a community of teachers as learners, or critical friends (Dunne, Nave, & Lewis, 2000; Wineburg & Grossman, 2000), will be a vital piece of successful implementation of the CCSS.

IN SUMMARY

Within this chapter, we have attempted to highlight critical features for successful implementation of the integrated instruction of ELA within disciplinary contexts (literature, history, and science) as per the CCSS. Ballute and Lent served as excellent models for scaffolding learning, both in planning and in instruction. First, throughout the module they designed lessons that followed a particular structure: using known and/or accessible content to teach new skills. This guaranteed that students were familiar with at least one aspect of the task, enabling them to focus their cognitive effort on the new task or skill.

In addition to the planned examples of scaffolding, Ballute made many on-the-spot instructional changes. As she perused the classroom and offered feedback to individual students, she identified patterns within their work that she used to address the whole class in a minilesson. This combination of planned and spontaneous scaffolds based on on-the-spot formative assessment proved to be a powerful instructional package and should be used as a model for other teachers.

Second, Ballute and Lent offered students multiple opportunities to prepare them with the skills necessary for the final task. In the essay, students were expected to argue for one side or another of the question of whether or not the Industrial Revolution was worth its costs to society. Students were offered repeated practice with this task of weighing of evidence, beginning with the introductory information, continuing through the Cornell Notes, and into the writing of the argumentative essay. The content of the task changed (students were asked to argue the benefits and disadvantages of inventions and the value of home-cooked versus fast food), but the goal was the same: to prepare them for close reading of texts, an analysis of the evidence, and an opportunity to argue their claims. This higher-order thinking and these learning skills are specifically valued within the CCSS (NGA/CCSSO, 2010) and the LDC framework for implementing the CCSS and are also considered integral to the traditions of integrated language arts and PBL (Thomas, 2000). Specifically, this integrated unit required students to wrestle with content by employing a full range of reading and writing skills: Students critically read texts, evaluated and synthesized the information, and constructed argumentative essays that demonstrated their knowledge of the content.

Ballute and Lent's instruction was particularly impressive because of the challenges experienced by their students. Their teaching demonstrates how thoughtful, intentional teaching can lead to critical thinking and engaged learning by students for whom the prognosis for deep learning is not always optimistic. Even though this model of integrated instruction comes with challenges, the results clearly outweigh any costs! A serendipitous outcome of this work is that it provides at least one demonstration that curriculum conceived within the framework of the CCSS can lead to ambitious instruction and at least a "start" along the journey to deeper learning.

REFERENCES

Billman, A., & Pearson, P. (2013). Literacy in the disciplines. *Literacy Learning: The Middle Years, 21*(1), 25–33.

Crawford, M, Galiatsos, S., & Lewis, A.C. (2011). *The 1.0 guidebook to LDC: Linking secondary core content to the Common Core State Standards.* Literacy Design Collaborative. Retrieved from http://www.literacydesigncollaborative.org/wp-content/uploads/2012/02/LDCBook_web.pdf.

Donovan, M.S., & Brandsford, J.D. (Eds.). (2005). *How students learn: Science in the classroom.* Washington, DC: National Academies Press.

Dunne, F., Nave, B., & Lewis, A. (2000). Critical friends: Teachers helping to improve student learning. *Phi Delta Kappa International Research Bulletin, 28*, 9–12.

Faber, J.E., Morris, J.D., & Lieberman, M.G. (2000). The effect of note taking on ninth grade students' comprehension. *Reading Psychology, 21*(3), 257–70.

Fang, Z., & Schleppegrell, M.J. (2010). Disciplinary literacies across content areas: Supporting secondary reading through functional language analysis. *Journal of Adolescent and Adult Literacy, 53*(7), 587–597.

Fitzgerald, J., & Shanahan, T. (2000). Reading and writing relations and their development. *Educational Psychologist, 35*(1), 39–50.

Frankel, K., Jaeger, E., & Pearson, P.D. (2013). Integrating reading and writing to serve the interests of striving readers. In E. Ortlieb & E. Cheek (Eds.), *Utilizing Informative Assessments toward Effective Literacy Practices* (pp. 3–20). Bingley, UK: Emerald.

Graham, S., & Hebert, H. (2010). *Writing to read: Evidence for how writing can improve reading.* [A report from the Carnegie Corporation of New York]. Washington, DC: Alliance for Excellent Education.

Halvorsen, A., Duke, N.K., Brugar, K.A., Block, M.K., Strachan, S.L., Berka, M.B., & Brown, J.M. (2012). Narrowing the achievement gap in second-grade social studies and content area literacy: The promise of a project-based approach. *Theory and Research in Social Education, 40*, 198–229.

International Reading Association & the *Eunice Kennedy Shriver* National Institute of Child Health and Human Development (IRA/NICHD). (2012). *The reading-writing connection.* Retrieved from http://www.reading.org/Libraries/resources/reading-writingconnection_final.pdf

Mason, L.H., Harris, K.R., & Graham, S. (2011). Self-regulated strategy development for students with writing difficulties. *Theory into Practice, 50*(1), 20–27.

National Governors Association Center for Best Practices & Council of Chief State School Officers. (2010). *Common Core State Standards for English language arts and literacy in history/social studies, science, and technical subjects.* Washington, DC: Authors.

Nelson, N., & Calfee, R.C. (1998). The reading-writing connection viewed historically. In N. Nelson & R.C. Calfee (Eds.), *Ninety-seventh yearbook of the National Society for the Study of Education* (Pt. 2; pp. 1–52). Chicago, IL: National Society for the Study of Education.

New Visions for Public Schools. (2013). New visions for public schools. Retrieved from http://www.newvisions.org

No Child Left Behind (NCLB). (2002). Act of 2001, PL 107-110, 115, Stat. 1425, 20 U.S.C. §§ 6301 *et. seq.*

Pauk, W. (1997). *How to study in college.* Boston, MA: Houghton Mifflin.

Pearson, P.D. (2013). Research foundations for the Common Core State Standards in English language arts. In S. Newman & L. Gambrell (Eds.), *Reading instruction in the age of Common Core State Standards.* Newark, DE: International Reading Association.

Pearson, P.D., DeStefano, L., & Garcia, G.E. (1998). Ten dilemmas of performance assessment. In C. Harrison & T. Salinger (Eds.), *Assessing reading 1: Theory and practice* (pp. 21–49). London, UK: Routledge.

Pearson, P.D., & Gallagher, M.C. (1983). The instruction of reading comprehension. *Contemporary Educational Psychology, 8*, 317–344.

Ravi, A.K. (2010). Disciplinary literacy in the history classroom. In S.M. McConachie & A.R. Petrosky (Eds.), *Content matters: A disciplinary literacy approach to improving student learning* (pp. 33–61). San Francisco, CA: Jossey Bass.

Shanahan, T., & Shanahan, C. (2008). Teaching disciplinary literacy to adolescents: Rethinking content-area literacy. *Harvard Educational Review, 78*(1), 40–59.

Strobel, J., & van Barneveld, A. (2009). When is PBL more effective? A meta-synthesis of meta-analyses comparing PBL to conventional classrooms. *Interdisciplinary Journal of Problem-Based Learning, 3*(1), 44–58.

Thomas, J.W. (2000). *A review of research on project-based learning.* San Rafael, CA: The Autodesk Foundation.

Tierney, R.J., & Shanahan, T. (1996). Research on the reading-writing relationship: Interactions, transactions, and outcomes. In R. Barr, M.L. Kamil, P.B. Mosenthal, & P.D. Pearson (Eds.), *Handbook of reading research* (Vol. 2; pp. 246–280). Mahwah, NJ: Lawrence Erlbaum Associates.

Urbani, J.M., Pearson, P.D., Ballute, S., & Lent, T.A. (2012). Report for new visions for public schools: Smoke test of the Industrial Revolution module. [Technical report.] Stanford, CA: Stanford Center for Assessment, Learning, and Evaluation (SCALE), Stanford University.

Wineburg, S., & Grossman, P. (2000). Scenes from a courtship: Some theoretical and practical implications of interdisciplinary humanities curricula in the comprehensive high school. In S. Wineburg & P. Grossman (Eds.), *Interdisciplinary curriculum: Challenges to implementation* (pp. 57–73). New York, NY: Teachers College Press.

Wineburg, S., Martin, D., & Monte-Sano, C. (2011). *Reading like a historian: Teaching literacy in middle and high school history classrooms.* New York, NY: Teachers College Press.

10

Do No Harm

Applications and Misapplications of Research to Practice

Dorothy S. Strickland

Several years ago, a friend and fellow educator shared the following observation with me: "Dorothy," he said. "Do you realize that we are educating today's children for jobs that don't exist today, to solve problems that don't exist today, and to use technology that doesn't even exist today?" That very simple, yet very profound, question has remained with me and caused me to have great concern about the kind and quality of literacy instruction that I continue to observe and that many well-meaning and caring teachers describe to me as research- or evidence-based. Indeed, these teachers are acquainted with key meta-analyses of reading research, and their schools have often purchased materials said to align with that research. Moreover, my observations indicate that the emphasis on discrete skills and strategies is more likely to occur in situations where students are considered to be *at risk* and in need of the "fundamentals" before they can move on to higher-level thinking with texts. My concern is not with the research itself but with its misapplication, which often results in instruction that is focused on disconnected instructional elements of literacy education without attention to students' abilities to think with texts or to apply what they learn in new and ever-changing situations. Harm is done when the following things happen:

- Students, including our youngest learners, are not taught in ways that encourage independent application of skills and strategies.

- Students are not taught to think analytically and critically with oral and written texts, whether traditional print or technology-based.

- Students are not provided with opportunities to build the background knowledge required to understand and apply literacy skills to a variety of contents, both known and new.

- Because of their socioeconomic or linguistic backgrounds, students are denied opportunities to engage in reading and writing that emphasizes *thinking* as a way of *learning.*

Keep in mind that the choice is not about whether or not to teach skills and strategies but is how to teach and assess skills and strategies to ensure that they are truly learned and applied effectively by the learner.

All too often the findings of major research reports have been distilled and disseminated in ways that foster teaching and learning that is devoid of meaningful application to situations where students must retrieve and successfully apply the appropriate skills and/or strategies from a repertoire of those they have learned. Fortunately, the Common Core State Standards (CCSS; National Governors Association Center for Best Practices & Council of Chief State School Officers [NGA/CCSSO], 2010) and the assessments that link to them (The Partnership for the Assessment of Readiness for College and Careers [PARCC], http://parcconline.org, and The Smarter Balanced Assessment Consortium [SMARTER], www.k12.wa.us/smarter) offer hope, because both require students to learn and apply skills and strategies to meaningful content in purposeful ways. Greater emphasis is placed on writing, along with reading and the other language arts. Students are not only expected to analyze information from a variety of sources, but they must also construct written responses that are based on the evidence provided and communicate effectively through explanations and arguments. Thus the field is presented with an opportunity to revisit the application of literacy research in the classroom in ways that provide students with the help they need to become independent learners and thinkers in an ever-changing world.

This chapter provides a brief overview of some of the most influential studies and meta-analyses of research in the field of reading, together with relevant examples from research on writing. An examination of concerns related to the application and misapplication of that research in instruction and assessment will be offered along with suggestions for possible solutions. The solutions connect to the CCSS and the new assessment systems linked to them. Concrete suggestions for effective curriculum and instruction are offered along with examples of the types of professional development opportunities required to implement them.

LINKING LITERACY RESEARCH TO PRACTICE: SOME CONCERNS

The findings of literacy research have been applied and misapplied in a wide assortment of ways. Key issues and concerns include 1) the application of research findings as discrete, unrelated skills and strategies; 2) the application of foundational skills as discrete precursors to be mastered before "real" reading occurs; 3) Assessment Based on Students' Knowledge of skills and strategies absent of attention to their application in meaningful contexts; and 4) practice-based test preparation centered on the repeated practice of skills and strategies in isolation and apart from the context of content under study. Following is a brief overview of each issue.

Research Findings as Discrete, Unrelated Skills and Strategies

Among the vast number of research reports in literacy education, several in the area of reading stand out in terms of their influence on the field. They include *Preventing Reading Difficulties in Young Children* (Snow, Burns, & Griffin, 1998), which addresses the development of reading in young children; the *Report of the National Reading Panel* (National Institute of Child Health and Human Development, 2000), which focuses on the key instructional components/methods associated with teaching children to read; *Reading for Understanding: Toward an R&D Program in Reading Comprehension* (Snow, 2002), which focuses on the knowledge base for learning and teaching reading comprehension; and *Developing Early Literacy: Report of the National Early Literacy Panel* (National Institute for Literacy, 2008), which focuses on the literacy development of young children as predictors of later success.

Although all these reports were received with considerable interest, no doubt the report of the National Reading Panel (NRP) received the most widespread attention in the field. The report of the National Early Literacy Panel (NELP) also received considerable attention, particularly among early literacy educators. Both of these reports are of great interest to practitioners because of their potential for informing curriculum and instruction. Indeed, the NRP report has had a long and lasting influence on what the field believes is important in the teaching of reading. There is no question that both reports contain information with which teacher educators, teachers, and those responsible for the administration and supervision of reading programs should be thoroughly familiar.

Both reports list key findings based on meta-analyses of existing research. In the case of NRP, five components of reading instruction—phonemic awareness, phonics, fluency, vocabulary, and comprehension—were found to be essential to effective reading instruction. The work of NELP yielded a list of strong to moderate predictors, among young children, of later success in reading and writing: alphabet knowledge, concepts about print, phonological awareness, oral language, writing name/writing, and rapid automatic naming/lexical access (RAN).

Both reports have been accompanied by materials designed to help teachers translate the research into practice. The components listed in the NRP report, in particular, have received wide attention by publishers of materials for the teaching of reading and curriculum guides, yet many problems remain. The tendency to think of the findings as a *list* of factors to be addressed, one-at-a-time and in a particular order, may lead to teaching and learning that compartmentalize rather than connect the components under study, rendering them less useful to the learner. In their book *Reading Research in Action: A Teacher's Guide for Student Success*, McCardle, Chhabra, and Kapinus (2008) acknowledge concern for the application of research results in reading. "When we discuss reading development and instruction, it is important to acknowledge the complexity of reading, not only as a set of individual components but also as instruction that involves teaching all reading components collectively" (p. 6).

Overall, writing has received less research attention than reading. However, works such as *Writing: Teachers at Work* (Graves, 1983), a seminal work that helped to spawn a large body of high-quality research in this area and important meta-analyses of research on writing such as *A Meta-Analysis of Writing Instruction for Adolescent Students* (Graham & Perin, 2007), have been highly influential. The work of Graham and Perin yielded a list of recommendations for writing instruction found to improve the writing abilities of adolescent students. Examples of effective instructional strategies include the following:

- Teach strategies for planning, revising, and editing compositions.

- Teach strategies and procedures for text summarization.

- Have students work together to plan, draft, edit, and revise compositions.

- Give clear and explicit writing goals.

- Enable the use of word processing as a primary writing tool.

- Teach students to write increasingly complex sentences.

Once again, although the evidence for teaching these strategies is strong, care must be taken to go beyond instruction that teaches the strategies in isolation to include opportunities to apply them in purposeful ways; thus students become *strategic* users of the strategy.

Meta-analyses of high-quality research have been highly influential on literacy instruction—and rightly so. Nevertheless, educators need to keep in mind that, although meta-analyses render important information about literacy skills and strategies in terms of *what* is important, they were not designed to give clear direction on *how* those skills and strategies are learned nor *how* they are best taught. Although there have been many attempts to help teachers put the important knowledge gained from literacy research to work in classrooms, there is much more to be done.

Foundational Skills as Precursors to Be Mastered Before "Real" Reading Can Occur

Among early childhood professionals, the notion of *preliteracy* actually refers to the time before children are exposed to formal instruction in reading and writing. The foundational skills, many of which are included in the findings of the NELP report, are major areas of attention in prekindergarten and kindergarten. Alphabet knowledge in particular is likely to receive considerable attention. This may be because teachers consider the alphabet to be a concrete set of knowledge and, thus, easy to teach and assess.

Too often, the focus on low-level foundational skills has resulted in curriculum that is linear and skills-based. Thus many teachers believe that comprehension—making meaning with print, and the essence of reading—cannot begin until the so-called *preliteracy* skills are learned. In such classrooms, children are seldom taught in ways that help them discern how the various "components" of our written language system connect to one another. Thus they may be unable to unlock the system on their own in order to apply the very foundational skills they are learning.

Literacy learning does indeed start from birth and involves all the components listed in the NELP report. Literacy learning is greatly influenced by oral language and continues to develop in conjunction with oral language. The two are interrelated and interdependent. When very young children are read to and engage in discussions about the content, language, and pictures in a book, they are developing both oral language and literacy. Moreover, they are building background knowledge about the world—something that is critical to reading comprehension.

When research is misapplied, the literacy program may be consumed with drills in specific areas in the belief that such knowledge will assure *readiness* for *real* reading and writing. Unfortunately, a focus on learning to think with print may be neglected. Our goal as educators must be to enable children to apply what they know in new and novel situations. This is the essence of *learning how to learn*—perhaps the most important outcome of schooling.

Assessment based on Students' Knowledge of Skills and Strategies with Little or No Attention to Their Application in Meaningful Contexts

As with curriculum and instruction, the results of highly credible research reports often form the basis for both formative and summative assessments. The results are used to inform the progress of students and, in part, to evaluate the success of schools and teachers. There is no question that assessment is an essential part of the curriculum. Effective teachers monitor students' achievements and use that information to make decisions about differentiating instruction and adjusting the curriculum.

In today's schools, much attention is given to *data-driven instruction,* a term that is often used to describe decision making based on test results. Unfortunately, attention to what is actually being assessed and how it links to the standards being addressed may be neglected.

Again, the importance of how students apply their knowledge of the skills and strategies they are learning is critically important. This may change, however, as more and more educators move to address the CCSS and the assessments that link to them. Both require demonstrations of knowledge and the ability to *meaningfully* apply what is known. Perhaps most important, this kind of knowledge and application is required throughout schooling, as students confront increasingly complex texts and tasks. Obviously, it is important to lifelong learning as well.

In addition to collecting assessment data that yields useful information about what students know and are able to do, today's educators must employ methods to record and analyze what they have learned and communicate that information and the actions taken to address apparent needs with others, such as parents and administrators.

Test Preparation as Repeated Practice of Skills and Strategies in Isolation and Apart from Content under Study

The growing use of assessment data to inform student achievement and teacher performance has caused a great deal of anxiety. In order to address these concerns, many districts have turned to the use of test preparation materials designed to assess specific skills and strategies in the form of test items. Unfortunately, although it may be satisfying to put materials into the hands of teachers and students in order to provide practice for "the test," the result may be counterproductive. Students may spend hours engaged in mindless practice with little or no actual teaching to help them successfully address the kinds of items included in the test practice booklets. Struggling students, who need the most help, may merely practice sample test items over and over again only to confirm their inability to handle the material. Too often, teachers assume that the problem is the need for more practice rather than the need for supportive instruction in the underlying tasks involved. No doubt, this kind of preparation was inadequate in the past; however, it will be even less relevant in the future as the new assessments linked to the CCSS will involve thoughtful analyses of complex texts and well-constructed responses. The texts will simulate content generally under study at the grade levels involved.

LINKING LITERACY RESEARCH TO PRACTICE: POSSIBLE SOLUTIONS

Despite the concerns offered here regarding the misapplication of research findings, new developments in the field of literacy offer hope for effective application of research-based approaches to instruction in reading and writing. Namely, the CCSS and the assessments that are linked to them—PARCC and SMARTER—offer hope for an increased focus on meaningful application of what is learned. The CCSS contribute to students' long-term achievement in reading and writing because they focus on independent, high-level thinking and application. The key considerations that accompany the standards require a curriculum that attends to foundational and higher-level skills and strategies in ways that are both distinct and interrelated. English language arts/literacy is taught within the context of meaningful content. What is learned must be demonstrated through and applied in meaningful situations. Equally important, the demonstration of those skills and abilities is carried out in the assessments (PARCC and SMARTER) that are linked to the CCSS.

The guidelines for planning curricula listed next are based on the design considerations offered in the CCSS (2010). They help provide clarity about how the CCSS for English language arts/literacy should be implemented through curriculum and instruction:

1. **An integrated model of literacy.** The language arts—listening, speaking, reading, and writing—should be integrated with each other and across the curriculum. Students are asked to read and/or listen to texts read aloud and respond critically through discussion and in writing. Responses may take the form of written or oral explanations and arguments. Emphasis is placed on critical thinking, problem solving, and collaboration with peers.

2. **A cumulative model of expectations.** Instruction should address grade-specific standards in tandem with the broader goals of college and career readiness. Sometimes referred to as *spiraling,* similar standards are expressed with increasing complexity from grade to grade, providing an ongoing and cumulative progression of mastery that is refined and applied at increasingly higher levels for various purposes and in a variety of contexts.

3. **Shared responsibility for students' literacy development.** Teachers in self-contained classrooms are generally responsible for the integration of curriculum. However, grade-level planning among groups of teachers could facilitate the process. In departmental settings, content-area teachers and language arts/literacy teachers should plan and work together, thus providing a more coherent program to support students' abilities to apply what they learn about language and literacy to actual content under study.

4. **Research and media skills blended into instruction as a whole.** Critical thinking with texts in all forms of media and technology is emphasized. Texts may be oral or written and may make use of a variety of types of media and graphics. Forms may be combined for a specific goal or purpose. A balance of literary and informational texts appropriate to the grade level is desirable.

5. **Greater use of on-grade-level texts.** Emphasis is placed on helping students become proficient in reading complex texts independently and in a variety of content areas. Models of instruction should include complex texts for reading aloud to students; closely guided/interactive instruction to build background knowledge, vocabulary, and concepts; and modeling of how good readers approach difficult texts. Texts representing a range of complexity should also be available for independent reading and response.

Linking Standards, Curriculum, Instruction, and Assessment in a Common Core State Standards-Based Curriculum

Curriculum planning that connects the standards for English language arts/literacy and those for content-area subjects under study allows for preplanning in order to address specific English language arts/literacy standards and their application in meaningful contexts. Planning would include the selection of a theme or topic of inquiry based on the local standards for each grade level in the target content area (e.g., science, social studies). Key content goals relevant to what students are expected to learn or know at the end of this inquiry (e.g., State Standards for Social Studies: Grade 4: Learning about Our State) would be addressed along with selected CCSS for English language arts/literacy. Planning would also take account of the selection of texts to be used, including a range of text complexities and media along with other resources. Major activities such as field trips, class projects, and guest speakers would also be planned ahead with instructional activities that address the CCSS (Strickland, 2012).

Assessment would take the form of instructional activities designed to determine how well students are learning and how well they can apply that information. Assessment may be informal or structured as measured against a specific list of criteria. In either case, students should have had numerous opportunities to engage in English language arts processes through scaffolded instruction involving teacher modeling and teacher-student collaboration, with gradual guidance toward independence.

The inclusion of periodic, formative assessments as an integral part of curriculum planning and instruction is an important component of an effective CCSS-based curriculum. The difference between this and the type of test preparation exercises described earlier is that this involves purposeful formative assessment that is embedded within the instructional process. Opportunities for assessment are thoughtfully planned in advance, connected to the content under study, and designed and implemented by teachers as a means to assess and adjust learning and teaching accordingly. The use of constructs for assessment that are known to be a part of the assessment consortium of which students will ultimately be tested give students an opportunity to demonstrate what they have learned about the English language arts with content that is currently under study.

Both consortia are reported to include an assortment of item types, including selected response, constructed response, technology-based, and complex performance tasks (Center for K–12 Assessment & Performance Management at Educational Testing Service, 2012). Students will be asked to read material in a variety of genres, analyze what is read, and respond in ways that demonstrate critical thinking and analysis. Students who have opportunities to engage in these processes as a routine part of their instruction will be able to better apply these skills in the far less routine and more challenging context of standardized assessment. Obviously, it also gives teachers an opportunity to assess the learning and teaching involved. Sample items for both consortia can be found on their web sites (http://parcconline.org; www.k12.wa.us/smarter).

Teachers should make use of what is known about the assessments proposed by the assessment consortium adopted by their state. Thus students will benefit from meaningful assessment of their learning relative to the key standards addressed in the unit of inquiry, and at the same time, they will engage in meaningful preparation for the types of items they will encounter in the future. Progress may be tracked in terms of 1) the student in relationship to him or herself, 2) the student in relationship to the group, and 3) the areas in need of attention across the group as a whole. The first two serve to inform differentiated instruction decisions for individuals and small groups. The third helps to inform needed adjustments to the curriculum.

IMPLICATIONS FOR POLICY AND PRACTICE: FOCUS ON PROFESSIONAL DEVELOPMENT

The importance of career-long, high-quality professional development is widely accepted among educators. Today's education professionals realize that excellence as a teacher is not attained upon graduation from a teacher preparation program followed by occasional participation in their district's in-service activities or through graduate course work alone (Strickland, Kamil, Walberg, & Manning, 2004). Ongoing professional development is indeed simply a part of the job. Even though this has always been true, reform efforts such as the CCSS and the assessments linked to them offer opportunities to engage in high-quality professional development that links standards, instruction, and assessment in ways that have the potential to improve teaching and promote student achievement. The need for professional development that is thoughtfully planned, long-term, collaborative, linked to classroom instruction, and designed to foster a community of learners has become widely accepted. It should be emphasized that, although collaboration and the building of learning communities is valued, it is equally important to develop professional development plans that embrace whole school needs and priorities as well as the individual needs of teachers. The list of recommendations for tailoring professional development offered next is based on the knowledge that the professional development needs of individual school staff members will differ. The report of the National Invitational Conference, *Improving Reading Achievement through Professional Development* (Strickland & Kamil, 2004), outlines a set of recommendations for planning professional development within the context of a broader, ongoing effort. Recommendations for tailoring professional development to meet diverse needs include the following:

- Professional development should be grounded in children's learning processes.

- The school's vision for reform should be shared by all in the school community, including principals, teachers, and other staff members.

- Professional development should be designed to attend to individual teacher needs and encourage teachers to reflect on and evaluate their teaching practices.

- Professional development should encourage the formation of teacher study groups in which teachers can discuss their goals, needs, and perceptions of student needs.

PROFESSIONAL DEVELOPMENT DESIGNED TO ADDRESS SCHOOL AND INDIVIDUAL NEEDS: SOME EXAMPLES

Professional Development to Support a Cohesive Early Learning Continuum from Preschool Through Grade 3

Educators, policymakers, and the general public increasingly view support for early learning as a strategic investment in the future of children, particularly those considered at risk. Many states increased their funding for prekindergarten education in particular and maintained that funding even in the face of budget crises. The hope, of course, is to mitigate serious learning gaps that are evidenced by grade 3 and that often persist throughout the grades. Interest in prekindergarten has also focused attention on issues of quality and sustainability. Over time, it became increasingly clear that simply providing access to prekindergarten was not enough. In order to replicate the gains demonstrated by model programs such as those described and studied in the research, prekindergarten programs must be of high quality. Indeed, even early gains may dissipate unless preschool is followed by consecutive years of quality schooling in the early years (Haynes, 2008).

Professional development that involves an ongoing program of regularly scheduled meetings that allow time for teachers from all levels—across the prekindergarten to grade-3 spectrum—to meet and discuss standards, curriculum, instructional strategies, and assessment is essential. A program of specific topics would be generated at the beginning of the year with teachers taking responsibility for planning and conducting the meetings, recommending related reading, preparing presentations, and guiding the discussion. Guests would be invited to speak and share information on topics of interest. Ideas and strategies for instruction and assessment would be shared and tried in classrooms. The expectation would be that what is learned would be the subject of group discussions regarding what worked and what presented a challenge. Emphasis would be placed on how instruction geared to address similar standards might "look" at different grade levels.

Opportunities would also be provided for teachers to share and discuss how they address the need for increased coordination with education and family support agencies throughout state and community systems. Preserving an early learning environment that is cognitively stimulating as well as socially and emotionally supportive would be the goal.

Professional Development to Support Collaboration Between Teachers of English Language Arts/Literacy and Content-Area Teachers

One of the key considerations of the CCSS is the goal of increased collaboration among educators. Certainly, the collaboration among teachers during the early learning years, as discussed previously, has much to recommend it. The need for greater collaboration in departmental settings is also of great importance. Much has been written about the need for attention to reading in the content areas (Alvermann, Phelps, & Gillis, 2013). Yet all too often, literacy instruction remains the domain of the English language arts instructor, and there may be little or no intentional or systematic application of what is learned to actual content under study.

A model of long-term professional development to address this need involves regularly scheduled meetings among both English language arts and content-area instructors within a particular grade level or across a span of grade levels in a middle school or high school. Ideally, this would also include a literacy coach. Administrators would work with teachers to plan time for regularly scheduled collaborative meetings throughout the year. The English language arts teachers might take responsibility for introducing several relevant strategies to the group at the beginning of the year. Both English language arts and content-area teachers would decide which strategies would be most helpful at the beginning of the term. At times, different strategies might be emphasized in a particular content area based on an expression of specific need. The strategies would be introduced in the language arts classroom and reintroduced in the content-area subjects along with assignments that involve their application. Teachers would meet regularly to discuss how they are approaching the strategies, those things that seem to be working well, and those that present challenges. Obviously, the need for planning well in advance is very important. Based on observations and discussion, the plans would be revised as needed. It is important to note that, although some English language arts teachers may tend to focus on literary rather than informational texts, their instruction will benefit from these discussions. The demands placed on listeners, speakers, readers, and writers are important for both literary and informational texts. For example, levels of meaning (literary texts) or purpose (informational texts), text structures and complexity, language use, and knowledge demands are among the key reader/task considerations across the spectrum of literacy learning (NGA/CCSSO, 2010). Perhaps most important is the fact that students would begin to experience a cohesive instructional program.

Although this kind of collaboration has always been important, it has become increasingly relevant as the CCSS and the assessments that link to them require students to engage in critical thinking across multiple content-area texts (see http://parconline.org and www.k12.wa.us/smarter). Professional development that involves interdisciplinary collaboration provides more attention to these types of skills and strategies.

Professional Development as Responsible Test Preparation

An alternative to mindless test practice discussed earlier is the implementation of a collaborative effort among teachers to plan and implement a test preparation program as part of an ongoing professional development effort designed to stimulate school change and reform. The use of periodic assessments that reflect classroom instruction and simulate statewide testing programs can serve as a catalyst for establishing a school-wide vision and grade-level goals that address the need for ongoing teacher education and improved student outcomes. Focused assessment that makes use of the constructs included in statewide assessments would be strategically embedded within the instructional program and applied to content under study. Instruction that makes use of scaffolding techniques in which teachers model the assessment constructs, collaborate with students on their use, and gradually guide them toward independence would be included. The use of school-wide workshops, teacher study groups, and individual action research projects would all be a part of the mix. Leadership teams composed of principals, supervisors, literacy coaches, and grade-level representatives would work together to plan and implement the program.

The plan would go well beyond the collection of data to include the recording of information in ways that inform teacher practice. As mentioned previously, student progress would be tracked in terms of each student in relationship to him or herself, each student in relationship to the group, and with attention to the areas of need across the group as a whole. Study groups among specific groups of teachers would share results and instructional strategies to meet common needs across the group and to assist teachers with specific concerns.

Warning: Literacy Learning and Teaching That Is Devoid of Thinking May Do Harm and That Harm May Be Both Grave and Cumulative for Students Considered at Risk

Today's educators know a great deal about the key instructional components associated with successful achievement among readers and writers. Yet there is much to be done to ensure that what is known is applied to classroom instruction in ways that "do no harm." All students must be given opportunities to learn and to think in ways that will help them apply what they know in the short term and in an ever-changing future. It becomes obvious that what is true for students is also true for teachers. The need for high-quality professional development that is ongoing and linked to instruction has the potential to help teachers apply what they have learned from the research in order to improve the quality of instruction in the classroom and ultimately the quality of students' learning throughout life.

REFERENCES

Alvermann, D.E., Phelps, S.F., & Gillis, V.R. (2012). *Content area reading and literacy: Succeeding in today's diverse classrooms* (7th ed.). Boston, MA: Allyn & Bacon.

Center for K–12 Assessment & Performance Management at Educational Testing Service. (2012). *Coming together to raise student achievement: New assessments for the common core state standards.* Princeton, NJ: Educational Testing Service.

Graham, S., & Perin, D. (2007). A meta-analysis of writing instruction for adolescent students. *Journal of Educational Psychology, 99*(3), 445–476.

Graves, D. (1983). *Writing: Teachers and children at work.* Exeter, NH: Heinemann.

Haynes, M. (2008, June). Building state early learning systems: Lessons and results from NASBE's Early Childhood Education Network. *The State Education Standard,* 13–16.

McCardle, P., Chhabra, V., & Kapinus, B. (2008). *Reading research in action: A teacher's guide to student success.* Baltimore, MD: Paul H. Brookes Publishing Co.

National Governors Association Center for Best Practices & Council of Chief State School Officers (NGA/CCSSO). (2010). *Common Core State Standards for English language arts and literacy in history/social studies, science, and technical subjects.* Washington, DC: Authors.

National Institute of Child Health and Human Development (NICHD). (2000). *Teaching children to read: An evidence-based assessment of the scientific research literature on reading and its implications for reading instruction.* (NIH Publication No. 00-4754). Washington, DC: U.S. Government Printing Office.

National Institute for Literacy. (2008). *Developing early literacy: Report of the National Early Literacy panel.* Washington, DC: National Center for Family Literacy.

Office of Superintendent of Public Instruction. (n.d.). Smarter balanced assessment consortium. Retrieved from http://www.k12.wa.us/smarter

Partnership for the Assessment of Readiness for College and Careers. (2013). Retrieved from http://parcconline.org

Snow, C.E. (Ed.). (2002). *Reading for understanding: Toward an R&D program in reading comprehension.* Washington, DC: RAND.

Snow, C.E., Burns, M.S., & Griffin, P. (Eds.). (1998). *Preventing reading difficulties in young children.* Washington, DC: National Academies Press.

Strickland, D.S. (2012, February/March) Planning curriculum to meet the Common Core State Standards. *Reading Today, 29*(4), 25–26.

Strickland, D.S., & Kamil, M.L. (Eds.). (2004). *Improving reading achievement through professional development.* Norwood, MS: Christopher Gordon Publishers.

Strickland, D.S., Kamil, M.L., Walberg, H.J., & Manning, J.B. (2004). Improving reading achievement through professional development. [Reports and recommendations from the National Invitational Conference.] In D.S. Strickland & M.L. Kamil (Eds.), *Improving reading achievement through professional development* (pp. vii–xi). Norwood, MS: Christopher Gordon Publishers.

Preparing for Change

The Intersection of
Theory, Measurement, and
Technology with Instruction

11

Measurement

Facilitating the Goal of Literacy

Joanna S. Gorin, Tenaha O'Reilly,
John Sabatini, Yi Song, and Paul Deane

R ecent advances in cognitive science and psychometrics have expanded the possibilities for the next generation of literacy assessment as an integrated domain (Bennett, 2011a; Deane, Sabatini, & O'Reilly, 2011; Leighton & Gierl, 2011; Sabatini, Albro, & O'Reilly, 2012a). In this chapter, we discuss four key areas supporting innovations in assessment for literacy instruction that focuses on reading, writing, and their connection. In particular, we describe how advances in 1) cognitive models, 2) task design, 3) automated scoring, and 4) psychometric modeling can work in concert to create a more effective assessment system. First, we argue that there is added value in leveraging the relatively separate theoretical research bases on reading, writing, and the emerging literature on their connection to create a unified assessment model for literacy. A common model of literacy then enables test designers to develop contextually rich tasks with items that not only can be sequenced to help improve summative scores but also can provide formative information for students and teachers alike. Coupled with recent advances in automated scoring, current multidimensional and Bayesian modeling techniques appropriate for the complex models can be applied to improve scoring efficiency, accuracy, and instructional utility. This chapter reviews advances and challenges in each of these areas that must be considered in concert for proper design of literacy assessment tools.

Assessment, when properly designed, scored, and interpreted, has the potential to play a key role in the educational process (Bennett, 2011a; National Research Council, 2001). Summative assessment is widely used to make inferences about individual and group proficiency at various points in the educational process. Broad initiatives, including Race to the Top (U.S. Department of Education, 2009), have emphasized the need for valid and reliable measures that provide accountability for what students have learned and can do at the end of each K–12 academic year. Many of these efforts have focused on research and development efforts focusing on summative assessment—status or growth assessment that documents the outcomes of instructional experiences. To a lesser extent, efforts have been made to improve the quality and utility of formative assessment tools—measurement, instructional, and professional development tools that use test scores, data, and reports to help inform the instructional process, thereby enhancing student learning. Whether developing formative or summative educational assessments, the success of the assessment in facilitating learning is based entirely on the alignment between the goals of the assessment (i.e., the intended use of the test) and its design and scoring (Gorin, 2006, 2012; Mislevy, 1994). All assessment development activities should proceed from a comprehensive model of the targeted skills that incorporates instructional practices and developmental theories about proficiency and expertise in the domain.

As evidence mounts to support the need for learning and instruction—including the reading–writing connection—in an integrated framework of literacy, our assessments must be reconceptualized and redesigned such that they are sensitive to this new purpose. Graham and Hebert (2010, 2011) conducted meta-analyses of empirical studies showing that writing about materials one reads can improve students' reading comprehension, reading fluency, and word reading. There are also theoretical and practical reasons as well as some evidence (e.g., Graham, 2000; Krashen, 1989) to suggest that reading instruction can also enhance writing skills. On the theoretical side, there is some scholarly exploration of social and cognitive models of reading and writing development and inclusion (e.g., Bazerman, 2008; Bereiter & Scardamalia, 1987; Hayes, 1996; Langer, 2002; Olson, 1990; Olson & Hildyard, 1983; Shanahan, 2006). On the practical side, there are many instances of inclusion within classroom practices—teachers assign students to write about what they read; students write documents modeled after examples they have read; peers critique each other's writing, and so forth. Despite this growing evidence base and the common sense observation that reading and writing are inextricably intertwined in one's language and literacy skills, reading and writing are often taught as separate subjects, and this practice is likely reinforced by requiring students to take separate high-stakes assessments. If we want an assessment to support instruction and research on students' reading and writing that not only accounts for but also leverages their connections, we must build an assessment system with four key aspects:

- A theoretical model of reading, writing, *and* their connections

- Tasks that provide behavioral evidence for claims about both reading and writing

- Automated scoring approaches that allow for efficient, valid, and reliable reporting for formative and summative purposes

- Complex psychometric models that account for the multidimensionality and dependencies that exist among reading and writing

AN INTEGRATED LITERACY CONSTRUCT MODEL

The driving engine for any educational assessment is the definition of the construct in which the desired inferences and claims about student abilities are laid out (Mislevy, 1994). Recently, the use of cognitive models has been advocated as a powerful tool for construct definition in the assessment design process (Gorin, 2006, 2007; Gorin & Embretson, 2012; Leighton & Gierl, 2011). When moving toward assessment of the reading–writing connection, it is critical that we begin with an appropriate cognitive model of the intended construct—that is, a model of the reading–writing connection itself. Assessments designed to measure reading, writing, and their relationship must therefore begin with an integrated model of the two constructs that includes the nature of the relationships between them and their development.

Deane, Sabatini, and O'Reilly (2011) have drawn on the reading–writing connections literature to develop an English language arts (ELA) competency model, a form of cognitive model, for assessment design that puts a strong emphasis on literacy practices as integrated, socially situated activity systems that should be assessed within the complex array of expressive, interpretive, and deliberative/reflective skills, which are hypothesized to call on shared, integrated mental representations.[1] Consider any relatively complex but commonplace literacy activity a student might be called on to perform—prepare for a class discussion, study for an exam, write a research report or argument, give a presentation on a topic or issue—and one will quickly observe a complex mixture of reading, writing, and thinking skills that must be deployed in each. Texts must be sourced, read, and comprehended. A full-fledged composition must be iteratively drafted, and during the writing process, ancillary writing skills should be deployed for such purposes as notetaking, glossing texts, creating lists, writing summaries or outlines, communicating with peers or querying web sources, and so forth. Throughout this process, reflection, deliberation, and discussion are deployed to reason, articulate, and communicate about ideas initially read, written, or thought. Thus one of the advantages and contributions of a combined ELA model is that it reinforces the common, shared, cognitive resources deployed in literacy activity systems, whether the channel/modality itself is primarily reading, writing, or reasoning. Drawing on this framework, one can design assessments that systematically probe reading, writing, and thinking, while providing insights into how these processes are related.

Let us consider a particular ELA skill that is often assessed separately in either reading or writing—argumentation. In reading, argumentation is generally defined as the ability to identify people's positions, arguments, and evidence; in writing, it is the ability to express one's own position, argument, and evidence (Graff, 2003; Hillocks, 2010, 2011; Kuhn, 2005; Newell, Beach, Smith, & VanDerHeide, 2011). The argument component of Deane and colleagues' (2011) integrated ELA competency model targets key argumentation skills in four critical aspects (i.e., building an appeal, taking a position, providing reasons and evidence, and framing a case) at five hypothesized developmental levels across the preK through college-student continuum. It not only specifies how the reading, writing, and critical thinking skills related to argumentation shift qualitatively as students achieve higher levels of sophistication, but it also identifies strategies that teachers could use to help scaffold students toward the next level—across both reading *and* writing. As skillful writing presupposes a baseline level of reading skill, the integrated argumentation model explicitly includes critical reading skills. In effect, the critical reading tasks specified in the design target interpretation skills that are prerequisites to successful completion of expressive writing tasks. More generally, critical evaluation of content is fundamental to argumentation and is necessarily involved in planning, writing, and revising processes. Effective writing requires that the writer think effectively and critically about the goal, audience, position, and argument. In essence, the integrated argumentation model captures the insight that successful writing is closely integrated with general literacy, including reading, writing, and thinking skills.

SCENARIO-BASED TASK DESIGN

Once a researcher or test developer specifies a construct model, the next crucial issue is task design. What item types or task types should appear in an assessment of ELA literacy?

---

[1]The framework is consistent with a broader initiative that connects assessment explicitly with best practices in instruction and what is known about student learning and development from the cognitive and learning sciences literatures. This initiative is termed *cognitively-based assessment of, for, and as learning*, or CBAL for short (Bennett, 2011; Bennett & Gitomer, 2009).

When considering item types for any assessment, one must take a step back and consider a more fundamental question: What are the behavior types that constitute the strongest evidence of the literacy skills to be measured? One must then create opportunities for such evidence to be observed via test questions and tasks. Of utmost concern are the two most commonly cited threats to validity: construct underrepresentation and construct irrelevant variance. If separate measures of reading and writing are used as a basis for decisions about an integrated literacy curriculum or to make summative conclusions, the most obvious threat to validity is underrepresentation of the more complex integrated literacy construct. By measuring reading and writing in an integrated assessment, these and other threats to validity can potentially be mitigated.

A commonly cited threat to validity for reading and writing assessments is a student's level of background knowledge on the topic of the texts and writing prompts. In short, students who know more about the topic of the passages and prompts understand and can write more than students who know very little about the topic (Benton, Corkill, Sharp, Downey, & Khramtsova, 1995; O'Reilly & McNamara, 2007; Shapiro, 2004); therefore, it is difficult to determine whether test scores reflect true reading and writing ability or the level of the students' background knowledge. A second threat to validity concerns the potential for narrowing the construct of reading and writing due to lack of a specific purpose for the assessment task. Reading and writing are purpose-driven activities that should represent the range of contexts in which students read and write (McCrudden, Magliano, & Schraw, 2011). However, in a typical reading assessment, the only purpose for reading is to answer multiple-choice questions correctly (Rupp, Ferne, & Choi, 2006). Clearly, people read and write for a wide variety of purposes. Sampling from a range of these in a joint reading and writing assessment not only improves construct coverage and the potential authenticity of the assessment but also helps clarify task demands.

A common solution to both challenges is to measure reading and writing skills jointly under the context of a scenario (Bennett, 2011b; Bennett & Gitomer, 2009). A scenario-based task includes an authentic purpose for reading about a collection of sources on a particular topic that culminates in an integrative writing task. For instance, students could be given multiple texts about e-waste, its sources, and opposing arguments about its consequences. The texts and readings become the common "background knowledge" that allows students to write on a more level playing field. The student is then asked questions about the content of the texts. Finally, the student is given a writing task—for example, to write to an electronics company about the potential dangers of e-waste and steps the company can take to reduce the amount of e-waste. The use of a scenario with carefully sequenced, related tasks may resolve several of our validity threats within a common ELA assessment framework. First, by introducing a critical reading task, we not only measure students' abilities to understand text but also give students content to consider (e.g., to summarize, to analyze, to synthesize, to evaluate) in preparation for writing, thus modeling the kinds of activity systems and processes we aim for students to learn. Further, this design not only builds up students' knowledge of the topic through reading, but it also isolates what parts they did or did not understand, which is useful for evaluating the quality of their essay. Research on the use of these integrated tasks on high-stakes assessment—for example, with the new Test of English as a Foreign Language (TOEFL)—confirms some of our hypotheses about the benefits of scenario-based task design. However, it also suggests that care must be taken when crafting the content and presentation of the scenario itself (e.g., controlling density of information), particularly when using the tasks for formative purposes (Cumming, Grant, Mulcahy-Ernt, & Powers, 2005).

HUMAN AND AUTOMATED SCORING

One of the most significant challenges to any assessment that includes a writing component is that of scoring. Issues of reliability, validity, cost, and time are among the potential limitations of human scoring. No matter how well defined the construct, or well constructed the task, if the scoring cannot be reliable, valid, cost-feasible, and sufficiently rapid, the instructional utility of the assessment scores is limited. Despite these challenges, most (if not all) state writing and reading assessments now include various types of constructed response items. This condition has been facilitated by technological advances that support automated scoring of constructed responses, including automated essay scoring systems such as *e-rater* and *c-rater* (Shermis & Burstein, 2013). These engines have been used to generate scores for summative assessments as well as feedback for students on their writing quality in formative assessment systems, such as the *Criterion* online writing evaluation system. A growing literature documents the reliability and validity of human and automated scoring of performance items (e.g., short and extended constructed response item) on either reading or writing assessment (see Shermis & Burstein, 2013). We briefly consider the issues of human and automated scoring of constructed responses to integrated literacy assessment.

Human Ratings

The relationship between reading skill and the ability to produce high-quality writing is complicated by several issues related to scoring—namely, the context sensitivity, cognitive encapsulation, and variety of factors that underlie judgments of writing quality (see Bejar, 2012, for more detailed discussion on rater cognition).

Context Sensitivity   As a construct, writing quality is mediated by the intended audience and, hence, by factors relevant to reading. A poem is not read the same way as an essay; nonfiction is not read the same way as fiction; technical manuals are not read the same way as newspapers; thus the judgments people make about the quality of a piece of writing when scoring it will be related to assumptions about its purpose, audience, and genre. These considerations provide reasons to expect linkage between the factors that contribute to text readability and those that indicate writing skill, but not in any simple way. For instance, use of relatively simple vocabulary may indicate quality writing (if it reduces the cognitive load on readers) or not (if the resulting language is inappropriately imprecise or informal given the task and audience). Conversely, use of relatively difficult vocabulary may indicate low writing quality (if it imposes unnecessary burdens on the reader), or it may reflect high writing quality (if the author's selection of difficult words is more precise and carries more appropriate connotations). This functional connection between reading and writing guarantees that there will be a large common substrate of abilities shared between reading and writing (Shanahan, 2006) but implies that they will not be deployed in the same way; in fact, features that predict that a text will present greater reading difficulty often also predict higher levels of writing skill (McNamara, Crossley, & McCarthy, 2010).

Cognitive Encapsulation   As a performance, skilled writing must take many different factors into account. But the more skilled a student becomes, the more likely that important subskills of reading and writing will be fluent—for example, both automatized and accurate (Kuhn, Schwanenflugel, Meisinger, Levy, & Rasinski, 2010; Logan, 1997; McCutchen, 2006). A rater is being asked to evaluate how well a reader or writer has controlled a variety of elements that are not normally available for conscious inspection. Such analysis exposes the rater to all the dangers of introspective analysis, which leads to low levels of interrater reliability and difficulty separating out traits on writing rubrics (Elliott, 2005).

Variety of Underlying Factors Judgments of writing quality are sensitive to a variety of properties of the text, ranging from easily measurable features such as spelling errors to much more global, inferred features such as rhetorical effectiveness and validity of arguments. In an early study of rater behavior, French (1962) identified six underlying factors; descendants of this kind of analysis inform scoring methods such as the 6-trait model (Spandel, 2004) to this day, identifying such writing traits as mechanics/conventions, word choice, organization, and content. The challenge for human raters, however, is that many of these factors appear to be directly linked to shared skills that may also be relevant to reading. For instance, mechanics-related writing abilities are closely linked to mastery of the ortho- graphic patterns needed for effective reading; word-choice-related writing abilities are closely related to vocabulary skills needed for effective reading comprehension, and so forth.

Automated Scoring Methods

Many but not all dimensions of writing quality are amenable to automated measurement through the use of automated scoring technologies, which in addition to the speed and cost-efficiency they offer, may resolve some of the previously listed challenges to human ratings. The kinds of analysis possible can be summarized by considering the kinds of features employed in a typical automated scoring engine. One, the *e-rater* scoring engine, is well documented (Attali & Burstein, 2006; Burstein, Chodorow, & Leacock, 2003) and can be used to stand in for the larger class. Quinlan, Higgins, and Wolf (2009) mapped individual *e-rater* features onto the dimensions of a 6-trait writing quality construct. Attali and Powers (2009) demonstrate a factor structure for these features in which many of the features map onto factors that roughly correspond to vocabulary (word choice), accuracy (mechanics/conventions), and fluency (organization and development). A regression model is built using these features to predict human-assigned scores. In general, such models provide strong predictions of human ratings (Burstein & Chodorow, 2010; Chodorow & Burstein, 2004; Powers, Burstein, Chodorow, Fowles, & Kukich, 2001).

Automated scoring offers a cost-effective, time-saving solution to many of the chal- lenges associated with scoring extended reading and writing constructed responses. Though the focus on much of their use has been on summative assessment, where the demands on precision and accuracy are the priority, they offer perhaps even more utility in lower-stakes contexts such as classroom and formative assessments, where the emphasis is on instructionally relevant feedback on process rather than status. Through the use of automated tutoring systems, computer-based classroom reading and writing exercises, and possibly simulation-based assessment, automated scoring engines can be used to provide meaningful feedback to students about their writing and to teachers about their instruc- tional effectiveness (Graesser, Hu, & Person, 2001; McNamara, Levinstein, & Boonthum, 2004). If assessment is to become an integral part of literacy instruction, further research on the use of these automated systems to provide timely and instructionally relevant feed- back for teachers from either classroom or large-scale assessments—not to mention reli- able and valid summative scores—is still needed. Specifically, research on differences in automated scoring approaches, their relationship to human scores, and the extent to which both approaches, human and automated, are affected by unintended sources of variance is warranted (Bejar, 2012).

ADVANCED PSYCHOMETRIC MODELS

Ultimately, in order to make inferences about our claims using observed evidence, the data must be translated into an interpretable form. As the constructs we measure and claims we want to make from our assessments increase in complexity, as is the case with an integrated literacy assessment, our analytic tools must also adapt (Gorin & Svetina, 2011; Gorin & Svetina, 2012; Rupp, 2012; Wilson & Moore, 2012). Psychometric approaches, ranging from classical true score theory to item response theory, offer a variety of methods for converting individuals' behaviors into estimated ability levels. In the traditional assessment paradigm, the focus is on transforming scored item responses into latent trait estimates (i.e., an estimate of the student's underlying ability on whatever skill you want to measure, taking into consideration the measurement error inherent in the test), traditionally on unidimensional latent trait scales. Unidimensional models that assume a single underlying latent trait affecting task performance are overly simple for highly contextualized tasks appropriate to measure literacy. With the increased computing power of the last several decades, we now have multidimensional alternatives that are likely exactly what is needed for assessing the reading–writing connection as we have described thus far. We briefly review multidimensional modeling approaches that offer the most promise for integrated literacy assessment: multidimensional item response theory and Bayesian inference networks (BINs).

Multidimensional item response theory (MIRT) allows for the contribution of two or more constructs to the solution for an item or set of items. MIRT decomposes the unidimensional person parameter into an item-dependent linear combination of latent traits (Junker & Sijtsma, 2001). One form of the MIRT model, compensatory MIRT, allows for an examinee to correctly respond to an item when some but not all the skills needed to answer the question are mastered. That is, a high level of ability on one skill may compensate for a lower level of ability on a different skill, both levels of which are associated with that same item. However, according to Junker and Sijtsma (2001), although these models have made advances in blending MIRT and cognitive assessment, they are not sensitive to all aspects of cognition. Thus noncompensatory MIRT approaches might be more appropriate. In these models, performance on tasks involves the conjunction of successful performances on multiple subtasks, where each subtask may be thought of as a unidimensional IRT model.

Though MIRT models allow simultaneous consideration of multiple abilities, these models still typically only model a single piece of observed data—an item-level score. If we follow the advice given up to this point in the chapter, the complex tasks for integrated literacy assessment would yield multiple scored behaviors, each of which might be related to one or more of the skills of interest. As the number of observable variables (scores) for an item increases, the use of the traditional IRT and MIRT models that typically handle one variable per item is insufficient. One approach that has had some success is the use of BINs (Jensen, 1996, 2001; Pearl, 1988). BINs are graphical models in which we transmit complex observational evidence within a network of interrelated variables—the skills of interest (unobservable variables) and the scores from the complex task (the observed variables). Conditional relationships between the observable variables, the unobservable variables, and characteristics of the task are graphically diagramed as a network. Then, using Bayes's theorem of conditional probabilities, the strength of the relationships and the fit of the overall model to the data can be tested. The key, of course, is to construct a BIN based on a nonarbitrary model of cognition and the tasks; hence the need for a strong theoretical model of the constructs and appropriately designed tasks that are aligned with one another.

CONCLUSION

As the role of assessment in education increases, it has the potential to guide instruction—for good or ill. For that reason, it is critical that our assessments be designed to measure constructs as we believe that they exist, develop, and are learned. The reading–writing connection requires a complex assessment with the explicit purpose of measuring both constructs within a single system. The development and relationship between students' reading and writing abilities should be measured by design. It is only in doing so that we can provide educators and researchers with the assessment tools necessary for them to improve reading and writing instruction and learning, an outcome that benefits us all.

Construct models, task design, scoring, and psychometric modeling are linked; advances in any one of these areas is only effective if advances are made in all areas. That is all the more reason for education researchers from a broad array of disciplines, ranging from developmental psychology to psychometrics to natural language processing, to work collaboratively and to consider both innovations and limitations in each discipline (for examples, see Sabatini, Albro, & O'Reilly, 2012a; 2012b). Many of the fundamental tools are in place, thanks in large part to the fast pace of technological advances in the cognitive and learning sciences. If properly coordinated, the result is a powerful assessment system that serves equally well as an instructional design mechanism for reading and writing classrooms.

REFERENCES

Attali, Y., & Burstein, J. (2006). Automated essay scoring with e-rater v. 2. *Journal of Technology, Learning, and Assessment, 4*(3). Retrieved from http://ejournals.bc.edu/ojs/index.php/jtla/article/view/1650/1492

Attali, Y., & Powers, D. (2009). *A developmental writing scale.* (ETS research report No. RR-08-19). Princeton, NJ: Educational Testing Service. Retrieved from http://www.ets.org/Media/Research/pdf/RR-08-19.pdf

Bazerman, C. (Ed.). (2008). *Handbook of writing research.* Hillsdale, NJ: Lawrence Erlbaum.

Bejar, I.I. (2012). Rater cognition: Implications for validity. *Educational Measurement: Issues and Practice, 31*(3), 2–9.

Bennett, R.E. (2011a, June). *Theory of action and educational assessment.* Paper presented at the National Conference on Student Assessment, Orlando, FL.

Bennett, R.E. (2011b). *CBAL: Results from piloting innovative K–12 assessments.* (ETS research report No. RR-11-23). Princeton, NJ: Educational Testing Service.

Bennett, R.E., & Gitomer, D.H. (2009). Transforming K–12 assessment: Integrating accountability testing, formative assessment and professional support. In C. Wyatt-Smith & J.J. Cumming (Eds.), *Educational assessment in the 21st century.* New York, NY: Springer.

Benton, S.L., Corkill, A.J., Sharp, J.M., Downey, R.G., & Khramtsova, I. (1995). Knowledge, interest, and narrative writing. *Journal of Educational Psychology, 87,* 66–79.

Bereiter, C., & Scardamalia, M. (1987). *The Psychology of Written Composition.* Hillsdale, NJ: Lawrence Erlbaum.

Burstein, J., & Chodorow, M. (2010). Progress and new directions in technology for automated essay evaluation. In R. Kaplan (Ed.), *The Oxford handbook of applied linguistics* (2nd ed.; pp. 487–497). Oxford, UK: Oxford University Press

Burstein, J., Chodorow, M., & Leacock, C. (2003). Criterion: Online essay evaluation: An application for automated evaluation of student essays. In *Proceedings of the fifteenth annual conference on innovative applications of artificial intelligence* (pp. 3–10). Acapulco, MX: Association for the Advancement of Artificial Intelligence.

Chodorow, M., & Burstein, J. (2004). *Beyond essay length: Evaluating e-rater's performance on TOEFL essays* (TOEFL research report No. RR-73; ETS research report No. RR-04-04). Princeton, NJ: Educational Testing Service.

Cumming, A., Grant, L., Mulcahy-Ernt, P., & Powers, D.E. (2005). *A teacher-verification study of speaking and writing prototype tasks for a new TOEFL.* (Monograph No. MS-26; ETS Monograph Series). Princeton, NJ: Educational Testing Service.

Deane, P., Sabatini, J., & O'Reilly, T. (2011). *English language arts literacy framework.* Princeton, NJ: Educational Testing Service. Retrieved from http://www.ets.org/s/research/pdf/ela_literacy _framework.pdf

Elliott, N. (2005). *On a scale: A social history of writing assessment in America.* New York, NY: Peter Lang.

French, J.W. (1961). *Schools of thought in judging excellence of English themes.* Reprint from Proceedings of Invitational Conference on Testing Procedures. Princeton, NJ: Educational Testing Service.

Gorin, J.S. (2006). Item design with cognition in mind. *Educational Measurement: Issues and Practice, 25*(4), 21–35.

Gorin, J.S. (2007). Test construction and diagnostic testing. In J.P. Leighton & M.J. Gierl (Eds.), *Cognitive diagnostic assessment in education: Theory and practice.* Cambridge, UK: Cambridge University Press.

Gorin, J.S. (2012). *Assessment as evidential reasoning.* [Paper commissioned by the Gordon Commission on the Future of Educational Assessment.] Retrieved from http://gordoncommission.org/ rsc/pdfs/gorin_assessment_evidential_reasoning.pdf

Gorin, J.S., & Embretson, S.E. (2012). Using cognitive psychology to generate items and predict item characteristics. In M.J. Gierl & T.M. Haladyna (Eds.), *Automatic item generation theory and practice* (pp. 136–156). New York, NY: Taylor & Francis.

Gorin, J.S., & Svetina, D. (2011). Test design with higher order cognition in mind. In G. Schraw & D.H. Robinson (Eds.), *Assessment of higher order thinking skills.* Charlotte, NC: Information Age Publishing.

Gorin, J.S., & Svetina, D. (2012). Cognitive psychometric models as a tool for reading assessment engineering. In J. Sabatini, E. Albro, & T. O'Reilly (Eds.), *Reaching an understanding: Innovations in how we view reading assessment* (pp. 169–184). Lanham, MD: Rowman & Littlefield Education.

Graesser, A.C., Hu, X., & Person, N.K. (2001). Teaching with the help of talking heads. In *Proceedings of the IEEE international conference on advanced learning technologies* (pp. 460–461). Los Alamitos, CA: IEEE Computer Society.

Graff, G. (2003). *Clueless in academe: How schooling obscures the life of the mind.* New Haven, CT: Yale University Press.

Graham, S. (2000). Should the natural learning approach replace traditional spelling instruction. *Journal of Educational Psychology, 92,* 235 247.

Graham, S., & Hebert, M.A. (2010). Writing to read: Evidence for how writing can improve reading. In *A Carnegie Corporation Time to Act Report.* Washington, DC: Alliance for Excellent Education.

Graham, S., & Hebert, M.A. (2011). Writing to read: A meta-analysis of the impact of writing and writing instruction on reading. *Harvard Educational Review, 81*(4), 710–744.

Hayes, J.R. (1996). A new framework for understanding cognition and affect in writing. In C.M. Levy & S. Ransdell (Eds.), *The science of writing: Theories, methods, individual differences, and applications* (pp. 1–27). Mahwah, NJ: Lawrence Erlbaum.

Hillocks, G., Jr. (2010). Teaching argument for critical thinking and writing: An introduction. *English Journal, 99*(6), 24–32.

Hillocks, G., Jr. (2011). *Teaching argument writing: Supporting claims with relevant evidence and clear reasoning.* Portsmouth, NH: Heinemann.

Jensen, F.V. (1996). *An introduction to Bayesian networks.* London, UK: University College London Press.

Jensen, F.V. (2001). *Bayesian networks and decision graphs.* New York: Springer-Verlag.

Junker, B.W., & Sijtsma, K. (2001). Cognitive assessment models with few assumptions, and connections with nonparametric item response theory. *Applied Psychological Measurement, 25,* 258–272.

Krashen, S.D. (1989). We acquire vocabulary and spelling by reading: Additional evidence for the input hypothesis. *The Modern Language Journal, 73*(4), 440–464.

Kuhn, D. (2005). *Education for thinking.* Cambridge, MA: Harvard University Press.

Kuhn, M.R., Schwanenflugel, P.J., Meisinger, E.B., Levy, B.A., and Rasinski, T.V. (2010). Aligning theory and assessment of reading fluency: Automaticity, prosody, and definitions of fluency. *Reading Research Quarterly, 45*(2), 230–251.

Langer, J. (2002). *Effective literacy instruction: Building successful reading and writing programs.* Urbana, IL: National Council of Teachers of English.

Leighton, J.P., & Gierl, M.J. (2011). *The learning sciences in educational assessment: The role of cognitive models*. Cambridge, UK: Cambridge University Press.

Logan, G.D. (1997). Automaticity and reading: Perspectives from the instance theory of automatization. *Reading and Writing Quarterly, 13*(2), 123–146. doi:10.1080/1057356970130203

McCrudden, M.T., Magliano, J., & Schraw, G. (Eds.). (2011). *Text relevance and learning from text*. Greenwich, CT: Information Age Publishing.

McCutchen, D. (2006). Cognitive factors in the development of children's writing. In C.A. MacArthur, S. Graham, & J. Fitzgerald (Eds.), *Handbook of writing research* (pp. 115–130). New York, NY: Guilford Press.

McNamara, D.S., Crossley, S.A., and McCarthy, P.M. (2010). Linguistics features of writing quality. *Written Communication, 27*(1), 57–86.

McNamara, D.S., Levinstein, I.B., & Boonthum, C.(2004). iSTART: Interactive strategy trainer for active reading and thinking. *Behavior Research Methods, Instruments, and Computers, 36*, 222–233.

Mislevy, R.J. (1994). Evidence and inference in educational assessment. *Psychometrika, 59*, 439–483.

Newell, G.E., Beach, R., Smith, J., & VanDerHeide, J. (2011). Teaching and learning argumentative reading and writing: A review of research. *Reading Research Quarterly, 46*(3), 273–304.

Olson, D.R. (1990). Literacy and objectivity: The rise of modern science. In D.R. Olson & N. Torrance (Eds.), *Literacy and orality* (pp. 149–164). Cambridge, UK: Cambridge University Press.

Olson, D.R., & Hildyard, A. (1983). Writing and literal meaning. In M. Martley (Ed.), *Psychology of written language: A developmental and educational perspective* (pp. 920–928). New York, NY: Wiley.

O'Reilly, T., & McNamara, D.S. (2007). Reversing the reverse cohesion effect: Good texts can be better for strategic, high-knowledge readers. *Discourse Processes, 43*(2), 121–152.

National Research Council. (2001). *Knowing what students know: The science and design of educational assessment*. Washington, DC: National Academies Press.

Pearl, J. (1988). Probabilistic reasoning in intelligent systems: Networks of plausible inference. San Mateo, CA: Kaufmann.

Powers, D.E., Burstein, J., Chodorow, M., Fowles, M.E., & Kukich, K. (2001). *Stumping e-rater: Challenging the validity of automated essay scoring* (GRE Board professional report No. 98-08bP; ETS Research Report No. RR-01-03). Princeton, NJ: Educational Testing Service. Retrieved from http://www.ets.org/Media/Research/pdf/RR-01-03-Powers.pdf

Quinlan, T., Higgins, D., & Wolf, S. (2009). *Evaluating the construct coverage of the e-rater scoring engine* (ETS research report No. RR-09-01). Princeton, NJ: Educational Testing Service. Retrieved from http://www.ets.org/Media/Research/pdf/RR-09-01.pdf

Rupp, A.A. (2012). Psychological vs. psychometric dimensionality in reading assessment. In J. Sabatini, E.R. Albro, & T. O'Reilly (Eds.), *Measuring up: Advances in how we assess reading ability* (pp. 135–152). New York, NY: Rowman & Littlefield Education.

Rupp, A., Ferne, T., & Choi, H. (2006). How assessing reading comprehension with multiple-choice questions shapes the construct: A cognitive processing perspective. *Language Testing, 23*, 441–474.

Sabatini, J., Albro, E., & O'Reilly, T. (Eds.). (2012a). *Measuring up: Advances in how we assess reading ability*. Lanham, MD: Rowman & Littlefield Education.

Sabatini, J., Albro, E., & O'Reilly, T. (Eds.). (2012b). *Reaching an understanding: Innovations in how we view reading assessment*. Lanham, MD: Rowman & Littlefield Education.

Shanahan, T. (2006). Relations among oral language, reading, and writing development. In D.A. MacArthur, S. Graham, & J. Fitzgerald (Eds.), *Handbook of writing research* (pp. 171–186). New York, NY: Guilford Press.

Shapiro, A.M. (2004). How including prior knowledge as a subject variable may change outcomes of learning research. *American Educational Research Journal, 41*, 159–189.

Shermis, M.D., & Burstein, J. (2013). *Handbook of automated essay evaluation: Current applications and new directions*. New York, NY: Routledge Academic.

Spandel, V. (2004). *Creating writers through 6-trait writing assessment and instruction*. Boston, MA: Pearson.

U.S. Department of Education. (2009). *Race to the Top Program executive summary*. Washington, DC: Author. Retrieved from http://www2.ed.gov/programs/racetothetop/executive-summary.pdf

Wilson, M., & Moore, S. (2012). An explanative modeling approach to measurement of reading comprehension. In J. Sabatini, E. Albro, & T. O'Reilly (Eds.), *Reaching an understanding: Innovations in how we view reading assessment* (pp. 147–168). Lanham, MD: Rowman & Littlefield Education.

12

The Many Possible Roles for Technology in the Reading–Writing Connection

Kim Atwill and Jay Blanchard

Much has been written about reading instruction, and it continues to be a focus of national and international attention (National Institute of Child Health and Human Development [NICHD], 2000; United Nations Educational, Scientific and Cultural Organization, 2010; U.S. Department of Education, 2012). However, this is not the case for writing instruction, as there are elements of writing instruction without a coherent knowledge base (Connor, Goldman, & Fishman, in press; Graham et al., 2012). One of these elements is the developmental relationship or interaction between reading and writing instruction and, thus, "when and how best to integrate these two critical areas of instruction" (International Reading Association & the *Eunice Kennedy Shriver* National Institute of Child Health and Human Development [IRA/NICHD], 2012, p. 1; see also Shanahan & Lomax, 1986). This is the case in the United States because reading and writing instruction have generally been treated as separate, unrelated curriculum focuses (Weiser & Mathes, 2011). This has also been true worldwide (i.e., Andrews, 2008).

Despite curricular separation and the lack of a knowledge base, some teachers have been connecting reading and writing instruction in their classrooms, and research has supported the efficacy of their efforts (Applebee & Langer, 2011; Biancarosa & Snow, 2006; Fitzgerald & Shanahan, 2000; Graham & Hebert, 2010). In addition, many school districts, governmental agencies, professional organizations, and foundations have provided performance standards that explicitly require students to demonstrate reading and writing connection skills and therefore support teachers as they connect reading and writing instruction in their classrooms (i.e., National Center for Education and the Economy, 1999; see Achieve, Inc., 2006, for historical perspective). Many of these performance standards have required students to use technology (i.e., International Society for Technology in Education, 2007; National Council of Teachers of English, 2007; North Central Regional Educational Laboratory, 2003). As a group, these technology-based standards have been commonly called 21st-century skills (for discussion, see Kay & Greenhill, 2012). Even though these 21st-century skills standards were never adopted across the United States, discussions about the need for students to meet workplace demands for technology-based skills such as communication and collaboration nevertheless clearly guided the development of the Common Core State Standards (CCSS; National Governors

Association Center for Best Practices & Council of Chief State School Officers [NGA/
CCSSO], 2010). As a result, the CCSS not only acknowledge the influence of technology
in reading and writing instruction but also prescribe student performance standards that
include technology within the reading–writing connection for skills such as communication and collaboration.

Furthermore, the CCSS prescribes *when* as well as *what* students should be able to do
with their technology-based reading and writing connection skills. However, the CCSS
purposefully does not address *how* teachers will integrate technology within the reading–
writing connection to meet the performance standards for all students. This means that
all teachers must learn how to teach the reading–writing connection using technology,
without much in the way of a clear understanding of how all the "connecting" will happen
nor perhaps which technology resources best enable the "connecting." Teachers will need
much ongoing support (for discussion, see Brenner, this volume).

A recent review of the research on technology implementation, even before the adoption of the CCSS, has suggested that it is an inherently complex, social, and developmental
process, with K–12 teachers constructing new and unique perceptions about the role of
technology in the classroom despite uncertain effects on skills such as reading and writing
and the connection or interface between them (Means, Toyama, Murphy, Bakia, & Jones,
2010; Purcell, Heaps, Buchanan, & Friedrich, 2013; Straub, 2009; Voogt & Knezek, 2008;
Wellings & Levine, 2009). Perhaps support for teachers will come! For example, as a result
of the U.S. *National Educational Technology Plan* (U.S. Department of Education, Office of
Educational Technology, 2010), the Department of Education is funding Communities
of Practice to help teachers learn about and understand the best practices, research, and
implementation strategies for technology use. In addition, the National Science Foundation
has begun funding projects under a new research arm, Cyberlearning: Transforming Education. Since its inception in 2010, there have been many projects funded, including a few
that have focused, at least partially, on the reading–writing connection. When the results
of these projects become widely available, they may support K–12 teachers' integration of
technology into the reading–writing connection.

TECHNOLOGY, READING, AND WRITING

Technology has played a role in classroom reading and writing instruction since the
late 1960s (Blanchard, 1999; Blanchard & Farstrup, 2011; Blanchard & Marshall, 2004;
Blanchard & Mason, 1987; Blanchard, Mason, & Daniels, 1987; Kamil, Intrator, & Kim,
2000; Mason & Blanchard, 1979; Mason, Blanchard, & Daniels, 1983; Tamim, Bernard,
Borokhovski, Abrami, & Schmid, 2011). Just over a decade ago, the National Reading
Panel (NICHD, 2000) and the National Commission on Writing (2003) concluded that
technology could be used effectively for instruction and that it had the potential to support
the reading–writing connection as a tool.

Since the publication of the National Reading Panel and the National Commission
on Writing reports, much has happened to reading and writing in the classroom courtesy of easily available and affordable digital technology (Barron et al., 2011; Blanchard &
Moore, 2010; Grimes & Fields, 2012; Guernsey, Levine, Chiong, & Stevens, 2012; Gutnick,
Robb, Takeuchi, & Kotler, 2010; Ito et al., 2013; National Commission on Writing, 2010;
Peterson-Karlan & Parette, 2007; Shuler, 2012; U.S. Department of Education, 2012; for
recent review, see Connor et al., in press). And much has happened outside of the classrooms too. All K–12 teachers know that today's children are awash in a world of learning
experiences courtesy of digital technology. At home, at school, and in between, even young

children (3- to 5-year-olds) in the United States spend from 28 to 35 hours a week with technology (including television), and the hours per week increase with age (Tandon, Zhou, Lozano, Christakis, 2011). With one seventh of the world's population actively using *Facebook*, children lead not only digital lives but Wi-Fi and Internet-connected lives as well. As a result, children's reading- and writing-connected experiences may well have transpired courtesy of technology. Evidence of this can be seen in their texting, blogging, chatting, and tweeting. Not surprisingly, these reading- and writing-connected experiences are often short, nonlinear, informal, episodic, and interactive—often just the opposite of traditional classroom reading and writing instruction.

The widespread availability of digital media, devices, and applications, when coupled with their infusion into the CCSS, is explicit acknowledgment that technology is at the center of virtually every aspect of children's daily lives, and teachers must leverage it to provide engaging and powerful learning experiences. The expanding role of technology in the CCSS is also an acknowledgment that today's digital world requires 21st-century skills with new forms of reading and writing connected by technology (Leu, O'Byrne, Zawilinski, McVerry, & Everett-Cacopardo, 2009). Thus any discussions about the possible roles of technology in the reading–writing connection, at least in the United States, must address the CCSS student performance standards.

> **BOX 12.1.** Nongovernmental efforts with an interest in technology integration that might support these K–12 teachers
>
> - Digital Media and Learning (www.macfound.org/programs/learning)
> - Alliance for Excellent Education (www.digitallearningday.org)
> - Center for Media Literacy (www.medialit.org)
> - Joan Ganz Cooney Center (www.joanganzcooneycenter.org)
> - The Inspired Classroom: Technology in the Classroom (www.theinspiredclassroom.com)
> - Teacher Engage (www.engage.intel.com)
> - Simple K–12 *YouTube* tutorials (www.youtube.com/user/simplek12team)

COMMON CORE, TECHNOLOGY, READING, AND WRITING

Anchor Standards

The CCSS prescribe a substantial role for technology in classroom reading–writing connection activities paralleling the way that 21st-century workers use technology. Workers routinely connect reading and writing with technology as they research, collaborate, problem-solve, and communicate in their jobs. Thus one requirement of the CCSS is that all students across all grade levels gradually improve their ability to use technology to connect reading and writing. What all this means for teachers is that, beginning in kindergarten and continuing through 12th grade, technology appears in the reading, writing, speaking, listening, and college and career readiness anchor standards, as well as 6th- through 12th-grade-level literacy in history/social sciences, science, and technical subject content-area standards. In these standards, technology is linked to the reading–writing connection, and the links can be seen in the following five anchor standards.

1. [Reading] Integrate and evaluate content presented in diverse media and formats, including visually and quantitatively, as well as in words.

2. [Writing] Use technology, including the Internet, to produce and publish writing and to interact and collaborate with others.

3. [Writing] Gather relevant information from multiple print and digital sources, assess the credibility and accuracy of each source, and integrate the information while avoiding plagiarism.

4. [Speaking and Listening] Integrate and evaluate information presented in diverse media and formats such as visual, quantitative, and oral.

5. [Speaking and Listening] Make strategic use of digital media and visual displays of data to express information and enhance understanding of presentations.

These five anchor standards explicitly require the use of technology in reading and writing.

Grade-Level Standards

What the general anchor standards mean for classroom lesson plans of teachers can be found in the specific grade-level standards (for a complete list, see www.corestandards .org). For example, beginning in kindergarten, students (with teacher assistance) are expected to "explore a variety of digital tools to produce and publish writing, including in collaboration with peers" (K–5 writing, standard #6; NGA/CCSSO, 2010). To achieve this outcome, teachers must provide these exploratory reading and writing opportunities in their classrooms early and often. Teachers also must help students understand and evaluate information presented from various technology sources as well as help students use this information to express their thoughts—individually or in collaboration with peers—using technology tools. This may prove to be quite a challenge for kindergarten teachers, given their classroom resources and the pedagogical skill required to accomplish technological integration.

Kindergarten teachers are not alone in these challenges, as all elementary teachers must begin integrating technology and instructing their students in the use of technology in reading, writing, and the reading–writing connection. Progressing in school up through fifth grade, another grade-level example maintains that children are expected to read, understand, and interpret informational text "presented visually, orally or quantitatively (e.g., in charts, graphs, diagrams, timelines, animations, or interactive elements on Web pages) and explain how the information contributes to an understanding of the text" (K–5 reading information text, standard #7; NGA/CCSSO, 2010). By fifth grade, they are also expected to read, understand, and interpret literature text as well as "analyze how visual and multimedia elements contribute to the meaning, tone, or beauty of a text (e.g., graphic novel, multimedia presentation of fiction, folktale, myth, poem)" (K–5 reading literature text, standard #7). In addition, by fifth grade, students are expected to write (produce and publish), using technology tools individually and in collaboration with peers, based on multiple sources that include technology sources. Again, this will be a challenge for teachers and their classroom resources.

Content-Area Standards

Of course, most upper elementary, middle, and high school teachers now know that sixth grade marks the beginning of the content-area grade-level standards (6th–12th)—namely, literacy in the history, social sciences, biological and physical sciences, and technical subjects. Thus the complete K–12 CCSS (NGA/CCSS, 2010) begin with the general anchor standards and end with the specific grade standards; taken together, they provide the directional nucleus for the role of technology in classrooms and with the reading–writing connection.

The content-area grade-level standards are clustered or grouped around grades 6–8, grades 9–10, and grades 11–12, each with an incremental increase in the sophistication of the reading–writing connection. The reading grade-level standards for literacy in history and social studies (similar, as well, for literacy in science and technical subjects) are generally consistent across content areas, with each stressing the role of technology:

- [Reading, grades 6–8] Integrate visual information (e.g., charts, graphs, photographs, videos, maps) with other information in print and digital texts.

- [Reading, grades 9–10] Integrate quantitative or technical analysis (e.g., charts, research data) with quantitative analysis in print and digital text.

- [Reading, grades 11–12] Integrate and evaluate multiple sources of information presented in diverse formats and media (visually, quantitatively, as well as in words) in order to address a question or solve a problem.

The writing grade-level standards for literacy in history and social studies as well as science and technical subjects also clearly stress technology (NGA/CCSSO, 2010):

- [Writing, grades 6–8] Write information/explanatory texts, including the narration of historical events, scientific procedures/experiments, or technical processes. Introduce a topic clearly, previewing what is to follow; organize ideas, concepts, and information into broader categories as appropriate to achieving purpose; include formatting (e.g., headings), graphics (e.g., charts, tables), and multimedia when useful to aiding comprehension.

- [Writing, grades 9–10] Write information/explanatory texts, including the narration of historical events, scientific procedures/experiments, or technical processes. Introduce a topic and organize ideas, concepts, and information to make important connections and distinctions; include formatting (e.g., headings), graphics (e.g., figures, tables), and multimedia when useful to aiding comprehension.

- [Writing, grades 11–12] Write information/explanatory texts, including the narration of historical events, scientific procedures/experiments, or technical processes. Introduce a topic and organize complex ideas, concepts, and information so that each new element builds on that which precedes it to create a unified whole; include formatting (e.g., headings), graphics (e.g., figures, tables), and multimedia when useful to aiding comprehension.

- [Writing, grades 6–8] Use technology, including the Internet, to produce and publish writing and present the relationships between information and ideas clearly and efficiently.

- [Writing, grades 9–10] Use technology, including the Internet, to produce, publish, and update individual or shared writing products, taking advantage of technology's capacity to link to other information and to display information flexibly and dynamically.

- [Writing, grades 11–12] Use technology, including the Internet, to produce, publish, and update individual or shared writing products, in response to ongoing feedback, including new arguments or information.

- [Writing, grades 6–8] Gather relevant information from multiple print and digital sources, using search terms effectively; assess the credibility and accuracy of each source; and quote or paraphrase the data and conclusions of others, avoiding plagiarism and following standard format for citation.

- [Writing, grades 9–10] Gather relevant information from multiple authoritative print and digital sources, using advanced searches effectively; assess the usefulness of each source in answering the research question; integrate information into the text selectively to maintain the flow of ideas, avoiding plagiarism and following standard format citation.

- [Writing, grades 11–12] Gather relevant information from multiple authoritative print and digital sources, using advanced searches effectively; assess the strengths and limitations of each source in terms of the specific task, purpose, and audience; integrate information into the text selectively to maintain the flow of ideas, avoiding plagiarism and overreliance on any one source and following standard format citation.

So what do all these CCSS mean for teachers concerned with using technology in effective reading and writing instruction, including instruction focused on the reading–writing connection?

ROLES FOR TECHNOLOGY IN THE READING–WRITING CONNECTION

Like any tool, when technology is integrated with quality instruction, it can—and does—enhance learning. As noted earlier, technology-based reading and writing opportunities have tended to be viewed from either the lens of reading instruction or the lens of writing instruction. The result has been reading or writing instruction that has focused on utilizing technological resources to maximize engagement during the presentation of information in order to increase student knowledge or skill (i.e., computer-assisted instruction, computer-based learning, computer-assisted learning, web-based learning, and application-based learning). However, today's CCSS require a paradigm shift away from learning *from* technology (via remediation or independent practice of isolated literacy skills) toward focusing on students (and teachers) researching, collaborating, problem-solving, and communicating *with* technology—functionally using technology (e.g., Blanchard & Farstrup, 2011; McKenna, Labbo, & Reinking, 2003; see also Tondeur, van Braak, & Valcke, 2007). Thus integrating technology into the reading–writing connection will require a transformation in the role technology plays in many classrooms. Unfortunately, teachers looking for effective classroom-tested strategies and practices that integrate technology within the reading–writing connection will be somewhat surprised to find few examples, especially for the lower grades. They will find numerous examples of technology-based reading or writing examples but not for the reading–writing connection (e.g., National Writing Project, www.digitalis.nwp.org; Reading Rockets, www.readingrockets.org; Read-Write-Think, www.reading.org). Nevertheless, the information that follows provides a few of the available examples that should allow you to gain a clearer picture of technology's possible roles in the reading–writing connection—roles that neatly align with the CCSS.

KINDERGARTEN: INTEGRATING TECHNOLOGY INTO THE READING–WRITING CONNECTION

In some of today's kindergarten classrooms, children can be found using multitouch-sensitive screens on desktops or tablets that support their emerging reading and writing skills as they document a classroom experience and print the results for all to see and read. In fact, both of this chapter's authors have used and are using tablets and other digital technology for similar emergent reading–writing connection activities in their U.S. Department of Education, Early Reading First projects. Here is a fictional account from 2007 of one kindergarten classroom that foreshadowed the experiences of the authors.

> It is an ordinary school day, as a group of kindergarten students gets off the bus. Suddenly, one of them spots an unusual bird high up in a tree. Running inside, they tell their teacher in excited voices that there is an owl in the tree. Armed with cameras, they run back outside with their teacher, who identifies the bird as a red-tailed hawk as students capture the bird digitally. Discussing the bird on their way back to the classroom, one student asks, "Can I Google red-tailed hawk?" He does so, sharing his findings with his classmates via large-screen projector. Using multimedia software, each student creates a small piece of illustrated writing about the hawk, some e-mailing what they have created to their parents. At the students' request, the teacher organizes the class to create a torn-paper collage of the red-tailed hawk, which is framed and displayed prominently in the classroom. (van 't Hooft, Swan, Cook, & Lin, 2007, p. 3)

Even if this fictional account would work for some kindergarten classrooms, would it work for all classrooms, as the CCSS would suggest? Is this type of classroom activity realistic for all kindergarten children and teachers? Kindergarten teachers know—maybe more than most teachers—that children learn by doing, especially when all five senses are involved. Kindergarteners are concrete thinkers (Piaget, 1983). As a result, when deliberating the possible advantages and disadvantages of integrating technology into their reading and writing lessons, there will be many questions. Chief among these questions will be whether 5-year-olds can handle the cognitive and psychomotor demands of technology use. Empirical research has found that they can (Ching, Wang, Shih, & Kedem, 2006; Yost, 2003). Common-sense observation of 5-year-olds using tablet apps, game consoles, television remote controls, or smart phones would seem to support this empirical research. However, children using technology outside the classroom is different from teachers linking technology to the reading–writing connection in their classrooms; teachers may remain skeptical.

George (2010), Gathers (2010), Keengwe and Onchwari (2009), and Suomi (2010) provide evidence that kindergarten teachers can be convinced to use technology in their classrooms once they see how it can be done. For example, kindergarten teacher and self-described technophobe Denyell Suomi (2010) successfully incorporated technology into her kindergarten classroom and has encouraged others to learn from her experiences. Ms. Suomi was wary of sacrificing instructional time to teach her students about the hardware and software but has no regrets now. Through trial and error, she learned what students typically already know, how intuitive they can be, and what she specifically has to teach in order for her students to "research" and "write" independently. Using a digital storytelling package, students began writing, sharing, revising, and publishing stories detailing their autobiographies and why they love their families. Students have also published a compilation of their favorite part about kindergarten so that next year's class would know what to expect. Ms. Suomi's kindergarten students have also been creating and collaborating on multimedia projects across the Internet using VoiceThreads (www.voicethread.com) in much the same way as the earlier fictional account illustrates. As a result of her experiences, she has suggested that teachers start searching for effective ways to integrate technology in much the same way that they search for other effective strategies and practices. Unfortunately, this search is not supported by the typical resources; there is no *What Works Clearinghouse* of instructional practices that effectively integrates technology into the classroom or, more specifically, that explains how to integrate technology into the reading–writing connection. Ms. Suomi and her peers must search teacher blogs and web sites such as those listed in this chapter as well as consult with their district's often lone technology instructor for ideas.

ELEMENTARY SCHOOL: INTEGRATING TECHNOLOGY INTO THE READING–WRITING CONNECTION

Explicit in the CCSS is the simple fact that children must become adept at integrating and evaluating information from technology sources such as the Internet. These skills do not come naturally; they must be taught. For example, Kuiper, Volman, and Terwel (2005) found that young students do not critically evaluate Internet information. Instead, they tend to focus on graphical elements, including font styles and images, rather than the text, and make immediate decisions to use information rather than taking time to read the information and evaluate it. Here is one example of an elementary teacher's strategy for helping her students develop Internet evaluation skills.

A fourth-grade teacher decided her students needed a systematic way to evaluate Internet information. Finding no existing resource, she decided to work with her students to develop an Internet evaluation tool: the *Research Resource Guide Sheet* (Baildon & Baildon, 2008). To develop the tool, the class first examined a variety of Internet sites that included a range of information presented via text, graphs, tables, and images. As they were reviewing information from the sites, the teacher asked her students what they were noticing and how they could determine whether the information was necessarily "true." The teacher guided the students to three general areas of consideration: readability (R), trustworthiness (T), and usefulness (U). Then the class worked together to develop critical evaluation questions in each of the three areas. From these questions, the class then developed a guide sheet that featured a total of 10 critical evaluation questions that should be answered about Internet information. Of interest, after implementing the guide sheet for several Internet projects, students progressed to a notetaking scheme that simplified the guide sheet and included only the letters "R-T-U" as a mnemonic device for critically evaluating Internet information (see teachers.net/lessons for other evaluation tools).

In another example, a fifth-grade teacher looking to embed activities to celebrate women's history month with the school's science curriculum was dismayed to find so few women listed in their textbooks. The teacher, a biology major as an undergraduate, developed a unit for her class to address this oversight. Students worked in groups to select historic female scientists to be included in their elementary school's *Addendum to Our Science Text: A Celebration of Women*. The students accessed the Internet to research facts about each scientist's activities. They e-mailed science experts in the field—primarily university professors and medical doctors—to gather images, details, and activities to expand their biographies. Students shared their writing across the groups to ensure interest and readability. Finally, using the publishing software preloaded on their classroom computer, the students produced a textbook-like addendum that the class then shared with the other fifth-grade classes in the school.

The authenticity in these examples demonstrates how teachers can use technology to support the reading–writing connection and satisfy the CCSS. Missing, however, is research documenting the outcomes of these innovative inclusions of technology into the reading–writing connection. The teachers provided the instruction and anecdotally observed their students' engagement and the quality of their products, yet whether or not and to what degree these examples have an impact on student achievement is unknown.

MIDDLE SCHOOL: INTEGRATING TECHNOLOGY INTO THE READING–WRITING CONNECTION

Even though technology use for all children has increased over the past decade, during the middle school years, total technology use increases by more than 4 hours per day to nearly 12 hours each day (Rideout, Foehr, & Roberts, 2010). Although teachers may be less than comfortable with the hours of technology use outside of their classrooms, they must acknowledge that students are entering their classrooms with many technology experiences, and these can be used to support traditional reading–writing connection activities. Here are a few examples.

A university professor worked with the language arts teachers in one middle school to implement a unit titled "Digital Storytelling with the iPad: Creating Book Trailers." Through this unit, students worked collaboratively to create "book trailers" for the novels they were to read for their eighth-grade class. They learned how to critique movie trailers in order to ensure that their trailers were of quality. They wrote the scripts for their trailers that transformed the often trite book summary into a teaser that would reveal enough of the story to garner interest without spoiling the story. The teachers summarized their struggles and successes on a blog linked on the National Writing Project web site (digitalis .nwp.org/resource/4341).

Equally innovative, a small group of teachers from two small towns that are states apart (i.e., New York and North Carolina) worked independently to include students' passion for role-playing games into reading–writing connection activities through the *World of Warcraft School Project* (n.d.). In a creative use of *gamification* (see Kapp, 2012 for discussion), these middle school teachers have integrated lessons on *The Hobbit* and *Beowolf* with the role-playing characters in the World of Warcraft (WoW) game scenario. The teachers, now a team, have also integrated poetry, riddles, and persuasive writing, as well as reading and responding to each of these genres, into the WoW format. For example, one of the teachers posted a WoW "quest" that required students to use the Internet to locate, review, and rate mission statements of real-world corporations in order to develop mission statements for their individual player "guilds." Students' mission statements had to incorporate what they learned from their reviews as evidenced by clear, concise presentations supporting their guild's existence and the purpose of its goals.

At the middle-school level, many teachers are experimenting with exciting and engaging ways to integrate technology in the reading–writing connection. Unfortunately, these teachers appear to be integrating technology on their own and not as part of school- or district-wide efforts.

HIGH SCHOOL: INTEGRATING TECHNOLOGY INTO THE READING–WRITING CONNECTION

As noted earlier, the CCSS expect that students will graduate from high school able to use technology to connect reading and writing across content areas. In the past, some high schools have been connecting technology, reading, and writing, but their efforts were focused on English language arts or the social sciences (i.e., National Writing Project, digitalis.nwp.org). Today, under the CCSS, that focus must be expanded to include all high school content areas. This will be a challenge! However, there are a few high school programs that are already connecting technology, reading, and writing; they offer a glimpse of how high schools might meet this challenge.

The Chicago Hive Learning Network (www.hivechicago.org) ensures that students have 24/7 technology-based access to museums, libraries, universities, and fine art venues as sources for their reading–writing connection activities. Connecting these resources to classroom experiences affords both opportunities and challenges for the teachers. The currently funded Hive projects are just beginning but already include numerous opportunities for including technology within the reading–writing connection for an authentic purpose. One example, Jamming for a Reason, brings together students throughout Chicago to create video public service announcements for a community issue of their choosing. Mentors who specialize in digital photography, video, animation, sound, and design have volunteered their expertise to support this project.

Another way that high school teachers are including technology with the reading–writing connection in the content areas is through blogs. A *blog*, short for *web log*, is an ongoing conversation via multiuser *posts* on a specific theme. Most high school teachers know that many of their students are blogging (and *vlogging*—video blogging) about a variety of non-school-related content. Capitalizing on students' blogging enthusiasm, a few teachers have successfully embedded content-area instruction that involves the reading–writing connection. Skipwith and Miranda (2012) have even provided lesson plans that introduce blogging as a format for connecting writing and reading in content areas. Hunt (2010), another high school teacher, has shared his suggestions on how to help fellow teachers in "Teaching Blogging Not Blogs," whereas Boardman (2010) reported on how reticent students become empowered and engaged by the expanded audience and asynchronous conversation format blogs afford. Other examples of high school content-area teachers sharing experiences and lesson plans about applications that could involve the reading–writing connection such as blogging to "bootstrap" learning of content-area knowledge can be found at the Connected Learning Research Network blog (clrn.dmlhub.net/blog) or Edublogs (edublog.com).

CONCLUSION

There are many possible and evolving future roles for technology in the reading–writing connection; however, for the present, the CCSS provide the clearest picture of what those possible evolving roles will look like in the classrooms. But there will be challenges! First, as noted earlier, technology integration necessarily involves inherently complex, social, and developmental processes with teachers constructing new and unique perceptions of the success and failure of technology—and they are costly. Second, the focus on reading–writing connection activities that integrate technology is a role change and will not happen at a school- or district-wide level without a conscientious and concerted effort by teachers, administrators, and policy makers. Third, a majority of students will need explicit instruction in the reading–writing connection and then how to integrate technology with the connection—and teachers will need to know how to do this efficiently and effectively. Technology, even the most innovative digital media, devices, or applications, will not replace the intangible social and psychological elements of quality teaching. Fourth, teachers will need resources. Although the National Center for Education Statistics reports a national average of about five students per classroom computer, this value has a standard deviation of almost eight, reflecting the wide disparity of technology access in classrooms. Some classrooms have one computer *per student* whereas others have one computer *per classroom* (Gray, Thomas, & Lewis, 2010). Finally, the substantial role of technology in the CCSS could accentuate the Matthew Effect so common in literacy achievement gap discussions, allowing full participation to students who have foundational reading, writing, and technology skills while denying access to those who struggle with these skills (i.e., the digital gap; Jenkins, Clinton, Purushotma, Robison, & Weigel, 2006). Conversely, technology could ameliorate the gaps by providing opportunities to effectively develop these foundational skills through activities anchored by the authentic connection of reading and writing.

REFERENCES

Achieve, Inc. (2006). *Closing the expectations gap 2006: An annual 50-state progress report on the alignment of high school policies with the demands of college and work.* Washington, DC: Author. Retrieved from http://www.achieve.org

Andrews, R. (2008). *Getting going: Generating, shaping, and developing ideas in writing.* Nottingham, UK: Department of Schools and Families.

Applebee, A., & Langer, J. (2011). *The national study of writing instruction: Methods and procedures.* Albany, NY: Center for English Learning & Achievement, New York State University at Albany.

Baildon, R., & Baildon, M. (2008). Guiding independence: Developing a research tool to support student decision making in selecting online information sources. *The Reading Teacher, 61*(8), 636–647. Retrieved from http://www.readingrockets.org/article/27428

Barron, B., Cayton-Hodges, G., Bofferding, L., Copple, C., Darling-Hammond, L., & Levine, M. (2011). *Taking a giant step: A blueprint for teaching children in a digital age.* New York, NY: Joan Ganz Cooney Center at Sesame Street Workshop.

Biancarosa, C., & Snow, C. (2006). *Reading next: A vision for action and research in middle and high school literacy* (2nd ed.). Washington, DC: Alliance for Excellence in Education.

Blanchard, J. (Ed.). (1999). *Educational computing in the schools: Technology, communication and literacy.* New York, NY: Haworth Press.

Blanchard, J., & Farstrup, A. (2011). Technologies, digital media, and reading instruction. In S. Samuels & A. Farstrup (Eds.), *What research has to say about reading instruction* (pp. 286–314). Newark, DE: International Reading Association.

Blanchard, J., & Marshall, J. (Eds.). (2004). *Web-based learning in K–12 classrooms: Opportunities and challenges.* New York, NY: Haworth Press.

Blanchard, J., & Mason, G. (Eds.). (1987). *The computer in reading and language arts.* New York, NY: Haworth Press.

Blanchard, J., Mason, G., & Daniels, D. (1987). *Computer applications in reading* (3rd ed.). Newark, DE: International Reading Association.

Blanchard, J., & Moore, T. (2010). *The digital world of young children: Impact on emergent literacy.* Mill Valley, CA: Pearson Foundation.

Boardman, D. (2010). *Amplifying student voices.* Retrieved from digitalis.nwp.org/resource/604

Ching, C., Wang, X., Shih, M., & Kedem, Y. (2006). Digital photography and journals in kindergarten-first grade classrooms: Toward meaningful technology integration in early childhood education. *Early Education and Development, 17*(3), 347–371.

Connor, C., Goldman, S., & Fishman, B. (in press). Reading and writing technology. In M. Spector, D. Merrill, & M. Bishop (Eds.), *Handbook of research on educational communications and technology.* Bloomington, IN: Association for Educational Communications and Technology.

Fitzgerald, J., & Shanahan, T. (2000). Reading and writing relations and their development. *Educational Psychologist, 35*(1), 39–50.

Gathers, C. (2010). *Using technology with kindergarten students.* Retrieved from http://4teachers.org/testimony/gathers/index.shtml

George, F. (2010). *Technology in kindergarten.* Retrieved from http://digitalis.nwp.org/collection/technology-kindergarten

Graham, S., Bollinger, A., Olson, C., D'Aoust, C., MacArthur, C., McCutchen, D., & Olinghouse, N. (2012). *Teaching elementary school students to be effective writers: A practice guide* (NCEE 2012-4058). Washington, DC: National Center for Education Evaluation and Regional Assistance, Department of Education.

Graham, S., & Hebert, H. (2010). *Writing to read: Evidence for how writing can improve reading* [A report from the Carnegie Corporation of New York]. Washington, DC: Alliance for Excellent Education.

Gray, L., Thomas, N., & Lewis, L. (2010). *Teachers' use of educational technology in U.S. public schools: 2009* (NCES 2010-040). Washington, DC: National Center for Education Statistics, Institute of Education Sciences, U.S. Department of Education.

Grimes, S., & Fields, D. (2012). *Kids online: A new research agenda for understanding social networking forum.* New York, NY: Joan Ganz Cooney Center at Sesame Street Workshop.

Guernsey, L., Levine, M., Chiong, C., & Stevens, M. (2012). *Pioneering literacy.* Washington, DC: New American Foundation.

Gutnick, A., Robb, M., Takeuchi, L., & Kotler, J. (2010). *Always connected: The new media habits of young children.* New York, NY: Joan Ganz Cooney Center at Sesame Street Workshop.

Hunt, B. (2010). *Teaching blogging not blogs.* Retrieved from http://digitalis.nwp.org/resource/1198

International Reading Association & the *Eunice Kennedy Shriver* National Institute of Child Health and Human Development (IRA/NICHD). (2012). *The reading-writing connection.* Retrieved from http://www.reading.org/Libraries/resources/reading-writingconnection_final.pdf

International Society for Technology in Education. (2007). *National educational technology standards for students: The next generation.* Washington, DC: Author.

Ito, M., Gutierrez, K., Livingstone, S., Penuel, B., Rhodes, J., Salen, K., . . . Watkins, C. (2013). *Connected learning.* Chicago, IL: MacArthur Foundation.

Jenkins, H., Clinton, K., Purushotma, R., Robison, A., & Weigel, M. (2006). *Confronting the challenges of participatory culture: Media education of the 21st century.* Chicago, IL: The MacArthur Foundation.

Kamil, M., Intrator, S., & Kim, H. (2000). Effects of other technologies on literacy and literacy learning. In M. Kamil, P. Mosenthal, P. Pearson, & R. Barr (Eds.), *Handbook of reading research* (Vol. 3; pp. 771–790). Mahwah, NJ: Erlbaum.

Kapp, K. (2012). *The gamification of learning and instruction: Game-based methods and strategies for training and education.* San Francisco, CA: Pfeiffer.

Kay, K., & Greenhill, V. (2012). *The leader's guide to 21st century education: 7 steps for schools and districts.* White Plains, NY: Pearson Education.

Keengwe, J., & Onchwari, G. (2009). Technology and early childhood education: A technology integration professional development model for practicing teachers. *Early Childhood Education Journal, 27*(1), 209–218.

Kuiper, E., Volman, M., & Terwel, J. (2005). The web as an information resource in K–12 education: Strategies for supporting students in searching and processing information. *Review of Educational Research Fall, 75*(3), 285–328.

Leu, D.J., O'Byrne, W.I., Zawilinski, L., McVerry, J.G., & Everett-Cacopardo, H. (2009). Expanding the new literacies conversation. *Educational Researcher, 38*(4), 264–269.

Mason, G., & Blanchard, J. (1979). *Computer applications in reading.* Newark, DE: International Reading Association.

Mason, G., Blanchard, J., & Daniels, D. (1983). *Computer applications in reading* (2nd ed.). Newark, DE: International Reading Association.

McKenna, M.C., Labbo, L.D., & Reinking, D. (2003). Effective use of technology in literacy instruction. In L. Morrow, L. Gambrell, & M. Pressley (Eds.), *Best practices in literacy instruction* (pp. 307–331). New York, NY: Guilford Press.

Means, B., Toyama, Y., Murphy, R., Bakia, M., & Jones, K. (2010). *Evaluation of evidence-based practices in online learning: A meta-analysis and review of online learning studies.* Washington, DC: U.S. Department of Education, Office of Planning, Evaluation, and Policy Development.

National Center for Education and the Economy. (1999). *New standards: Reading grade by grade and writing.* Washington, DC: Author.

National Commission on Writing. (2003). *The neglected R: The need for a writing revolution.* New York, NY: College Board.

National Commission on Writing. (2010). *Writing, learning and leading in the digital age.* New York, NY: College Board.

National Council of Teachers of English. (2007). *21st century literacies: A policy research brief.* Urbana, IL: Author.

National Governors Association Center for Best Practices & Council of Chief State School Officers (NGA/CCSSO). (2010). *Common Core State Standards.* Washington, DC: Authors.

National Institute of Child Health and Human Development (NICHD). (2000). *Teaching children to read: An evidence-based assessment of the scientific research literature on reading and its implications for reading instruction.* (NIH Publication No. 00-4754). Washington, DC: U.S. Government Printing Office.

North Central Regional Educational Laboratory. (2003). *enGauge 21st century skills: Literacy in the digital age.* Naperville, IL: Author.

PBworks. (n.d.). World of Warcraft in School. [Wiki]. Retrieved from http://wowinschool.pbworks.com/w/page/5268731/FrontPage

Peterson-Karlan, G., & Parette, H. (2007). *Supporting struggling writers using technology: Evidence-based instruction and decision-making.* Normal, IL: Special Education Assistive Technology Center, Illinois State University.

Piaget, J. (1983). Piaget's theory. In P. Mussen (Ed.), *Handbook of child psychology* (4th ed.; Vol. 1). New York, NY: Wiley.

Purcell, K., Heaps, A., Buchanan, J., & Friedrich, L. (2013). *How teachers are using technology at home and in their classrooms.* Washington, DC: Pew Research Center. Retrieved from http://pewinternet.org/Reports/2013/Teachers-and-technology

Rideout, V., Foehr, U., & Roberts, D. (2010). *GENERATION M2: Media in the lives of 8- to 18-year-olds.* Menlo Park, CA: Kaiser Family Foundation.

Shanahan, T., & Lomax, R. (1986). An analysis and comparison of theoretical models of the reading-writing relationship. *Journal of Educational Psychology, 78,* 116–123.

Shuler, C. (2012). *What in the world happened to Carmen Sandiego? The edutainment era: Debunking myths and sharing lessons learned.* New York, NY: Joan Ganz Cooney Center at Sesame Street Workshop.

Skipwith, S., & Miranda, A. (2012). *Youth blogging: Tutoring as collaboration and coauthoring.* Retrieved from http://digitalis.nwp.org/collection/youth-blogging-tutoring-collaboration-co

Straub, E. (2009). Understanding technology adoption: Theory and future directions for informal learning. *Review of Educational Research, 79*(2), 625–649.

Suomi, D. (2010). *Technology and kindergarten: Is it possible?* Retrieved from http://digitalis.nwp.org/resource/640

Tamim, R., Bernard, R., Borokhovski, E., Abrami, P., & Schmid, R. (2011). What forty years of research says about the impact of technology on learning: A second-order meta-analysis and validation study. *Review of Educational Research, 81*(1), 4–28.

Tandon, P., Zhou, C., Lozano, P., & Christakis, D. (2011). Preschoolers' total daily screen time at home and by type of child care. *Journal of Pediatrics, 158*(2), 297–300.

Tondeur, J., van Braak, J., & Valcke, M. (2007). Toward a topology of computer use in primary education. *Journal of Computer Assisted Learning, 23*(3), 197–206.

United Nations Educational, Scientific and Cultural Organization. (2010). *EFA global monitoring report, 2008: Education for all by 2015—Will we make it?* Oxford, UK: Oxford University Press.

U.S. Department of Education. (2012). *Just write guide!* Washington, DC: Office of Vocational and Adult Education.

U.S. Department of Education, Office of Educational Technology. (2010). *National Educational Technology Plan* [Executive summary]. Washington, DC: Author. Retrieved from http://www.ed.gov/technology/netp-2010

van 't Hooft, M., Swan, K., Cook, D., & Lin, Y. (2007). What is ubiquitous computing? In M. van 't Hooft & K. Swan (Eds.), *Ubiquitous computing in education: Invisible technology, visible impact* (pp. 3–17). Mahwah, NJ: Lawrence Erlbaum Associates.

Voogt, J., & Knezek, G. (Eds.). (2008). *International handbook of information technology in primary and secondary education.* New York, NY: Springer.

Weiser, B., & Mathes, P. (2011). Using encoding instruction to improve the reading and spelling performance of elementary students at risk for literacy difficulties: A best-evidence synthesis. *Review of Educational Research, 81*(2), 170–200.

Wellings, J., & Levine, M. (2009). *The digital promise: Transforming learning with innovative uses in technology.* New York, NY: Joan Ganz Cooney Center.

Yost, N. (2003). Computers, kids, and crayons: A comparative study of emergent writing behaviors. *Proceedings of the International Federation for Information Processing Working Group 3.5: Open Conference on Young Children and Learning Technologies, 34,* 107–112.

13

Why We Should Care About Literacy Models

Models of Reading and Writing and How They Can Elucidate the Connection Between Reading and Writing

Yusra Ahmed,[1] Young-Suk Kim, and Richard K. Wagner[2]

Although historically most research and pedagogy has separated reading and writing instruction (Shanahan, 2006), interrelations between reading and writing have been studied over the past couple of decades. Theoretically, children's reading skill has been hypothesized to be a component skill of writing development (Berninger, Abbott, Abbott, Graham, & Richards, 2002) and to draw on common knowledge and overlapping cognitive processes (Fitzgerald & Shanahan, 2000). Most studies find that reading and writing are highly related (e.g., Abbott & Berninger, 1993; Berninger et al., 2002; Jenkins, Johnson, & Hileman, 2004; Juel, 1988; Juel, Griffith, & Gough, 1986; Loban, 1963; Shanahan, 1984; Tierney & Shanahan, 1996), and neuroimaging studies have shown that reading and writing activate overlapping brain regions (Pugh et al., 2006). Furthermore, interventions that have focused on transfer of skills show that reading instruction can have a positive effect on writing (Shanahan, 2006) and writing instruction on reading (Graham & Hebert, 2011; Tierney & Shanahan, 1996; Weiser & Mathes, 2011). However, less is known about how these interrelations might change as children develop their reading and writing skills. In the following sections, we review previous studies using various models of literacy, and we describe new ways that can be used to determine whether 1) what a student learns about reading affects writing development, 2) what a student learns about writing affects reading development, 3) both, or 4) neither.[3]

INTERRELATIONS BETWEEN READING AND WRITING

Various approaches have been used to investigate the relation of reading and writing development over time. One frequently used approach was latent variable modeling or structural equation modeling (SEM). Latent variables can be conceptualized as *supervariables*, which are hypothesized constructs. They represent the commonality among similar tests

---

[1] University of Houston and Texas Institute for Measurement, Evaluation and Statistics

[2] Kim and Wagner, Florida State University and Florida Center for Reading Research

[3] This chapter does not focus on experimental designs, where a randomly selected group of students are given intensive instruction on reading or writing. It focuses instead on the codevelopment of reading and writing in the context of the general education framework.

143

(e.g., between two or more tests of spelling) minus the variability that is due to each specific test (e.g., errors in administering the test).

Shanahan and Lomax's (1986, 1988) studies are among the earliest examples of latent variable modeling used to examine bidirectional reading–writing relations. Their studies included three aspects of reading (word analysis, vocabulary, and comprehension) and four aspects of writing (spelling, vocabulary diversity, syntax, and story structure). Their results were that reading influenced writing and writing influenced reading. In other words, reading and writing were related reciprocally.

Lerkkanen, Rasku-Puttonen, Aunola, and Nurmi (2004) reported results from a longitudinal study of reading and writing development in Finnish. The study included 83 first-grade Finnish students who were assessed four times during grade 1. Finnish is a transparent orthography and has more consistent letter sound correspondences than English. Their reading-related measures were letter naming, word list reading, and reading comprehension. Their writing-related measures were spelling and writing fluency (in which children were asked to write as many words or sentences as they could—or a story—about a given picture). Their results were that reading and spelling were reciprocally related during the first semester, but in subsequent semesters, reading predicted spelling, and writing fluency predicted reading.

Although these studies and several others show that relations between reading and writing appear to be bidirectional (Shanahan & Lomax, 1986; Lerkkanen et al., 2004; Abbott et al., 2010; Graham & Hebert, 2011), other studies suggest that the relation might be largely unidirectional. Some studies have reported that writing influences reading (e.g., Berninger et al., 2002; Caravolas, Hulme, & Snowling, 2001; Cataldo & Ellis, 1988), particularly for spelling predicting word reading for children in earlier stages of reading–writing development. In addition, a review conducted by Graham and Hebert (2011) showed that intensive writing instruction improves reading comprehension, reading fluency, and word reading, and increasing how much students write enhances their reading comprehension. On the other hand, most of the studies that find bidirectional relations suggest that reading-to-writing relations are stronger than writing-to-reading relations (e.g., Shanahan & Lomax, 1986).

LEVELS OF LANGUAGE APPROACH

Recent studies have analyzed the separate contributing skills of reading and writing based on levels of language (e.g., word, sentence, and passage). Although these levels are typically not related in a one-to-one fashion for reading and writing (Abbott et al., 2010; Berninger et al., 2002; Whitaker, Berninger, Johnston, & Swanson, 1994), they provide a way to compare components of each that are similar. This approach is supported by the finding that differences exist in how individual children perform at different levels of language (word, sentence, and text) for reading (e.g., Vellutino, Tunmer, Jaccard, Chen, & Scanlon, 2004) as well as writing (Abbott & Berninger, 1993; Whitaker et al., 1994). Some children can be adequate in decoding but not in reading comprehension or adequate in spelling but not in sentence or text writing.

Decoding and Encoding Words

Alphabetic writing systems rely on a relatively small number of orthographic units or letters that map roughly onto the phonemes of speech. The alphabetic principle holds that there is a rough correspondence between phonemes and the letters in an alphabetic system of writing, and we rely on this grapheme-phoneme correspondence in order to read and write words. Fitzgerald and Shanahan (2000) suggest that writers rely on graphophonics, which requires phonological awareness, grapheme (letters and letter combinations) awareness, and morphology (Shanahan, 2006). For example, for decoding the beginning of the word "sure," a reader chooses between the potential phonological representations /s/, /z/, /sh/, or a silent letter. For encoding the same word, however, a writer chooses from the s, sh, or ch orthographic paths (Shanahan, 2006; Sprenger-Charolles, Siegel, Bechennec, & Serniclaes, 2003). Most researchers suggest that encoding is not a reversal of decoding, although both rely on knowledge of the alphabetic principle (Abbott et al., 2010; Foorman, Arndt, & Crawford, 2011; Shanahan, 2006).

Sentence Reading and Writing

The grammatical rules and punctuations used in creating sentences are attributes of syntax (Shanahan, 2006). Both readers and writers rely on meaningful syntactic orderings of words as well as the knowledge of punctuation marks to create sentence boundaries. Several studies have shown that children are sensitive to linguistic constraints in oral language as well as written language (e.g., Bates & Goodman, 1999; Rode, 1974), even at the preschool level (Puranik & Lonigan, 2010). Most of the syntactic structures found in written language are learned through many years of schooling (Beers & Nagy, 2011), during which children are also learning to read. Research on combining sentences suggests that writers first acquire syntax and semantics at the level of the clause, but they are unable to form larger units of meaning without error (Rode, 1976). Research on syntactic complexity of writing has shown that syntactic complexity generally increases as children develop their writing skills (Scott & Windsor, 2000), although how this development occurs is still unknown, as most research has focused on the development of writing at the text level or has used cumulative measures of writing (Beers & Nagy, 2011; Berninger et al., 2010).

Text Reading and Writing

Recent studies have shown that the correlations between passage comprehension and text composition range from moderate to high for both children and adults (Berninger et al., 2002; Kim, Park, & Park, under review) and that reading comprehension and composition are mutually predictive over time (Abbott et al., 2010). Readers apply a series of inferences and construct propositions based on the information provided by the text (Foorman et al., 2011; Kintsch & Mangalath, 2011). In addition, they form mental models of the text that represent the situation described in the text. Analogous to reading comprehension, composition is also a complex process, requiring translation of ideas as well as transcription skills (e.g., handwriting and spelling; Hayes & Berninger, 2010). However, the pattern of reasoning is different for each process: While readers focus on gaining support for their interpretations, writers focus on strategies to create meaning (Langer, 1986).

The important conclusion from the levels-of-language framework is that, although reading and writing are not inverse processes, they rely on similar cognitive mechanisms that allow for simultaneous growth as well as transfer of knowledge. However, whether this theory holds for all levels of language is still unknown. A recent study by Abbott, Berninger, and Fayol (2010) modeled the longitudinal development of reading and writing across levels of language. Their study placed emphasis on integrating levels of language by specifying several bidirectional models. In contrast to the studies discussed earlier, their study used single observed variables instead of latent variables and included data from two cohorts of children who were tested longitudinally from grades 1 through 5 and from grades 3 through 7. The first model was a subword/word-level model that included handwriting, spelling, and word reading. The results showed a significant bidirectional relation between word reading and spelling across grades 2 through 7. For grade 1, however, only the spelling-to-reading pathway was statistically significant.

Their second reading–writing bidirectional model included pathways between word- (word reading and spelling) and text-level (reading comprehension and written composition) measures. Similar to the first subword/word-level model, the results for the word/text-level model showed significant bidirectional relations between word spelling and reading for grades 2 through 7. For grade 1, however, only the path from word reading to spelling—but not the other way around—was significant. Overall, their results indicate that spelling is an important predictor for both reading and writing development, and this relation is unidirectional in grade 1 and bidirectional in subsequent grades, possibly because other factors (such as verbal ability or exposure to print) contribute to the development of reading and writing in grade 1. Their findings suggests that spelling should be taught from the beginning of schooling, and poor spellers should be identified and provided spelling instruction because of its important role in reading and writing development in middle elementary grades.

LATENT CHANGE SCORE MODEL OF READING AND WRITING

In this section, we present results from a recent study using a new approach to examine change in reading and writing over time. We present preliminary results here, but more comprehensive results can be found in Ahmed, Wagner, and Lopez (in press). This approach uses a type of model called a *latent change score model* that allows one to determine whether improvement in reading is related to later improvement in writing and vice versa (McArdle, 2009). Following the levels of language approach, we looked at relations between growth in reading and writing at the word, sentence, and text levels (see Figures 13.1–13.3).

Participants in this study included 316 boys and girls who were assessed annually in grades 1 through 4. Following the Sunshine State Standards, schools in Florida prepare students for increasing their reading and writing skills by providing instruction on phonological awareness, phonics, fluency, vocabulary, comprehension, and writing (Florida Department of Education [FLDOE], 2013). Specifically, students' writing is expected to improve on focus, organization, support, and conventions.

Several standardized reading and writing tests were administered.[4] Students were also asked to write for 10 minutes on a topic provided by the tester. In the text-level model presented here, the total number of words children wrote was used as an indicator of compositional fluency. Nelson and Van Meter (2007) report that total word productivity is a robust measure of developmental growth in writing. However, it should be noted that compositional fluency is a dissociable construct from writing quality (Kim, Al Otaiba, Folsom, Gruelich, & Puranik, in press).

---

[4]Word reading included two forms of the Test of Word Reading Efficiency (Torgesen et al., 1999). Sentence reading included two forms of the Test of Silent Reading Efficiency and Comprehension (Wagner et al., 2010). Passage comprehension included the Woodcock-Johnson-III passage comprehension subtest (Woodcock et al., 2001), and the Woodcock Reading Mastery Test-Revised passage comprehension subtest (Woodcock, 1987). Spelling subtests were included from the Wide Range Achievement Test-3 (Wilkinson, 1993) and the Wechsler Individual Achievement Test-II (Psychological Corporation, 2002).

Sentence writing was measured by the Combining Sentences subtest from the Wechsler Individual Achievement Test-II (Psychological Corporation, 2002).

Findings suggested that a reading-to-writing model better describes the data for the word and text levels. For the sentence level, growth in reading predicted later growth in writing, and growth in writing predicted later growth in reading (see Ahmed, Wagner, & Lopez, in press, for additional details). Figures 13.1–13.3 present the unstandardized regression coefficients for the pathways between reading and writing variables. The regression coefficients from reading to writing variables are interpreted as the rate of change in writing skills at given reading skill levels. Overall, children who made larger gains were those who were low on reading or writing achievement the previous year. At the word level (see Figure 13.1), change in spelling was predicted by earlier decoding, suggesting that skilled readers made improvements in spelling more than did less skilled readers. Change in spelling was also predicted by change in decoding, suggesting that children who improved on decoding between grades improved on spelling between subsequent grades. These findings are in line with theories of reading and spelling development (e.g., Aarnoutse, van Leeuwe, &

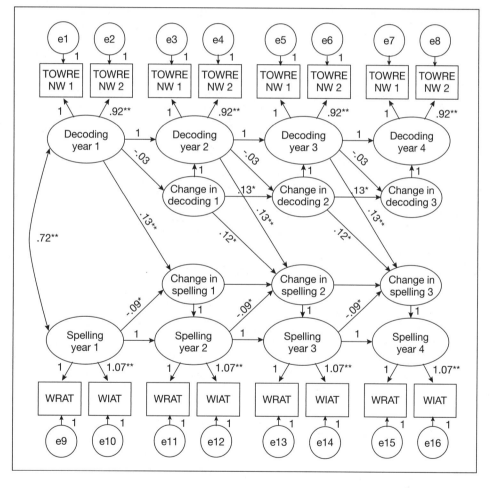

Figure 13.1. Unstandardized estimates for the word-level reading-to-writing model. Acronyms stand for the following: Test of Word Reading Efficiency (TOWRE); Wide-range achievement test (WRAT); and the Wechsler Individual Achievement Test (WIAT). (Adapted from Ahmed, Y., Wagner, R.K., & Lopez, D. [in press]. Developmental relations between reading and writing at the word, sentence and text levels: a latent change score analysis. *Journal of Educational Psychology.*)

* $p < 0.05$
** $p < 0.001$

Verhoeven, 2005; Babayigit & Stainthorp, 2011; Berninger et al., 2002; Juel, 1988; Shana-han & Lomax, 1986; Sprenger-Charolles et al., 2003) and suggest that the ability to read words correctly may facilitate writing them correctly, via mastery of phoneme-grapheme relations that are learned through reading (Ehri, 2005). The finding that an improvement in decoding leads to an improvement in spelling is also consistent with spelling interven-tions that are based on word and pseudoword reading (Shanahan, 2006).

We also found that sentence reading fluency influenced change in sentence combining (Figure 13.2; but see Berninger et al., 2011). Thus our findings suggest that the ability to read sentences facilitates writing them. One possible explanation is that an individual who is fluent at reading sentences is more familiar with sentence structures and syntax com-pared to an individual who is not fluent. Writing sentences requires syntactic knowledge, which includes grammatical rules and punctuation rules used to form clauses. Further-more, sentence construction requires considerable cognitive effort, as it is dependent on word choice, syntax, clarity, and rhythm (Saddler & Graham, 2005). Our results suggest

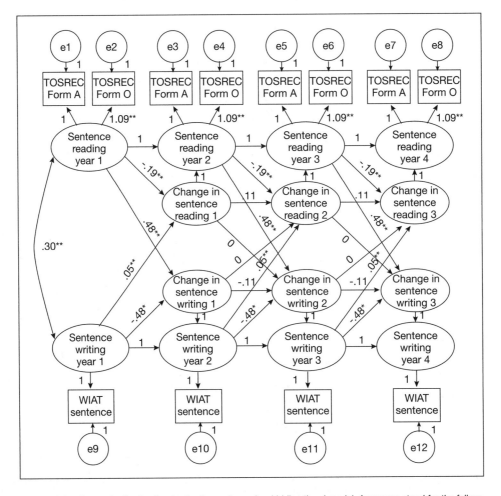

Figure 13.2. Unstandardized estimates for the sentence-level bidirectional model. Acronyms stand for the follow-ing: Wechsler Individual Achievement Test (WIAT) and Test of Silent Reading Efficiency and Comprehension (TOS-REC). (Adapted from Ahmed, Y., Wagner, R.K., & Lopez, D. [in press]. Developmental relations between reading and writing at the word, sentence and text levels: a latent change score analysis. *Journal of Educational Psychology*.)

* $p < 0.05$
** $p < 0.001$

that the knowledge underlying sentence comprehension facilitates sentence writing and that the reading-to-writing relation is strongest at the sentence level. Similarly, the significant—albeit small—effect of sentence writing on sentence reading suggests that writing sentences correctly also facilitates reading them; combining sentences requires knowledge of syntax and structures of sentences, which in turn facilitates reading sentences.

At the text level, reading comprehension facilitated growth in compositional fluency (see Figure 13.3). One possible explanation is that children who read for comprehension are more familiar with the format of larger texts and story structures and are better at writing stories. On the other hand, change in reading comprehension negatively predicted change in compositional fluency, suggesting a discrepancy between reading and writing development such that less skilled readers grew more on compositional fluency. One possible explanation is that students who did not improve on reading comprehension used more words to communicate ideas, whereas students who improved on reading comprehension wrote more concisely.

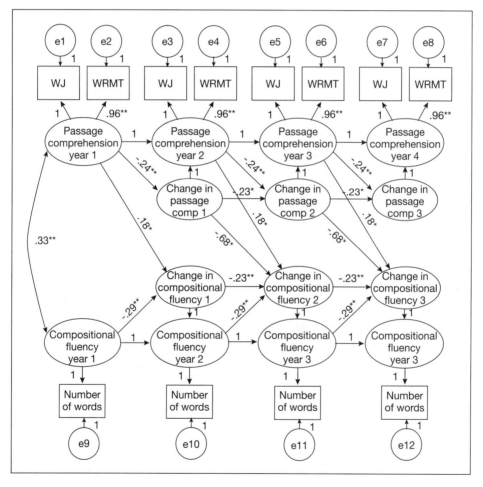

Figure 13.3. Unstandardized estimates for the text-level reading-to-writing model. Acronyms stand for the following: Woodcock-Johnson (WJ) and Woodcock Reading Mastery Test (WRMT). (Adapted from Ahmed, Y., Wagner, R.K., & Lopez, D. [in press]. Developmental relations between reading and writing at the word, sentence and text levels: a latent change score analysis. *Journal of Educational Psychology*.)

*$p < 0.05$
**$p < 0.001$

Although early correlational studies provided evidence for a general association between reading and writing by showing that the shared variability between reading and writing exceeded 50% in primary grades (Shanahan, 2006), our study found that reading-to-writing models were superior to writing-to-reading and bidirectional models, especially for the word and text levels of writing. At the sentence level, a bidirectional model was superior, although the writing-to-reading relations were very weak. Our findings suggest that, in the presence of both reading and writing instruction, students who are growing on writing are those who apply knowledge of reading skills to their writing. Thus it is possible that strategies used for reading are also useful for writing. Simply put, writing requires good reading skills, whereas reading may not necessarily require good writing skills.

Why reading affects writing more than writing affects reading may reflect how much time is spent on reading and writing instruction. Reading instruction is more widespread than writing instruction in the United States, particularly in primary grades. Thus it is possible that, in the presence of rigorous writing instruction, bidirectional or writing-to-reading models may be accurate. Some evidence of this possibility comes from a study of Chinese reading and writing development that found that learning to read Chinese depended on writing ability (Tan, Spinks, Eden, Perfetti, & Siok, 2005). Learning to read Chinese requires mastery of thousands of characters, and character copying is the major approach to learning them. So unlike reading instruction in the United States, writing is a larger component of learning to read Chinese. It also is possible that we might have found more of an effect of writing on reading in English had we studied younger children. Initial teaching of the alphabet often involves considerable copying and other writing-related activities.

TEACHERS SHOULD CARE ABOUT LITERACY MODELS

Our results show that typically developing children use the shared knowledge between reading and writing to improve on their writing skills. Thus, although it is important to teach each individual literacy skill (word decoding, sentence reading, passage comprehension, spelling, sentence writing, and text writing), general instruction and targeted interventions can also utilize the shared knowledge underlying reading and writing skills to teach children how to write. Specifically, children's word reading skills can be used to influence their spelling because children who improved on spelling were those who improved on word reading. Thus strategies used for strengthening the word reading skills of poor spellers can be beneficial for improving spelling skills. Although further research needs to be conducted on specific aspects of sentence-level literacy (e.g., syntax, grammar, and punctuation) as well as text-level literacy (e.g., conveying of overall meaning, structure of text), our results show that, overall, children who are adequate at reading sentences and paragraphs make improvements on writing. Thus it might be useful to teach specific aspects of sentence- and text-level comprehension in the context of literacy as opposed to reading and writing individually.

REFERENCES

Aarnoutse, C., van Leeuwe, J., & Verhoeven, L. (2005). Early literacy from a longitudinal perspective. *Educational Research and Evolution, 11*(3), 253–275.

Ahmed, Y., Wagner, R.K., & Lopez, D. (in press). Developmental relations between reading and writing at the word, sentence and text levels: A latent change score analysis. *Journal of Educational Psychology.*

Abbott, R.D., & Berninger, V.W. (1993). Structural equation modeling of relationships among developmental skills and writing skills in primary- and intermediate-grade writers. *Journal of Educational Psychology, 85*(3), 478–508.

Abbott, R.D., Berninger, V.W., & Fayol, M. (2010). Longitudinal relationships of levels of language in writing and between writing and reading in grades 1 to 7. *Journal of Educational Psychology, 102*(3), 281–298.

Babayigit, S., & Stainthrop, R. (2011). Modeling the relationships between cognitive-linguistic skills and literacy skills: New insights from a transparent orthography. *Journal of Educational Psychology, 103*(1), 169–189.

Bates, E., & Goodman, J. (1999). The emergence of grammar from the lexicon. In B. MacWhinney (Ed.), *The emergence of language* (pp. 27–80). Mahwah, NJ: Lawrence Erlbaum Associates.

Beers, S.F., & Nagy, W.E. (2011). Writing development in four genres from grades three to seven: Syntactic complexity and syntactic generation. *Reading and Writing, 24,* 183–202.

Berninger, V.W., Abbott, R.D., Abbott, S.P., Graham, S., & Richards, T. (2002). Writing and reading: Connections between language by hand and language by eye. *Journal of Learning Disabilities, 35*(1), 39–56.

Berninger, V., Abbott, R., Swanson, H.L., Lovitt, D., Trivedi, P., Lin, S., & Amtmann, D. (2010). Relationship of word- and sentence-level working memory to reading and writing in second, fourth, and sixth grade. *Language, Speech, and Hearing Services in Schools, 41,* 179–193.

Berninger, V., Nagy, W., & Beers, S. (2011). Child writers' construction and reconstruction of single sentences and construction of multi-sentence texts: Contributions of syntax and transcription to translation. *Reading and Writing, 24,* 151–182.

Caravolas, M., Hulme, C., & Snowling, M. (2001). The foundations of spelling ability: Evidence from a 3-year longitudinal study. *Journal of Memory and Language, 45,* 751–774.

Cataldo, S., & Ellis, N. (1988). Interactions in the development of spelling, reading and phonological skills. *Journal of Research in Reading, 11,* 86–109.

Ehri, L.C. (2005). Development of sight word reading: Phases and findings. In M.J. Snowling & C. Hulme (Eds.), *The science of reading* (pp. 135–155). Oxford, UK: Blackwell.

Fitzgerald, J., & Shanahan, T. (2000). Reading and writing relations and their development. *Educational Psychologist, 35*(1), 39–50.

Florida Department of Education (FLDOE). (2013). Bureau of K–12 Assessment. Retrieved from http://fcat.fldoe.org

Foorman, B.R., Arndt, E.J., & Crawford, E.C. (2011). Important constructs in literacy learning across disciplines. *Topics in Language Disorders, 31*(1), 73–83.

Graham, S., & Hebert, M. (2011). Writing to read: A meta-analysis of the impact of writing and writing instruction on reading. *Harvard Educational Review, 81*(4), 710–744.

Hayes, J.R., & Berninger, V. (2010). Relationships between idea generation and transcription: How act of writing shapes what children write. In C. Bazerman, R. Krut, K. Lunsford, S. McLeod, S. Null, P. Rogers, & A. Stansell (Eds.), *Traditions of writing research* (pp. 166–180). New York, NY: Taylor & Frances/Routledge.

Jenkins, J.R., Johnson, E., & Hileman, J. (2004). When is reading also writing: Sources of individual differences on the new reading performance assessments. *Scientific Studies of Reading, 8*(2), 25–151.

Juel, C., Griffith, P., & Gough, P. (1986). Acquisition of literacy: A longitudinal study of children in first and second grade. *Journal of Educational Psychology, 78,* 243–255.

Juel, C. (1988). Learning to read and write: A longitudinal study of 54 children from first through fourth grades. *Journal of Educational Psychology, 80,* 437–447.

Kim, Y.-S., Al Otaiba, S., Folsom, J.S., Greulich, L., & Puranik, C. (in press). Evaluating the dimensionality of first grade written composition. *Journal of Speech, Language, and Hearing Research.*

Kim, Y.-S., Park, C., & Park, Y. (under review). The unique relations of listening comprehension and oral expression to reading comprehension and written composition: Evidence from first-grade Korean-speaking children.

Kintsch, W., & Mangalath, P. (2011). The construction of meaning. *Topics in Cognitive Science, 3,* 346–370

Langer, J. (1986). Reading, writing and understanding: An analysis of the construction of meaning. *Written Communication, 3,* 219–267.

Lerkkanen, M., Rasku-Puttonen, H., Aunola, K., & Nurmi, J. (2004). The developmental dynamics of literacy skills during the first grade. *Educational Psychology, 24,* 793–810.

Loban, W.D. (1963). *The language of elementary school children.* Urbana, IL: National Council of Teachers of English.

McArdle, J.J. (2009). Latent variable modeling of differences and changes with longitudinal data. *Annual Review of Psychology, 60*, 577–603.

Nelson, N.W., & Van Meter, A.M. (2007). Measuring written language ability in narrative samples. *Reading and Writing Quarterly, 23*, 287–309.

Pugh, K.R., Frost S.J., Sandak, R., Gillis, M., Moore, D., Jenner, A.R., & Mencl, W.E. (2006). What does reading have to tell us about writing? Preliminary questions and methodological challenges in examining the neurobiological foundations of writing and writing disabilities. In C.A. MacArthur, S. Graham, & J. Fitzgerald (Eds.), *Handbook of writing research* (pp. 433–448). New York, NY: Guilford Press.

Puranik, C., & Lonigan, C. (2010). From scribbles to scrabble: Preschool children's developing knowledge of written language. *Reading and Writing: An Interdisciplinary Journal, 24*, 567–589.

Rode, S.S. (1974). Development of phrase and clause boundary reading in children. *Reading Research Quarterly, 10*(1), 124–142.

Saddler, B., & Graham, S. (2005). The effects of peer-assisted sentence combining instruction on the writing performance of more and less skilled young writers. *Journal of Educational Psychology, 97*, 43–54.

Scott, C.M., & Windsor, J. (2000). General language performance measures in spoken and written narrative and expository discourse of school-age children with language learning disabilities. *Journal of Speech, Language and Hearing Research, 43*, 324–339.

Shanahan, T. (1984). Nature of reading-writing relations: An exploratory multivariate analysis. *Journal of Educational Psychology, 76*, 466–477.

Shanahan, T. (2006). Relations among oral language, reading, and writing development. In C.A. MacArthur, S. Graham, & J. Fitzgerald (Eds.), *Handbook of writing research* (pp. 171–183). New York, NY: Guilford Press.

Shanahan, T., & Lomax, R.G. (1986). An analysis and comparison of theoretical models of the reading-writing relationship. *Journal of Educational Psychology, 78*, 116–123.

Shanahan, T., & Lomax, R.G. (1988). A developmental comparison of three theoretical models of the reading-writing relationship. *Research in the Teaching of English, 22*(2), 196–212.

Sprenger-Charolles, L., Siegel, L.S., Bechennec, D., & Serniclaes, W. (2003). Development of phonological and orthographic processing in reading aloud, in silent reading, and in spelling: A four-year longitudinal study. *Journal of Experimental Child Psychology, 84*, 194–217.

Tan, L.H., Spinks, J.A., Eden, G., Perfetti, C.A., & Siok, W.T. (2005). Reading depends upon writing, in Chinese. *Proceedings of the National Academy of Sciences, 102*, 8781–8785.

Tierney, R.J., & Shanahan, T. (1996). Research on the reading-writing relationship: Interactions, transactions, and outcomes. In R. Barr, M.L. Kamil, P.B. Mosenthal, & P.D. Pearson (Eds.), *Handbook of reading research* (Vol. 2; pp. 246–280). Mahwah, NJ: Lawrence Erlbaum Associates.

Vellutino, F.R., Tunmer, W.E., Jaccard, J., Chen, R., & Scanlon, D.M. (2004). Components of reading ability: Multivariate evidence for a convergent skills model of reading development. *Scientific Studies of Reading, 11*(1), 3–32.

Weiser, B., & Mathes, P. (2011). Using encoding instruction to improve the reading and spelling performance of elementary students at risk for literacy difficulties: A best-evidence synthesis. *Review of Educational Research, 81*(2), 170–200.

Whitaker, D., Berninger, V., Johnston, J., & Swanson, L. (1994). Intra-individual differences in levels of language in intermediate grade writers: Implications for the translating process. *Learning and Individual Differences, 6*, 107–130.

Wilkinson, G.S. (1993). *WRAT3 Wide range achievement test: Administration manual.* Wilmington, DE: Wide Range.

Woodcock, R. (1987). *Woodcock reading mastery test—revised.* Circle Pines, MN: American Guidance Service.

Woodcock, R.W., McGrew, K.S., & Mather, N. (2001). *Woodcock Johnson III tests of cognitive abilities and achievement.* Itasca, IL: Riverside Publishing.

14

In Summary

What Can We Agree On?

Peggy McCardle, Richard Long, and Brett Miller

Reading and writing are connected—both are language-related abilities, and together they form what we refer to as literacy. Indeed, it seems intuitively obvious that reading and writing are related, complementary, and might even be considered two sides of the same coin. Yet we know little about the specific nature of this connection or relationship with regard to typical development, learning, and student achievement (Fitzgerald & Shanahan, 2000; International Reading Association & the *Eunice Kennedy Shriver* National Institute of Child Health and Human Development [IRA/NICHD], 2012; Parodi, 2007). Research has not yet clearly delineated how learning in one influences or alters learning in the other, in what direction (i.e., reading to writing or writing to reading) such an influence might be strongest, how interactions between reading and writing might influence learning in both, or how the instructional processes for them relate and might optimally be integrated. At a more basic science level, there remains a need for additional research on reading and writing theory, modeling of the developmental processes involved in both skills, enhancements to measurements of these processes (both for research and for practice), and development of novel and more efficient technologies to support measurement and learning. Then we need to be able to use what we learn to help teachers and students realize greater successes in reading and writing.

Section 1 of this volume addresses how we approach reading and writing today, separately or as two sides of the same coin. In addressing these issues, the authors not only give us a current picture but also call for additional research. Connor, Ingebrand, and Dombek (Chapter 2) highlight the importance of writing to reading instruction and assessment, noting that better writers are more likely than weaker writers to reread their recently composed sentences and that writing seems more likely to be influenced by high-quality instruction that includes components of reading such as decoding or spelling. These authors highlight the importance of research on the role of writing in strengthening literacy overall as well as writing outcomes specifically, both for student success and for meeting the goals of the Common Core State Standards (CCSS; National Governors Association Center for Best Practices & Council of Chief State School Officers [NGA/CCSSO], 2010). In their parallel chapter, Costa and colleagues (Chapter 3) address the same issues from the writing side. They discuss cognitive models of writing, writing interventions, and shared instructional benefits of reading and writing. In examining the co-occurrence of reading and writing difficulties, they found that, by third and fourth grade, more than 40% of students at risk for writing problems also had reading problems. They note that research is needed to document whether similar rates of co-occurrence might be seen when beginning with a sample of students with reading difficulties. These authors also note that struggling writers in first grade have more than two and a half times the odds of struggling with both reading and writing in third grade as compared to first-grade children who are not classified as struggling writers. The authors call for additional work on how the overlapping cognitive abilities that underlie both reading and writing evolve across development of these literacy skills and how interventions for one may influence development in the other. Despite their preliminary data on at-risk students indicating that reading and writing should be treated differently in terms of instruction, they note the importance of the reading–writing connection and call for continued work on this connection regarding etiology, prognosis, response to intervention, and how reading and writing converge and diverge over the course of development.

Harris and Graham (Chapter 4) laud the increased recent attention to writing and the reading–writing connection, attributing this, in part, to the advent of the CCSS. They also note, however, that the CCSS have increased pressure in schools to implement instruction in ways that enable reading and writing to support each other. Harris and Graham thus address how to use one to support the other and how to teach them together. They lament the smaller research base available on writing instruction compared to that for reading but encourage educators to use what we do know to enhance instruction. They cite challenges to the implementation of the CCSS but also point out the positive aspects of this movement and encourage researchers and educators to work together toward the implementation of reading, writing, and integrated reading–writing instruction under the CCSS. Their optimism is clear and is echoed by others in this volume, as is the call for continuing to embrace evidence-based practice in schools.

Section 2 discusses applying what we know. It begins with McCardle and Miller (Chapter 5) discussing the last two decades' push toward evidence-based practice, where that evidence can be found, and how we can continue to build that evidence base in ways that are useful to educators. At the same time that we are conducting research, we need to determine how best to apply what we know and, in the current education climate, how that information can relate to and assist with the implementation of the CCSS in literacy and language arts. And as we do this, additional research on instruction and intervention—including randomized controlled trials, work studying students as they learn and grow over time (longitudinal studies), and what teachers need to know to be able to effectively implement instruction aligned with the CCSS—will be crucial to student success.

Brenner (Chapter 6) discusses the connection between reading and writing from a teacher education point of view, raising one of the key issues that teachers are most often concerned with—whether they are well prepared to teach the areas for which they are being held responsible. This is especially true for writing, given how few teacher preparation courses appear to address writing instruction; adding to this challenge is whether teachers are prepared to practically implement what they have learned, whether they will get the ongoing professional development support they may need to be able to teach reading and writing in an integrated way. Teachers must also be able to recognize when integrating reading and writing in instruction is most effective and when the two should be taught separately. As Brenner notes, studies that follow teachers from their preservice programs to the classroom, study their implementation, and relate it to student outcomes are relatively few. She outlines what we do know about strong teacher preparation programs—they teach content as well as pedagogical techniques and offer opportunities to observe strong models and to get hands-on experience in the presence of a mentor with constructive feedback as well as have their field experiences connected directly with their coursework. Brenner mentions some practices and technologies that are emerging to support teachers that are changing how we all read and write; she outlines how these technologies and practices can better prepare teachers for both teaching and understanding the reading–writing connection. Although we do know what generally makes for strong teacher preparation programs, Brenner emphasizes the importance of work that still must be done to identify how best to prepare teachers for the reading–writing connection, to evaluate emerging practices, to know what they can and cannot do, and to improve the craft of those who prepare teachers through preservice and professional development in ways that will benefit both teachers and their students.

Developmentally, listening and speaking precede reading and writing, but they continue to develop in complexity alongside literacy skills. In Chapter 7, Washington, Brown, and Rhodes address the role of linguistic differences—nonmainstream dialects of English and learning English as a second language—and present them in perspective with regard to reading, writing, and the intersection of these literacy skills. They call for specific attention to cultural and linguistic differences in the design of education interventions, especially those aimed at reducing achievement disparities. They also note that basing policies on the results of population-based interventions must take into account ethical, cultural, and linguistic issues if those policies are to succeed.

Reasoning and critical thinking involve listening, speaking, reading, and writing, and they are an area of emphasis within literacy instruction in the CCSS. Carlisle, Dwyer, and Learned (Chapter 8) lay out a logical progression for how teachers can use oral discussion to teach students to reflect on and analyze text as well as read and write using these skills of reasoning and analysis. These techniques are drawn from research, yet there is a need to study how they might be most effectively included in the various curricula that teachers are asked to use and what foundational knowledge teachers need in order to be able to skillfully, effectively, and flexibly adapt these techniques in real time in the classroom.

Similarly, Urbani, Pearson, Ballute, and Lent (Chapter 9) offer an example of how teachers might collaborate to implement the inclusion of reading, writing, and discussion to actively engage students in complex disciplinary text. Citing the emphasis of the CCSS on literacy skills in content areas, they present a case study of how teachers and students experienced simultaneous teaching and learning of history and literacy/language arts. They are encouraged by the outcomes they noted but also are clear that this is a significant cognitive load for teachers, requiring a lot of planning and teamwork. These authors advocate establishing communities of teachers as learners and see this as critical to successful implementation of the CCSS. This type of implementation, and the effort it would take, should be studied to identify how best to support the formation of such teams, how the work might differ by content area, and what the effect is on both teachers and students over time. Even though one would hope that gains made would be sustained, it may be that they require additional supports over time in order to maintain momentum and build on the learning that both teachers and students accomplish. So although this case study has had some successes, additional research that could help codify what aspects of their process worked best, under what circumstances, would make such procedures more transferrable to other settings and contexts.

In Chapter 10, Strickland discusses the role of the CCSS in helping schools and districts ensure that students are given the skills, strategies, and learning opportunities they need to move forward in the 21st century with choices for higher education and meaning-ful, gainful employment. She discusses the application and misapplication of research in instruction and assessment in both reading and writing and connects these to the CCSS and the new assessment systems linked to these standards. Strickland points out the need for integrated instruction rather than a narrow focus on discrete skills, pointing out that learning to think and to be able to apply what one knows in new and novel situations is "the essence of *learning how to learn*." Although asserting the importance of assessment, she clearly indicates that tests should not be the content of instruction and that well-constructed assess-ments challenge students to use what they have learned rather than produce rote informa-tion. In this, Strickland sees hope—hope that there will be an increased focus on meaning, on having students demonstrate the ability to use what they have learned. She outlines the guidelines for curriculum planning and urges that new curricula connect the English lan-guage arts standards and the content-area subject standards. Like Urbani and colleagues, she highlights the need for well-planned professional development that will foster commu-nities of teachers as learners, that is collaborative and supportive, and that embraces both student and teacher needs. Strickland offers both recommendations and examples for how to accomplish this. She offers both hope and a warning that, although we must continue to produce useable research and promote its use, we must do so planfully and thoughtfully, in ways that do not harm our learners—both teachers and students.

The third section of the volume, Preparing for Change: The Intersection of Theory, Measurement, and Technology with Instruction, takes on the topic of assessment that Strickland has already invoked in Chapter 10 as important. Accountability is critical for any education investment, yet assessment can also serve purposes of informing instruction and guiding the development of interventions. Gorin, O'Reilly, Sabatini, Song, and Deane (Chapter 11) discuss in more technical terms some important innovations in assessment for literacy instruction. These authors highlight the important role that assessment can play in the educational process, especially if the burden of administration and scoring is reduced by well-thought-out designs and the judicious application of technology. They begin with an integrated model of the literacy construct—of reading and writing and their relation-ship to one another. They discuss scenario-based task design, human and automated scor-ing, and advanced psychometric models, giving us a window into the internal workings of assessment development and providing reassurance that they are indeed seeking to assess what Strickland calls essential: how well individuals can use what they have learned and how well the assessment itself can serve as an instructional design mechanism for reading and writing.

Technology runs through current issues on reading, writing, and assessment. Atwill and Blanchard (Chapter 12) discuss the possible roles it can play in the connection between reading and writing and in the development and implementation of the CCSS. This is another area of the CCSS where teachers are learners, and Atwill and Blanchard discuss various efforts and resources that are becoming available to help teachers learn about, access, and accomplish the implementation of technology into their classrooms and their instruction. In their chapter, these authors walk us through anchor standards of the CCSS in reading and writing as well as reading, writing, and technology in content-area subjects and technical subjects. They cover all grade levels, including kindergarten, with some key examples. Atwill and Blanchard also discuss the challenges, including cost, complexity, the need for school- or district-level coordination, the need for resources (hardware and soft-ware), and the need for explicit instruction for students on how to include technology with the reading–writing connection. There is also the challenge of using technology to reduce, rather than increase, the digital gap—making sure that those who struggle with technology, reading, writing, or all three get the opportunities and instruction they will need to develop these foundational skills.

Finally, this section ends with Ahmed, Kim, and Wagner (Chapter 13) addressing literacy models. They discuss various approaches to statistical modeling, explaining how these work and why we should care about them. Their models demonstrate that children do use the shared knowledge between reading and writing to improve their writing skills, thus indicating that teachers should not only teach individual literacy skills but should also focus on general instruction to help students use that shared knowledge underlying reading and writing in learning to write. The authors note the need to further research specific aspects of both sentence-level and text-level literacy and to further target specific aspects of comprehension instruction. The work of Ahmed and colleagues—and others—clearly demonstrates the potential that statistical modeling holds for practice—that is, by providing empirical data to inform models for instructional change.

LOOKING FORWARD

Throughout the three sections of this volume, and in every chapter, the need for ongoing research is clear. Such a research enterprise will need to be inclusive of mixed-methods approaches to examining the reading–writing connection with the emphasis on a tight fit between the research approach utilized and the question to be answered, how the processes involved in the connection might change longitudinally, individual differences that might be present between learners, and how to include evidence across research approaches (i.e., behavioral, genetic, and neurobiological) to inform instruction and improve outcomes for all learners.

Although the CCSS have created the basis for curriculum development that will hopefully lead to the implementation of coherent, systematic programs of instruction, the field has not yet clearly determined what would constitute a complete or effective integrated literacy program in elementary or middle school. Further, in reading and writing instruction, it is not clear what needs to be addressed separately for each and what aspects may be most effectively taught if taught in combination. Other crucial questions include what the earliest predictors are of later reading and writing success or problems and how early we can intervene in ways that can prevent later difficulties in reading and writing and to obtain optimal student outcomes.

As new information is learned, new theories will need to be developed and existing theories tested and challenged—this process is a critical step in the scientific enterprise. Novel approaches to assessment will also be needed, both for research and as existing and newly developed information is applied to instruction. From a research perspective, assessments provide us our link between observable behavior that we can measure and latent constructs represented in theories, thus providing us a vehicle to evaluate theory. From a practice perspective, assessments can provide ongoing information to inform dynamic instructional change; summative assessments in particular can be used to more broadly evaluate the impact of a change or intervention over time. As we seek to more closely link theory and assessment, sophisticated statistical modeling techniques will be useful to test these theories and to guide both assessment and instruction.

As the individual chapters in this book indicate, there are several issues—theory, measurement/assessment, instruction and intervention, and the use of technology—that require more in-depth examination. Theory should guide not only research on instruction and intervention but also approaches to assessment. Assessment has historically been more about accountability than about dynamically guiding instruction, although in some ways writing instruction has used formative assessment, sometimes systematically and sometimes less systematically; more recently assessment has been gaining traction as a means of gathering data that can guide the tailoring of instruction (e.g., Connor, Morrison, Fishman, Schatschneider, & Underwood, 2007) and to document progress, as in Response to Intervention models. Studies are needed of the interconnectedness of reading and writing, of integrated instruction and how focused instruction in each domain can support the other, and of the interplay between reading and writing in assessment. Such studies can also help us tease apart the attributes and aptitudes that characterize students who struggle with one of these skills and better describe the factors that characterize students who struggle in both reading and writing.

Additional research will be needed on an ongoing basis; overall, there is a need to better understand the reading–writing connection across the developmental trajectory from preschool through high school and beyond, and indeed to more clearly delineate that developmental trajectory. Longitudinal work will be essential to increase our understanding of the complex developmental trajectory of writing, including how such development is linked with or independent of reading development. Such research will increase our understanding about how to support the growth of students' reading–writing developmental trajectories. Longitudinal studies can help us understand and thus guide what occurs in preschool experiences in early writing and its precursors. Because reading and writing are associated, learning in the two may be more closely associated during the preschool years than in later years and may change over time in nonlinear ways. These associations in the preschool years remain tentative at present, so it is critical that research efforts address the separate developmental trajectories of reading and writing, from assessment, intervention, and assessment-intervention perspectives.

In addition to documenting trajectories—longitudinal and cross-sectional— experimental research on intervention is also needed to address how best to instructionally support the development of effective writing and reading across genres from K through grade 12. This is critically important for those at risk for reading and writing difficulties and for those students with manifest learning disabilities. We need to more fully understand how learning trajectories and the ability to respond to different instructional approaches might differ for those students who struggle with reading, writing, or both reading and writing.

We also should not underestimate the need to create a clearer understanding of the relationship between these two historic areas of instruction—reading and writing instruction. They may well have more in common than is currently understood. In addition, students whose learning needs are greater should not become permanent remedial reading–writing students whose instruction will only bring them to the beginning of comprehension; research and theory building must include the expectation that high-need students can achieve.

How both reading and writing instructional strategies are responsive to and implemented within the Common Core Standards for Language Arts (NGA/CCSSO, 2010), how they are addressed within response-to-intervention approaches in the classroom and in special education more generally, and the results of these changes are current issues that require further scientific inquiry, as are approaches to implementing what is known both at home and in the classroom. This includes early parenting support and early identification of potential problems. It also includes guiding teachers in assessing (or seeking services for assessment), interpreting the results, and delivering writing instruction/intervention. This would likely require teachers to integrate writing with reading/language arts instruction to have students read and write more and would necessitate instructional engagement around varied types of documents. Taken together, new knowledge informing new actions should lead to stronger student reading and writing achievement. The connection, or interface, of the reading–writing connection is a dynamic issue that can offer exciting areas for further research that have the potential to inform how we help today's students become better readers and writers. This is, then, not only an opportunity to expand and improve instruction but also an opportunity to support the improvement of students' lives as they enter a postsecondary education world that requires deeper understanding of more complex areas of learning or as they enter careers for which understanding complex systems that now constitute most work environments is the norm. Education and learning science, however, must continue to develop the empirical bases for the varied facets of this connection or relationship between reading and writing. These efforts undoubtedly will drive evidence-based assessment, instruction, and intervention as well as push public policy in education that will support the advancement of reading and writing for all students.

REFERENCES

Connor, C.M., Morrison, F.J., Fishman, B.J., Schatschneider, C., & Underwood, P. (2007). The early years: Algorithm-guided individualized reading instruction. *Science, 315*(5811), 464–465.

Fitzgerald, J., & Shanahan, T. (2000). Reading and writing relations and their development. *Educational Psychologist, 35*(1), 39–50.

International Reading Association & the *Eunice Kennedy Shriver* National Institute of Child Health and Human Development (IRA/NICHD). (2012). *The reading-writing connection.* Retrieved from http://www.reading.org/Libraries/resources/reading-writingconnection_final.pdf

National Governors Association Center for Best Practices & Council of Chief State School Officers (NGA/CCSSO). (2010). *Common Core State Standards: English language arts standards.* Washington, DC: Authors.

Parodi, G. (2007). Reading-writing connections: Discourse-oriented research. *Reading and Writing: An Interdisciplinary Journal, 20,* 225–250.

Index

Tables and figures are indicated by *t* and *f*, respectively.